Trade Liberalization among Industrial Countries

Published volumes in
"The Atlantic Policy Studies"

Trade Liberalization among Industrial Countries:

Objectives and Alternatives

BELA BALASSA

A volume in the series
"The Atlantic Policy Studies"

Published for the Council on Foreign Relations by

McGRAW-HILL BOOK COMPANY

New York   Toronto   London   Sydney

Trade Liberalization among Industrial Countries

Library of Congress Catalog Card Number: 67-16296

First Edition   03547

To my wife

The Atlantic Policy Studies

The Atlantic Policy Studies is a series of major works on the future of the Atlantic Community. The project was undertaken by the Council on Foreign Relations on the basis of a grant from the Ford Foundation. Mr. Balassa's book, the eighth to be published in the series, is an analysis of the political and economic effects of trade liberalization in general and of various trade policies in particular. The main concern here is with trade in industrial materials and manufactured goods among the industrial nations.

Undertaken out of a conviction that a re-examination of U.S. relations with and policies toward Western Europe is urgently needed, the Atlantic Policy Studies are an attempt to come to grips with basic questions about the future of America's Atlantic relations.

The studies are policy-oriented, seeking not only to describe and forecast but also to prescribe. Each of the ten studies is the responsibility of its author, but considers its special problems in the light of the general aim of the program as a whole. The program is under the guidance of a Steering Committee, of which Charles M. Spofford is chairman.

The Atlantic Policy Studies are divided into four broad categories, dealing respectively with the broad strategic problems of the Atlantic Alliance; with economic relations among the Atlantic countries and between them and less developed countries; with the external environment of the West; and with Atlantic political relations.

Mr. Balassa's book is one of four studies of economic problems. A second, *Atlantic Agricultural Unity: Is It Possible?* by John O. Coppock, was published in 1966. John Pincus's volume *Trade, Aid and Development: The Rich and Poor Nations,* which discusses the role Atlantic trade and aid can play in the economic growth of the developing countries, was published in January 1967. In a fourth volume dealing essentially with economic issues, Richard N. Cooper of

Yale University will examine international financial arrangements and monetary policies among the industrialized nations.

Two studies of the Atlantic world's external environment have been made: *Alternative to Partition* by Zbigniew K. Brzezinski of Columbia University was published by McGraw-Hill in May 1965. A study by Theodore Geiger of the National Planning Association, *The Conflicted Relationship: The West and the Transformation of Asia, Africa, and Latin America,* examines the nature of the great transition now going on throughout the three continents in which development is hoped for—not always realistically. The implications of the changes in these areas for the future of political relations with the Western world are also explored.

Atlantic military problems are considered in their political context in Henry A. Kissinger's *The Troubled Partnership: A Re-appraisal of the Atlantic Alliance,* which McGraw-Hill published in April 1965.

Political relations among the Atlantic nations are the subject of three studies. Miriam Camps of Chatham House and the Council on Foreign Relations wrote a volume on the future of European unity, *European Unification in the Sixties: From the Veto to the Crisis,* published in 1966. In the spring of 1965 Stanley Hoffmann of Harvard University gave at the Council a series of lectures that reviewed the principal constraints, particularly the domestic constraints, on U.S. action in Atlantic affairs; the lectures will be published as a volume in the Atlantic Policy Series. A third political volume, by the Director of the Atlantic Policy Studies, *The Atlantic Idea and Its European Rivals,* published late in 1966, addresses the question of the future shape of political relations among the Atlantic countries.

HAROLD VAN B. CLEVELAND
Director, Atlantic Policy Studies
Council on Foreign Relations

Preface

During the last decade, rapid economic growth and the establishment of the Common Market have changed economic power relations in the Atlantic area to a considerable extent. In the atmosphere of *détente* between East and West, these developments have contributed to demands on the part of Europeans to share more fully in the making of decisions affecting their interests in political, economic, and military questions. The new situation facing the United States calls for a reappraisal of American policies regarding U.S.–European relationships and a rethinking of the objectives these policies may serve.

The subject of this book is trade policy—the choice among alternative trade arrangements, regional as well as multilateral. But such an investigation cannot be restricted to a comparison of the economic effects of possible alternatives. Rather, trade arrangements should be evaluated from the standpoint of the political and economic objectives they are supposed to serve. It is necessary, therefore, to make explicit what these political objectives are and what benefits trade liberalization can bring to the industrial countries.

At the same time, we cannot limit the discussion to trade relations between the United States and Western Europe, since trade between them affects the interests of Canada and Japan, and the United States has important interests in both countries. Furthermore, in evaluating alternative trade arrangements among the industrial countries, one should take account of the possible repercussions of these arrangements for developing nations whose economic well-being and political stability are major policy objectives of the United States. This study will accordingly consider the choices facing the United States and the other industrial countries in regard to trade policies and will attempt to evaluate the desirability of trade liberalization and its various alternatives on the basis of political and economic objectives—internal as well as external—for the countries concerned.

This study is a result of research on trade liberalization among the industrial countries, carried out in the framework of the Atlantic Trade Project, which is part of the Atlantic Policy Studies sponsored by the Council on Foreign Relations and directed by Harold van B. Cleveland. The Trade Project, directed by the author, has been undertaken with the collaboration of eight economists from six industrial countries.

The collaborators have prepared country studies dealing with the problem of trade liberalization from the viewpoint of individual countries and country-groupings; these include the United States (Mordechai Kreinin), Canada (Ronald J. Wonnacott), the European Common Market (F. Hartog), the United Kingdom (Sidney J. Wells), Scandinavia (Staffan B. Linder), and Japan (Kiyoshi Kojima), as well as studies on nontariff barriers (William B. Kelly, Jr.) and on the implications of intercountry differences in fiscal and social security systems for trade and foreign investment (Douglas Dosser). These papers are published under the title *Studies in Trade Liberalization* by the Johns Hopkins University Press.

In the writing of this book I have incurred obligations to many people. I am greatly indebted to Harold van B. Cleveland for his counsel and suggestions on a wide range of matters and to William Diebold, Jr., Senior Research Fellow at the Council on Foreign Relations, for valuable comments on successive drafts of the manuscript. The members of the Study Group of the Council, under the able chairmanship of William Butler, challenged me on a number of points and gave me the benefit of their criticisms. They were: Henry G. Aubrey, Richard N. Cooper, William Diebold, Jr., H. Edward English, Isaiah Frank, David M. Freudenthal, Theodore Gates, Theodore Geiger, Joseph A. Greenwald, Peter B. Kenen, Lawrence B. Krause, Irving B. Kravis, Sperry Lea, Francis McIntyre, Alfred C. Neal, Bernard Norwood, Walter S. Salant, and Ralph I. Straus.

While I cannot list them individually, I owe an especial debt to officials and fellow economists in the United States and other countries who have contributed to my understanding of problems of trade policy. I have further benefited from discussions with my collaborators in this project. In the section on nontariff barriers, I relied to a considerable extent on the studies by Douglas Dosser and William Kelly, while part of the methodology underlying the calculations of Chapter 4 was worked out jointly with Mordechai Kreinin.

Some findings of the study have appeared in article form in the *American Economic Review, Banca Nazionale del Lavoro Quarterly Review, Journal of Political Economy, Manchester School of Economic and Social Research, Moorgate and Wall Street Review,* and (jointly with M. E. Kreinin) *Review of Economics and Statistics.* The Institut d'Etudes Européennes of the Unversité Libre de Bruxelles included my lectures "Some Considerations on Trade Liberalization in the Atlantic Area" in its publication series. The publishers of these periodicals have kindly given permission for the use of published material.

I wish to express my appreciation to my secretary, Loretta Tallon, for uncomplainingly retyping several drafts of the various chapters. In my work I was also aided by a changing roster of research assistants who may remain nameless.

BELA BALASSA

April, 1966

Contents

Trade Liberalization among Industrial Countries

Introduction

Trade Policy in the Postwar Period

In an effort to benefit domestic producers at the expense of foreign competitors, the industrial nations substantially raised tariffs and other barriers to trade during the depression of the 1930s. But since one country's imports are another's exports, the general application of such "beggar-my-neighbor" policies restricted the extent of international specialization without stimulating the activity of domestic industries. As the failure of these policies became apparent, Cordell Hull, Roosevelt's Secretary of State, put forward new proposals designed to stem the tide of protectionism and to reduce tariffs on a multilateral basis. Political and economic uncertainties prevented the realization of these goals in the years preceding the Second World War, however, and tariff disarmament could not be undertaken until after the war.

Armed with authority from Congress under the Reciprocal Trade Agreements Act to reduce tariffs by 50 per cent, the U.S. Administration sought to find in the proposed International Trade Organization (ITO) an appropriate vehicle to carry out multilateral tariff reductions. After the failure of the ITO, this purpose was served by the General Agreement on Tariffs and Trade (GATT). Under the most-favored-nation clause, the contracting parties to GATT assumed the obligation to extend to one another tariff concessions accorded to any country, whether a party to the agreement or not. Another central feature of tariff negotiations under the aegis of GATT is the principle of reciprocity: mutual tariff concessions are designed to lead to equivalent increases in the exports and imports of each participant. But the principles of nondiscrimination and reciprocity often come into conflict since the agreed-upon tariff reductions are extended to countries which are not obliged to reciprocate.

To lessen the chances of giving a free ride to third countries, tariff bargaining was carried out on an item-by-item basis in the postwar period. This procedure contributed to the maintenance of high duties on the actual and potential export products of the developing countries but it proved difficult to avoid a spillover in the case of products that are of interest chiefly to the industrial nations because they export largely the same range of products. Thus, although parallel negotiations were carried out by a number of countries, the item-by-item approach to tariff bargaining limited the scope of tariff reductions and, after initial successes, the progress of multilateral trade liberalization slowed down. A contributing factor was the near exhaustion of the negotiating authority accorded by Congress to the President of the United States. Mention may also be made of the American "no injury" philosophy, which excluded a number of commodities from the negotiations and raised the threat that tariff reductions would be rescinded through the application of escape clauses.

More comprehensive reductions in trade barriers have taken place in the European Economic Community (EEC) and the European Free Trade Association (EFTA). The establishment of EEC and EFTA was made possible by Article 24 of the General Agreement, which provides for an exception to the principle of nondiscrimination. Countries that mutually agree to abolish tariffs in the framework of a free trade area or a customs union are not required to extend these concessions to other parties. Whereas multilateral reductions in duties are nondiscriminatory in character, the elimination of duties on internal trade and their maintenance on imports from outsiders in an integrated area involves discrimination against non-member countries. On the other hand, the scope of economic integration extends further than multilateral tariff reductions since it entails an irrevocable commitment to eliminate duties and other types of trade restrictions and may also be accompanied by integration in other spheres of economic (and political) life.

While the United States had long upheld the principle of nondiscrimination, it nevertheless encouraged exceptions to this rule in postwar Europe. Largely on the basis of political considerations, the United States championed the cause of European integration and took a position in favor of smaller but tighter preferential groupings that seemed to hold out the promise of political unification. Following the establishment of the European Common Market and the division of Western Europe into two trading blocs, attention has again focused on multilateral trade liberalization. In 1962, the U.S. Congress gave authority to the President to negotiate multilateral tariff reductions up to 50 per cent on an across-the-board basis and to eliminate duties on commodities of which the United States and the Common Market, taken together, supplied at least 80 per cent of world exports originating outside the Sino-Soviet Area.[1]

The Trade Expansion Act of 1962 has brought about some important modifications in the traditional method of tariff bargaining. For one thing, the replacement of bilateral negotiations by across-the-board reductions in duties, with exceptions in the case of especially sensitive industries, makes it possible to proceed with trade liberalization on a broad front. For another, the Act has provided for adjustment assistance to supplement, or supplant, the use of protective measures under the escape clause and has limited the conditions for the application of this clause.

At the time of writing, it is not yet clear whether—and to what extent—the Kennedy Round of tariff negotiations will be successful. Nevertheless, the time appears propitious for a reappraisal of American policy on trade with the industrial countries and for a consideration of alternative arrangements for trade liberalization. The Common Market has emerged as a bargaining partner of comparable strength to the United States; despite efforts to reach an accommodation between the EEC and EFTA, Western Europe is still divided into to trading blocs; Canada and Japan are reappraising their place in world trade; and the less developed countries clamor for access to the markets of the industrial nations.

But questions of trade policy cannot be profitably discussed without clarifying the political and economic objectives that can be served by lowering trade barriers. And, whatever trade arrangements may be regarded as realistic alternatives at the present or may enter our horizon in the future, there is need to examine the economic effects of reductions in barriers to trade for individual countries and country groupings. Also, given the interdependence of trade and direct foreign investment, it is appropriate to consider the repercussions of trade liberalization on foreign investment and the reciprocal influence of investment on trade.

[1] Without Britain's entry into the Common Market, however, the applicability of this rule is limited to a few commodities such as margarine and aircraft.

If trade liberalization is judged desirable on political and economic grounds, the next question concerns the alternative strategies that can be employed to further this objective. Four alternatives are considered in this study: (A) an Atlantic Free Trade Area; (B) periodic tariff reductions in accordance with the most-favored-nation (MFN) principle; (C) a trade arrangement among industrial countries that excludes the Common Market; and (D) European integration.

Future tariff disarmament may take the form of periodic negotiations on an across-the-board basis with the application of the most-favored-nation clause (Alternative B—in effect, a succession of "Kennedy Rounds"). Another—more revolutionary—solution would be to make use of the GATT rules by establishing a free trade area among the industrial countries of North America, Western Europe, and Japan. With some disregard of geography, I shall use the expression Atlantic Free Trade Area to designate this alternative (Alternative A).

A third alternative which has been proposed in recent years would involve establishing a trade arrangement—in the form of a free trade area or of preferential tariff reductions—including the United States, Canada, the members of the European Free Trade Association, and possibly Japan (Alternative C). Finally, in examining possible alternatives for trade liberalization among the industrial countries, one needs to consider the possibility that further economic integration would take place in Europe without involving tariff reductions on trade with other industrial countries (Alternative D).

This study will thus examine the effects of trade liberalization in general, and its various forms in particular, from the point of view of the political and economic objectives of the industrial countries. The investigation is restricted to manufactured goods and industrial materials, which account for more than 80 per cent of trade among the industrial countries. This procedure has been adopted because of the special characteristics of the protection of food and fuels. In the case of foodstuffs, fixed and variable duties, subsidies and quantitative restrictions applied in the importing countries, and price-support measures used by the major exporters greatly affect the pattern of trade. Because of the political and social issues involved in the protection of domestic agriculture, it may be difficult substantially to alter the policies presently applied or even to speculate on the forms changes in these policies may take. Similar considerations apply to fuels, where modifications in the system of protection would involve a reappraisal of national energy policies. On the other hand, industrial materials and manufactured goods are protected largely by tariffs, and these commodities have been in the center of trade negotiations in the postwar period.

To provide a background for the study, Chapter 1 examines changes in economic power relations among the industrial countries since the turn of the century. It also provides information on the dependence of the industrial nations on international trade and on the geographical and commodity composition of this trade. In turn, Chapter 2 considers the political objectives of trade liberalization and the political feasibility of alternative trade arrangements, with particular attention to the implications of these alternatives for integration in Western Europe and for the Atlantic alliance.

The discussion of the economic effects of trade liberalization begins in Chapter 3 with an analysis of the existing system of protection in the industrial countries. Attempts to measure the restrictive effects of tariffs on imports are dealt with there, and preliminary consideration is given to the possible impact of eliminating duties on international specialization. The character and forms of nontariff barriers to trade are also briefly examined.

The economic consequences of trade liberalization can be classified as static and dynamic effects. The static effects relate to changes in trade flows that would follow reductions in duties on the assumption that methods of production remained unchanged. Chapter 4 includes a calculation of the probable magnitude of these static effects under alternative assumptions. Attention is further given to the possible impact of trade liberalization on the balance of payments and on the industrial structure of the major industrial countries.

The dynamic effects of trade liberalization are dealt with in Chapter 5. Dynamic effects are the consequence of the widening of markets through trade: cost reductions due to economies of scale and improvements in production methods resulting from increased foreign competition. The claim made in Western Europe that their large size, financial power, and research facilities give advantages to American firms over European companies is also examined in this chapter. In turn, Chapter 6 focuses attention on the possible effects of tariff reductions on direct foreign investment and on the economic and political implications of international capital flows.

The concluding chapter considers, for each of the principal industrial countries, the relative importance of political and economic considerations in liberalizing trade. It also provides an evaluation of
alternative approaches to trade liberalization in the light of stated
political and economic objectives. Finally, an appendix to this chapter
examines some of the implications of trade liberalization for the coordination of national economic policies following reduction of duties.

CHAPTER ONE

The Economic Background

The Postwar Setting

The first half of the twentieth century brought considerable changes in economic power relations among the industrial countries.[1] Within Western Europe, shifts in the relative position of the individual countries accompanied alternating periods of peace and war, while Europe's position vis-à-vis the United States deteriorated more or less steadily throughout the period. As a result of these developments, the United States, a young industrial nation at the turn of the century, emerged as the dominant economic power on the world scene.

The U.S. economy experienced rapid increases in labor force as well as in productivity during the first decade of the century, and its lead over European economies increased considerably in the course of the two world wars. According to estimates prepared by the British National Institute of Economic and Social Research, U.S. national income grew at an average annual rate of 4 per cent in war periods and the years immediately following the two wars (1913–1922 and 1938–1950). During this time the national incomes of the three largest industrial countries in Western Europe (France, Germany, and the United Kingdom) remained, on balance, unchanged.[2]

Incomes rose faster in the major European countries than in the United States during the interwar period, but not rapidly enough to compensate for the wartime lag. Between 1899 and 1950 the gross domestic product of the United States grew at an average annual rate of 3.2 per cent, while growth rates were slightly below 1 per cent in the United Kingdom and Germany and 1.6 per cent in France. Thus,

[1] The United States, Canada, the member countries of the European Economic Community and the European Free Trade Association, and Japan.

[2] D. C. Paige, "Economic Growth: The Last Hundred Years," *National Institute Economic Review,* July 1961, pp. 24–49.

in a period of five decades, the United States GDP rose fivefold, as against an increase of 60 to 65 per cent in the United Kingdom and Germany and 130 per cent in France.

Substantial gains were made also in several of the smaller industrial countries that started out with a relatively undeveloped industrial base (Canada and Japan) or benefited from their neutrality in the course of the two world wars (Sweden and Switzerland). But the U.S. growth rate was exceeded only in Canada, and the share of the United States in the combined gross domestic product of the industrial countries increased during much of the period. The U.S. share rose from 38.5 per cent in 1899 to 52.8 per cent in 1929, and—after a decline to 50.3 per cent during the depression of the thirties—to 58.1 per cent in 1950 (Table 1.1).

TABLE 1.1   Estimates of Gross Domestic Products
in the Industrial Countries
($ billion at 1955 prices) [a]

	1899	1913	1929	1937	1950	1955	1964
United States	59.0	97.0	168.0	171.0	294.0	362.5	477.0
Canada	3.4	7.2	10.3	10.1	20.0	24.8	34.7
Common Market	46.1	60.0	74.9	78.2	100.6	136.1	215.0
of which							
France	14.0	16.0	25.0	22.4	32.4	40.0	62.5
Germany [b]	20.5	27.2	28.4	32.4	33.7	51.9	85.0
United Kingdom	34.0	42.0	42.0	50.0	54.7	63.5	81.9
Continental EFTA	8.0	10.6	13.9	17.8	25.9	30.8	46.2
Japan	2.8	4.8	9.1	12.9	11.1	16.5	40.1
Total	153.3	221.6	318.2	340.0	506.3	634.2	894.9

Sources: 1899–1955: Alfred Maizels, *Industrial Growth and World Trade* (Cambridge University Press, 1963), p. 531.
1955–1964: Organization for Economic Cooperation and Development, *National Accounts Statistics, 1955–1964* (Paris, 1966).

Notes: (a) Domestic factor prices converted by the use of purchasing power parities shown in Maizels, *Industrial Growth and World Trade,* p. 546.
(b) Present territory of Western Germany.

Changes in the relative position of the United States in world trade were not commensurate with developments in the field of production during the first four decades of the century, but the United States assumed increasing importance in world trade during and in the years immediately after World War II. By 1950, the United States accounted for 31.0 per cent of the combined exports of the industrial countries, as compared to a share of about one-fifth at the turn of the century and 23.1 per cent in 1937.[3]

Since, in countries at similar levels of economic development, the ratio of foreign trade to national income is as a rule inversely related to the volume of national income, it is not surprising that the United States had a smaller share in the exports of the industrial countries than in their combined output. At the same time, the relatively slow rise of the U.S. share during the period up to World War II can be explained by the inward orientation of the American economy. Subsequently, the proportion of exports supplied by the United States increased partly by default: the destruction suffered during the war hindered the countries of Western Europe and Japan in supplying their traditional markets, and they themselves required imports from the United States for purposes of reconstruction.

Parallel to these developments, the structure of U.S. foreign trade underwent considerable changes: raw materials assumed increasing importance in imports and manufactured goods came to predominate in exports. Thus manufactures accounted for more than 55 per cent of U.S. foreign sales in 1950, as against 30 per cent five decades earlier. Over the same period the share of the United States in the exports of manufactures originating in the industrial countries more than doubled: from 11 to 12 per cent around the turn of the century it rose to 27.5 per cent in 1950.[4]

The growth of the U.S. economy and the losses suffered by major European countries during the two wars further contributed to changes in creditor-debtor relationships. A debtor before the First World War, the United States became the major creditor nation after World War II, while the credit balances of the United Kingdom declined substantially and several European countries became net debtors. The share of the United States in world gold reserves, too, increased to a considerable extent, and its gold holdings grew from $3.8 billion in 1928 to $14.6 billion in 1938 and to $22.8 billion in 1950.[5]

[3] A. Maizels, *Industrial Growth and World Trade* (Cambridge: University Press, 1963), pp. 426–27, and United Nations *Statistical Yearbook,* New York 1952.

[4] Maizels, cited, pp. 426–28. The data refer to commodity classes 5 to 8 of the United Nations Standard International Trade Classification and do not include exports from Austria, Denmark, Norway, and Portugal.

[5] Robert Triffin, *Gold and the Dollar Crisis* (New Haven: Yale University Press, 1961), pp. 72–73.

These data point to the increasing importance of the United States within the industrial-country group—and in the world economy—during the first half of the century. With three-fifths of the gross domestic product of the industrial countries and one-third of their combined exports, the United States dwarfed any of her competitors and reached the peak of her economic power in the years following World War II. Her large credit balance in long-term investments and the possession of 46 per cent of the world's gold stock further enhanced the U.S. position. In turn, European countries were handicapped by wartime losses in productive equipment and the fragmentation of the continent into national states. The implications of this asymmetry were apparent in the role played by the United States in shaping the "rules of the game" in international trade and finance.[6]

The charter of the stillborn International Trade Organization largely reflected the views of U.S. officials who championed the cause of nondiscriminatory tariff reductions and looked with disfavor at preferential arrangements, especially Commonwealth preference. The United States also had a dominant influence on the tariff negotiations carried out under the auspices of the General Agreement on Tariffs and Trade, which assumed the functions of the ITO. Further, in preference to the Keynes plan, the ideas put forward by H. D. White, an official of the U.S. Treasury, served as a basis for the Articles of Agreement of the International Monetary Fund, and the Agreement gave expression to the U.S. objectives of limiting the scope of operation of the Fund and safeguarding the interests of the creditor countries. Finally, the United States was assured an influence commensurate with its financial contribution in the affairs of the International Bank for Reconstruction and Development.

Economic Growth and Integration in Western Europe

In the early postwar years it was widely assumed that this asymmetry in economic power relations would persist and might further be accentuated. Some doubted the recovery potential of the European economy; others asserted that in international trade the United States would derive an enduring advantage from her technological superiority over Western Europe. Theoretical explanations based on the maintenance of the technological lead of the United

[6] The political and the military implications of the asymmetry in economic power relations will be considered in the next chapter.

States were put forward to explain the allegedly permanent dollar shortage,[7] and pessimistic appraisals of Europe's chances in economic competition with the United States carried well into the 1950s. However, rapid growth in continental Europe and the establishment of the European Common Market have led to changes in the economic power structure and have diminished the dominant position of the United States in the world economy.

To begin with, considerable disparities appeared in regard to the rate of increase of the gross domestic product: in the 1950–1964 period, the average annual rate of growth of GDP was 3.5 per cent in the United States, as compared to 4.0 per cent in Canada, 4.7 per cent in Western Europe, and 9.6 per cent in Japan. The share of the United States in the combined gross domestic product of the industrial countries declined from 58.1 per cent in 1950 to 53.3 per cent in 1964. Canada's share remained unchanged at 3.9 per cent, Western Europe's rose from 35.8 to 38.3 per cent, and Japan's from 2.2 to 4.5 per cent (Table 1.1).

We also find substantial differences in the growth performance of the individual European countries during this period. While the United Kingdom placed behind the United States with a 50 per cent increase in the gross domestic product between 1950 and 1964, national incomes more than doubled in the countries participating in the European Common Market. As a result, Germany's national income surpassed that of the United Kingdom and, in 1964, the gross domestic products of the Common Market countries, taken together, reached 45 per cent of the United States GDP as against a ratio of 34 per cent in 1950.[8]

Gross domestic product is one of several indicators that can be

---

[7] Cf., Erik Hoffmeyer, *Dollar Shortage and the Structure of U.S. Foreign Trade* (Copenhagen: Ejnar Munksgaard, 1958).

[8] Table 1.1 also compares the situation existing in 1963 with that in 1929, the last "normal" year before the depression of the thirties. It appears that, over the period as a whole, the share of the United States in the combined gross domestic product of the industrial countries hardly changed, the gains made during the war being largely offset by the deterioration of the U.S. position after 1950 and, to a lesser extent, during the depression of the thirties. In turn, large gains were made in countries that had been at a lower level of industrial development in 1929 (Japan, Canada, Continental EFTA), while the United Kingdom was the main loser: the British share in the combined gross domestic product of the industrial countries declined from 13.3 per cent in 1929 to 10.8 per cent in 1950, and to 9.1 per cent in 1964.

used to assess the economic power of individual countries and country groupings. A comparison of gross domestic products may provide an appropriate indication of the capacity of individual countries to undertake military spending or to provide foreign aid, for example. But, from the point of view of bargaining power at trade negotiations, domestic production for internal consumption is hardly relevant and the volume of international trade assumes importance. Here we find that the U.S. share in the combined exports of the industrial countries declined from 31.0 per cent in 1950 to 24.5 per cent in 1963 and the proportion supplied by Britain fell from 18.5 to 11.5 per cent. In the same period the share of the Common Market countries rose from 28.3 to 39.7 per cent, and that of Japan from 2.5 to 6.2 per cent.[9]

Among institutional factors the establishment of the European Economic Community is the primary consideration. The bargaining power of the Common Market countries has increased by reason of their rising share in the world market and, more importantly, the progress made toward coordinating their commercial policies. While the member states have continued to follow independent policies in regard to trade with the Communist countries and at the United Nations Conference on Trade and Development, they have increasingly taken concerted action in their dealings with other industrial economies. The Community participates as a single bargaining unit at tariff negotiations carried out within the framework of GATT, and the EEC Commission also represents the member governments in negotiating the association of individual countries with the Common Market.

This is not to say that the road toward concerted action on matters of commercial policy would be smooth. Positions taken jointly are more often than not the result of hard bargaining among the EEC countries themselves and, in the case of Britain's application for entry, one country—France—singlehandedly put an end to the negotiations. Yet, even though the common position is frequently the outcome of much haggling within the EEC, the unified stand taken by the Community at the negotiating table contributes to its bargaining strength.

The increased bargaining power of the Common Market was apparent in the Dillon Round of tariff negotiations and, more dramatically, in the EEC's swift retaliation to President Kennedy's action to raise duties on carpet and plate glass. In the past, instead of retaliation, the adversely affected country (in this case, Belgium) would

9 United Nations *Statistical Yearbook,* various issues.

have asked for compensation through GATT, and while such a step was successful in the case of the famous cheese incident,[10] this has been the exception rather than the rule. One may also wonder if the outcome of the "chicken war," in which the United States sought unsuccessfully to prevent the Common Market from raising duties on imports of chicken, would not have been different had the United States faced only a single country.

U.S.–EEC bargaining appears to be the dominant feature of the Kennedy Round of tariff negotiations. Indeed, the origins of the Kennedy Round can be traced to the creation of the Common Market. Integration in Europe gave an impetus to the rethinking of trade policy in Washington and provided an inducement for seeking multilateral tariff cuts that would diminish the extent of discrimination associated with the removal of internal tariffs in the European Economic Community. At the same time, it is rather doubtful that President Kennedy would have received from Congress the wide powers entrusted to him in the Trade Expansion Act without the stimulus provided by the establishment of the EEC. Should the Geneva negotiations be successful, the creation of the European Common Market will have contributed, albeit inadvertently, to multilateral trade liberalization.

One may object to this analysis on the ground that, by giving emphasis to the establishment of the Common Market, the other European integration project, the European Free Trade Association, has been neglected. Indeed, tariff reductions within EFTA have proceeded at about the same rate as within the EEC, and the external trade of the EFTA is only slightly smaller than that of the Common Market. In 1964, the extra-area exports of EFTA amounted to $18.7 billion, as against $24.2 billion for the EEC and $26.2 billion for the United States. The comparable import figures are $22.4 billion for EFTA, $24.0 billion for the Common Market, and $18.3 billion for the United States (Appendix Table 1.1).[11]

From the point of view of commercial policy, however, one can hardly regard the European Free Trade Association as a unit. Under a free-trade-area arrangement, participating countries maintain their

[10] In the early fifties, GATT authorized retaliation after the United States repeatedly imposed quotas on cheese, first under the Defense Production Act and later under the Agricultural Production Act.

[11] For their bargaining power at trade negotiations, the extra-area rather than the total (intra- and extra-area) trade of the Common Market and EFTA is relevant.

own tariffs on products imported from outside the area and preserve the freedom to pursue independent policies. Accordingly, while the Common Market countries present a unified stand at the tariff negotiations, the member countries of EFTA continue to participate independently and often take different positions at the bargaining table.

The circumstances in which the European Free Trade Association was established largely explain the lack of coordination of commercial policies among the member countries. Whereas the founders of the Common Market aimed at economic and political integration, EFTA was regarded as a second-best solution by some of its participants and as a temporary expedient by others. It was formed after negotiations for an all-European Free Trade Area—proposed by the British in a large part to avoid EEC discrimination—had broken down, its main purpose being to serve as a counterweight to the Common Market and to provide a bargaining device for reaching an all-European solution at some future time.

Hopes for an accommodation with the EEC have not been realized so far, and the cohesion of EFTA has been impaired by the unilateral actions of the British government. While Britain had favored the establishment of the European Free Trade Association, in part to reduce the attraction of the Common Market for the smaller European countries, a few years later she decided to go it alone and to apply for entry into the EEC. Several of the continental EFTA countries followed Britain in applying for membership in or association with the Common Market, but the absence of joint action was conspicuous. The United Kingdom application for entry remained the center of attention; at the same time, the British showed more interest in obtaining favorable treatment for Commonwealth countries than in easing the way of their EFTA partners into the Common Market.[12]

The European Free Trade Association was given a new lease on

[12] According to the communiqué of the London agreement, signed by the countries participating in EFTA on June 29, 1961, the association would be maintained until "satisfactory arrangements have been worked out . . . to meet the various legitimate interests of all members of EFTA, and thus enable them to participate from the same date in an integrated European market." The reference to simultaneous entry was missing from later British statements, however, and it is generally assumed that Britain would have entered the Common Market even if an association agreement with the neutral countries (Austria, Sweden, and Switzerland) could not have been worked out. Cf. Miriam Camps, *Britain and the European Community, 1955–63* (Princeton, N.J.: Princeton University Press, 1964), pp. 497–99.

life following the breakdown of British negotiations with the EEC. The member countries continued to follow independent commercial policies, however, and EFTA received a serious setback in October 1964 when Britain applied a 15 per cent surcharge on imports of manufactures without consulting her partner countries. It is also apparent that Britain again seeks participation in an integrated Europe through membership in the Common Market rather than through the fusion of EEC and EFTA.[13]

Given her interest in reaching an accommodation with the Common Market and maintaining ties with the Commonwealth, Britain judges it advantageous to retain her freedom of action. Yet, in the absence of the coordination of commercial policies with the EFTA countries, the bargaining power of the United Kingdom has declined to a considerable extent. There has been a continuing fall in the United Kingdom share in world trade, and Britain's importance as a trading unit is overshadowed by that of the Common Market. In GATT, the decline in the relative importance of the United Kingdom was manifest during the Dillon Round of tariff negotiations and has further been accentuated in the Kennedy Round. In fact, in the public eye, the Kennedy Round has increasingly assumed the character of bilateral bargaining between the United States and the European Economic Community.

Mention should also be made of the balance of payments problem and the deterioration of the liquidity position of the United States and the United Kingdom. The United States ran an annual balance of payments deficit of about 2 or 3 billion dollars between 1958 and 1964, and her net monetary reserves fell by $12.6 billion during this period. Britain also experienced balance of payments difficulties and repeatedly employed deflationary measures to avoid a deterioration in the position of the pound sterling. In the same period continuing balance of payments surpluses led to an increase of $10.6 billion in the net reserves of the Common Market.[14]

[13] An early statement to this effect was made in London on January 25, 1966, by British Foreign Secretary Michael Stewart who declared that "we do regard wider European economic unity as essential [and] we shall continue to seek to work for it. Under the right conditions and at an appropriate time, we should be ready and willing to pursue this through membership of the EEC, together with such of our EFTA partners who wish to join us" (*EFTA Reporter*, January 31, 1966).

[14] International Monetary Fund, *International Financial Statistics,* Supplement to 1965–66 issue. Net monetary reserves have been defined as the differ-

Changes in reserves and balance of payments deficits will affect chiefly the bargaining strength of individual countries in international financial negotiations. Nevertheless, developments in the financial sphere will also influence the positions taken at trade negotiations. Despite the rise in long-term foreign asset holdings, the financial vulnerability of the United States and the United Kingdom may be judged by their increased short-term indebtedness, and other countries may attempt to use this situation to their own advantage in negotiating tariff reductions.

The Pattern of International Trade in 1964

It has been indicated that while the United States dominated the trade negotiations in the early postwar period and Britain was first in importance among European countries, the United States now faces a bargaining partner of comparable strength in the Common Market and the position of the United Kingdom has greatly weakened. But what of the future? What does the present pattern of international trade suggest about the interests of the various industrial countries in trade liberalization? To explore these questions, it will be useful to examine briefly the dependence of the individual countries and country groupings on foreign trade and the geographical and commodity composition of this trade.

A commonly used indicator of the relative importance of foreign trade is the share of exports and imports in the gross domestic product. However, GDP includes the activities of the service sector, the products of which are not traded; I have therefore chosen to compare the value of trade to value added in the sectors producing traded goods (agriculture, mining, and manufacturing).[15] On the basis of the average share of exports and imports, Canada and the Continental EFTA countries appear to be the most dependent on foreign trade, followed by the United Kingdom, the Common Market countries, Japan, and (at some distance) the United States (Table 1.2). The

---

ence between the gross gold and foreign exchange assets of the reporting country's monetary authorities and its indebtedness to foreign monetary authorities.

[15] Further adjustment would have to be made by adding service inputs, as well as the amount of imports used as inputs, to value added in the production of traded goods, so as to compare the value of trade to the value of production. In the absence of input-output tables for 1964 these adjustments could not be carried out.

TABLE 1.2   The Share of Foreign Trade in Value Added
in the Production of Traded Goods, 1964
(per cent)

		Export Share	Import Share	Average Share
United States		12.6	9.7	11.1
Canada		54.6	53.4	54.0
European Common Market	(a)	35.4	37.3	36.3
	(b)	20.0	22.3	21.1
European Free Trade Association	(a)	42.6	53.3	47.9
	(b)	33.2	43.4	38.3
United Kingdom	(a)	38.5	48.0	43.2
	(b)	33.6	42.7	38.1
Continental EFTA	(a)	48.1	60.5	54.3
	(b)	32.6	44.4	38.5
Japan		27.1	32.2	29.6

Sources: Value added (at market prices for France, Germany, and the
United States; at factor prices for others). Organization for Economic
Cooperation and Development, *General Statistics,* January 1965, and *National Accounts Statistics, 1955–1964,* Paris, 1966. Our estimates for
Sweden and Switzerland.

Foreign trade (exports at f.o.b. prices, imports as c.i.f. prices).
OECD, *Foreign Trade, Statistical Bulletins,* 1964. Our estimates for
U.S. and Canadian imports at c.i.f. prices.

Notes: (a) Total trade.
(b) Extra-area trade.

ranking changes somewhat if, in the case of the European Common
Market and the European Free Trade Association, we consider only
trade with nonmember countries. Still, extra-area trade amounts to
more than one-fifth of value added in the production of traded goods
in the EEC—approximately double the U.S. figure. The corresponding ratios are 54 per cent for Canada, 38 per cent for the United
Kingdom and the Continental EFTA countries, and 30 per cent for
Japan.[16]

Since this study focuses on trade liberalization among the industrial countries, we also need information on the relative importance

[16] In the case of the Continental EFTA countries, trade with the United
Kingdom was regarded as internal trade; the ratio rises to 44.5 per cent if trade
with all countries outside of Continental EFTA is considered.

for these countries of their trade with each other. Canada leads in this respect inasmuch as she carries out 85 per cent of her trade with industrial economies, followed by the Continental EFTA countries (80 per cent) and the countries of the European Common Market (70 per cent). The relevant proportions are 55 per cent in the case of the United States and about 45 per cent for the United Kingdom and Japan (Appendix Table 1.1).

These figures include, however, trade within the two European trading groups, EEC and EFTA. Intra-area exchange is especially important in the European Common Market; in 1964 the member countries carried out more than 43 per cent of their trade with each other.[17] Next in importance for the EEC is trade with the countries of the European Free Trade Association. The EFTA countries provided markets for 21 per cent of EEC exports in 1964 ($8.8 billion) and supplied 15 per cent of their imports ($6.5 billion). In the same year Common Market exports to the United States amounted to only $2.9 billion, although the United States weighs more heavily on the import side ($4.5 billion). Finally, the trade of the Common Market with Canada and Japan did not reach one-half of one billion dollars in either direction.

Intra-area trade is of lesser importance for the countries of the European Free Trade Association; it amounted to less than one-fourth of their combined exports and imports in 1964. Considerable differences are shown within EFTA, however. While trade between the United Kingdom and Continental EFTA accounted for only 12 to 13 per cent of the total exports and imports of each, the Continental EFTA countries carried out an additional 17 per cent of their trade with each other.

In the case of the United Kingdom, the nonindustrial Commonwealth countries had the largest share in both exports and imports in 1964 (35 per cent) with the Common Market following (18 per cent), but these comparisons have to be supplemented by information on changes over time. If we consider that United Kingdom exports to the EEC more than doubled between 1958 and 1964, whereas exports to the nonindustrial Commonwealth countries hardly changed, it will be apparent that the Common Market is rapidly gain-

[17] But this result also reflects the impact of the Common Market's establishment on trade flows. On this point see Bela Balassa, "Trade Creation and Trade Diversion in the European Common Market," *Economic Journal*, March 1967.

ing in importance over the Commonwealth in Britain's trade. Finally, the United States accounted for about one-tenth of United Kingdom exports and imports, Canada for 6 per cent, and Japan for hardly more than 1 per cent.

The trade of the Continental EFTA countries is concentrated primarily in Western Europe. Despite the distortions in trade patterns resulting from the establishment of two trading groups, the Common Market has remained their largest trading partner. Out of total exports of $11.7 billion and total imports of $13.9 billion in 1964, the exports of these countries to the EEC amounted to $3.9 billion and to their EFTA partners $3.7 billion, the corresponding import figures being $6.6 billion and $3.7 billion. During the same year, imports from the United States reached one billion dollars while exports were slightly lower. Finally, trade with Canada and Japan did not exceed $200 million in either direction.

The data point to the importance of intra-European trade for the countries of Western Europe: these countries carry out about three-fifths of their trade with each other while trade with the United States, Canada, and Japan taken together hardly exceeds one-tenth of their total- exports and imports. Intracontinental trade is of considerable importance also for Canada; in 1964, the United States provided 70 per cent of Canadian imports and took 54 per cent of her exports. At the same time, Canada is the single largest trading partner of the United States although, given the difference in the size of the two countries, it accounts for only about one-fifth of U.S. trade.

The industrial countries of Western Europe had 27 per cent of U.S. exports and imports in 1964, while Japan's share was slightly below 10 per cent. The United States looms large in Japan's trade, however, accounting for nearly one-third of her exports and imports. Japan trades relatively little with the other industrial countries; they accounted for only 14 per cent of Japanese exports, and for 15 per cent of imports, in 1964. In contrast, Japan carries out one-third of her trade with the countries of Southeast Asia and Oceania.

Since the prospects for trade liberalization among the industrial countries differ between commodity groups, the commodity composition of their mutual trade is also of interest. In providing information on the relative shares of the four major product groups,[18] internal

---

[18] Food, beverages, and tobacco (SITC classes 0 and 1), fuels (SITC 3), industrial materials (SITC 2+4+ unwrought metals), and manufactured goods (SITC 5+6+7+8=unwrought metals).

trade in the EEC and EFTA has been excluded because tariffs on this trade will be eliminated, regardless of the success of multilateral trade liberalization. The relevant data are shown in Appendix Table 1.2.

Among the major commodity groups, food, beverages, and tobacco account for about one-sixth of the exports of the United States, Canada, and Continental EFTA to the industrial countries, while the Common Market, the United Kingdom, and Japan are large importers of food. The former group of countries thus has a considerable interest in freer trade in foodstuffs; yet, as I noted in the introduction to this volume, the prospects for trade liberalization with regard to these products appear rather bleak.

Similar considerations apply to fuels, where quantitative restrictions have come to be applied to the imports of petroleum and petroleum products in the United States and to imports of coal in Western Europe. But since the industrial countries rely on petroleum imports from less developed areas, in their trade with each other these restrictions inhibit mainly U.S. coal exports to Western Europe and Canadian petroleum exports to the United States.

In contrast, industrial materials and manufactured goods are protected chiefly by tariffs that have been reduced on several occasions since the Second World War. These commodities are also in the center of current efforts to liberalize trade. But tariffs on manufactured goods are substantially higher than on industrial materials; therefore, multilateral reductions in duties among the industrial countries would tend to improve the balance of payments of countries that are large exporters of manufactures and importers of industrial materials and other primary products.

This is the case in Japan and, to a lesser extent, in the Common Market and the United Kingdom. All these countries have a substantial export surplus in manufactured goods and a high proportion of their imports consists of food, fuels, and industrial materials. In contrast, industrial materials provide 43 per cent of export earnings in Canada and 22 per cent in Continental EFTA; at the same time, the imports of manufactured goods are about double the exports of manufactures in both cases. Finally, although primary products provide more than 40 per cent of U.S. export earnings, the United States has an export surplus in trade in manufactured goods with the industrial countries.

Conclusion

This chapter has sketched the economic background for the subsequent discussion of trade liberalization among the industrial countries. Data on gross domestic products and on foreign trade have been used to indicate changes in the relative position of the industrial countries in the world economy, with special emphasis given to their bargaining strength at trade negotiations. It has been shown that, in the first half of the century, the United States made considerable gains over European economies and established itself as the dominant economic power on the world scene. The situation has changed in the period following the Second World War: rapid growth in continental Europe and the establishment of the European Economic Community have contributed to a deterioration in the relative position of the United States.

The largest trading nation at the turn of the century, the United Kingdom has steadily lost ground during the period under consideration. Following the establishment of the Common Market, Britain has come to play a secondary role in trade negotiations dominated by the United States and the EEC. The creation of the European Free Trade Association was a stopgap measure for Britain and, with the decline of its bargaining power and the decrease in the importance of Commonwealth trade, participation in the Common Market has become increasingly attractive.

Data on trade flows also indicate the interest of the Continental EFTA countries in reaching an accommodation with the EEC; in turn, while the countries of EFTA are the main trading partners of the Common Market nations. The countries of Western Europe carry on about three-fifths of their trade among themselves, whereas trade with the United States, Canada, and Japan, taken together, hardly exceeds one-tenth of their combined exports and imports. Distortions in trade flows due to the existence of the two trade blocs provide a further inducement for trade liberalization in Western Europe.

In turn, with the United States taking 54 per cent of her exports and providing 70 per cent of imports, the liberalization of trade in the North American area is of especial importance for Canada. The United States also accounts for two-thirds of Japanese trade with the industrial countries. But, for Japan, trade with the countries of Southeast Asia and Oceania is of comparable importance—hence her interest in trade liberalization in the Pacific region.

While much of the trade of the countries of Western Europe, as well as that of Canada and Japan, is regionally oriented, the U.S. trading interests are geographically more divided. The United States carries out more than one-fourth of its trade with Western Europe, 20 per cent with Canada, and nearly 10 per cent with Japan. Correspondingly, the United States has an interest in liberalizing trade in the entire industrial-country group. This conclusion is strengthened if we consider the effects on American exports of tariff discrimination in EEC and EFTA.

CHAPTER TWO

Political Considerations in the Liberalization of Trade

American Attitudes toward Integration in Western Europe

In the preceding chapter I examined the changes that have taken place in the economic position of the main industrial countries since the turn of the century. In this chapter I shall consider questions relating to the political objectives of trade liberalization for the industrial nations. Attention will be given to American attitudes toward integration in Western Europe and to the sharing of decision-making powers within the alliance. Further, the possible conflicts between national and international objectives and the implications of European integration for the Atlantic alliance will be discussed.

During the first half of the century, changes in political and military power relations by and large paralleled those occurring in the economic sphere. Two victoriously fought wars greatly strengthened the position of the United States, while losses suffered in times of war, and in the process of decolonization, weakened victors and vanquished alike in Western Europe. The military posture of the United States was further enhanced by the possession of nuclear weapons and the dependence of the countries of Western Europe on American power for protection against possible Soviet encroachment.

Changes in the political and military situation also led to a drastic revision of American attitudes toward European integration. Prior to 1945, proposals for integration in Western Europe were greeted with suspicion in the United States. Between the two wars, plans for the creation of a European union were considered detrimental to U.S. economic interests. Further, during the Second World War, American plans for establishing a new world order in collaboration with the Soviet Union left little room for regional arrangements.

A reappraisal of the issue of European integration occurred as the period of unqualified optimism concerning the continuation of wartime alliances gave place to mistrust of Soviet motives and policies. Whereas a few years earlier the U.S. government had resisted attempts to create a European regional organization within the framework of the United Nations, by 1948 the Administration not only accepted the idea of European integration but also became its leading champion. The shift in the American position is exemplified by the U.S. reaction to British attitudes toward European organizations. At the end of the war, British suggestions for political and economic arrangements among the non-Communist countries of Europe encountered heavy criticism in the United States and were regarded as a manifestation of the pursuance of selfish interest on the part of the United Kingdom. A few years later, however, Britain's insistence on limiting European arrangements to intergovernmental cooperation came to be considered the main obstacle in the way of realizing American designs for the integration of Western Europe.[1]

The change in the American position reflects the influence of several factors. First, a negative consideration, the objective of resisting the presumed Soviet threat. Given the increased prestige of the Soviet Union after the defeat of the German armies and the uncertainties associated with political developments in war-devastated Europe, it was feared that without integration the individual countries of Western Europe might come under Soviet domination and the balance of power altered in favor of the Soviet Union. Moreover, European integration was assumed to lessen the chances for a renewed conflict between France and Germany.

The economic advantages of integration received considerable attention from the European Cooperation Administration, set up by the U.S. Congress to administer aid to Western Europe under the Marshall Plan. To begin with, a joint effort for economic recovery was assumed to be more effective than measures undertaken by each country acting on its own. Further, it was suggested that economic integration would contribute to higher living standards in the European countries by reducing the U.S. advantage with respect to the size of domestic markets. But while economic considerations were foremost in the minds of the ECA officials, political and military objectives dominated State Department thinking.

Military considerations assumed special importance at the time of

[1] For an interesting discussion see Max Beloff, *The United States and the Unity of Europe* (Washington: The Brookings Institution, 1963).

the 1948 Berlin crisis and the Korean war. The United States wanted to prepare for a Korean-type conflict in Western Europe while the development of atomic weapons in the Soviet Union necessitated a transformation in Western military strategy. With the American atomic monopoly broken, conventional forces were thought necessary to form the first line of defense, and integration appeared as a means of sharing the burden of establishing these forces with European countries. By providing safeguards against the unilateral employment of German forces, integration also offered a solution to the problem of German participation in the defense of Western Europe.

The military advantages of European integration were emphasized by General Eisenhower, who expressed the view that "it would be difficult to overstate the benefit, in these years of stress and tension, that would accrue to NATO if the free nations of Europe were truly a unit." [2] Republican leaders joined the Truman Administration in supporting the establishment of a European army, and U.S. officials played a leading role in the negotiations for a European Defense Community. Subsequently, during the Eisenhower Administration, the EDC became the cornerstone of Dulles' policy in Western Europe.

The United States and the Common Market of the Six

The defeat of the EDC Treaty in the French parliament was a setback for Dulles, who accepted with reluctance the British-sponsored scheme for a Western European Union as a partial substitute for the European Defense Community. The American attitude toward European integration nevertheless remained favorable; there was, however, a change in emphasis with regard to the underlying objectives. With the economic recovery of Western Europe and the passing of the immediate Soviet military threat, the U.S. preoccupation with integration became predominantly political, closely related to the expected continuation of the cold war.

A united Europe was to play an important part in the system of world-wide alliances, the establishment of which was the major objective of American foreign policy at the time of Dean Acheson and, particularly, John Foster Dulles. One of the basic tenets of this policy was that integration would strengthen the U.S.-led forces of the Western world by increasing the cohesion of Western Europe. The general

[2] Dwight D. Eisenhower, speech before the English-Speaking Union in London, July 3, 1951, reported in *The New York Times,* July 4, 1951.

presumption was that, rather than following an independent policy, a united Europe would continue to accept American leadership.

The predominance of political objectives also explains the U.S. preference for closer ties among a small number of European countries over larger but looser groupings. This policy has been followed since the early fifties when successive British governments—Labour as well as Conservative—expressed their hostility to integration schemes that would infringe on British national sovereignty. In line with this policy, U.S. officials played an important role in convincing West Germany to take part in the European Coal and Steel Community. After the fiasco of the EDC, the United States favored the establishment of the European Economic Community and the European Atomic Energy Community. Early American support of the proposal for creating a Common Market in the face of British opposition might have contributed to the success of this scheme, while the decision to provide fissionable materials and technical assistance in nuclear matters was instrumental in the conclusion of the Euratom treaty.

Political considerations further account for the rather unsympathetic attitude of the U.S. government toward the establishment of the British-sponsored all-European Free Trade Area. The political advantages of the loose trade grouping envisaged in the Free Trade Area proposal appeared negligible to U.S. policy-makers; at the same time, some Administration officials shared the opinion expressed in French circles that the United Kingdom had advanced this scheme in order to weaken the Common Market.

Nor did the United States assume a more positive attitude toward the European Free Trade Association after negotiations for a free trade area embracing all OEEC countries had broken down. According to a former State Department official, "the contrast between the strong and outspoken United States government support for the Common Market of the Six and the relatively noncommittal official American attitude toward the proposed Outer Seven Free Trade Area project was explainable by the overriding political importance of the Common Market as a stage in the development of the political unity of the Six whereas the Free Trade Area was viewed as a purely commercial arrangement." [3]

The United States also opposed early efforts at "bridge-building"

[3] Isaiah Frank, *The European Common Market: An Analysis of Commercial Policy* (New York: Praeger, 1961), pp. 127–28.

between the EEC and EFTA. For one thing, it was felt that the political benefits of such an arrangement would not compensate for the increased discrimination against U.S. exports. For another, Administration officials apparently believed that the negotiations aimed at reaching an accommodation between the two trade groups—successful or not—would interfere with the process of consolidation in the Common Market that was at the time the principal American policy objective in Western Europe.

Subsequently, the United States supported the British decision to apply for entry into the Common Market largely on its political merits. Britain's entry would have furthered the cause of integration in Western Europe and it was assumed that British membership would strengthen U.S. influence in the EEC.[4] In turn, political considerations led the United States to take a stand against the association of the neutral EFTA countries—Austria, Sweden, and Switzerland—with the Common Market. The U.S. view appears to have been that the Common Market would be diluted through association agreements with neutral countries and that the latter should not enjoy the economic advantages of integration without accepting the political implications of the Community. In this respect, the American position was more rigid than that of several EEC countries that valued trade ties with Austria, Sweden, and Switzerland and were less sensitive to the political implications of their continuing neutrality.

American efforts aimed at enlarging the Common Market were frustrated when General de Gaulle decided to block British entry. In fact, the arguments marshaled by the United States in favor of Britain's entry into the EEC are likely to have contributed to the French opposition to it. Thus, according to De Gaulle, "the cohesion of all of [the] members [of a larger Community], who would be very numerous and very diverse, would not hold for long and . . . [at] the end

[4] According to Max Beloff, "it was felt in Washington that on the great issues of East-West relations, disarmament, and attitudes to the developing countries, the British position might prove nearer to that of the United States than the positions of Western Germany or France, and that Britain's voice would consequently tend to urge the European Community as a whole along lines satisfactory to the United States. Britain might also help to check tendencies in the Six to become too protectionist and inward. Finally, with Britain in the Community, the preeminent significance of the Atlantic alliance was unlikely to be overlooked, and the United States could proceed in its endeavors to construct an Atlantic Community." Max Beloff, cited, p. 16.

there would appear a colossal Atlantic Community under American dependence and leadership which would soon completely swallow up the European Community." [5]

British Prime Minister Harold Macmillan's decision to accept the Polaris missiles offered by President Kennedy at their Nassau meeting on December 18–19, 1962, might also have been instrumental in the breakdown of the Brussels negotiations. This decision, taken without previous consultation with France at the time the United Kingdom applied for membership in the EEC, was regarded by De Gaulle as a manifestation of Britain's policy of relying on the United States for her defense and of limiting her ties with continental Europe to purely economic questions. While opinions differ as to whether the Nassau agreements prompted De Gaulle's refusal to British entry into the EEC, it may be assumed that he would have acted differently had Macmillan expressed willingness to concert the efforts of the two countries in matters of nuclear defense. [6]

Thus, in their endeavor to reach an agreement with regard to nuclear weapons, Kennedy and Macmillan appear to have contributed to the failure of their common objective of ensuring British entry into the Common Market. The position taken by the United States and the United Kingdom seems to indicate a lack of adequate consideration of the interrelationships of political, military, and economic integration. The interdependence of decisions in these three areas was emphasized in France by Gaullists and non-Gaullists alike, and it was restated by Jean Monnet a few months after the breakdown of the Brussels negotiations. In an interview published in *The New York Times* on April 18, 1963, Monnet expressed the opinion that "it is difficult to conceive that the peoples of Europe will engage themselves toward a common economic destiny without engaging themselves to-

[5] Press conference on January 14, 1963, reprinted in *Major Addresses, Statements and Press Conferences of General Charles de Gaulle, May 19, 1958–January 31, 1964* (New York: French Embassy, Press and Information Division), p. 214.

[6] In an *aperçu* of De Gaulle's seven-year reign, *Le Monde* (November 27, 1965) noted that "the Nassau accords appear to have played a decisive role in De Gaulle's attitude toward the British candidacy. In the course of Macmillan's visit to Rambouillet a few days before Nassau, the General had made a suggestion to him, which the Prime Minister left unanswered, concerning the joint production of strategic missiles; instead, Macmillan hastened to negotiate with Kennedy with the exclusion of France the replacement of Skybolt missiles . . . by the Polaris."

ward a common political destiny and, necessarily, that leads them to have a common defense."

The British view, too, appears to be changing. Macmillan's successor, Sir Alec Douglas-Home, stated two years after the breakdown of the Brussels negotiations: "When the time comes to cement an agreement with Europe, it will be economic and political and in due course will cover security, for these three must go together." [7] And while Prime Minister Harold Wilson's position on this issue has not been made clear, there is little doubt that a Labour government, too, would have to consider problems of economic integration together with Europe's political future, and political cooperation would sooner or later be followed by a review of defense arrangements.

The United States and Atlantic Partnership

The breakdown of the Brussels negotiations marked the end of a phase in U.S.–European relations characterized by unchallenged American superiority in economic and political matters. Just as the Second World War strengthened the dominant position of the United States in the world economy, the fragmentation of Western Europe into national states and their dependence on the military power of the United States against the presumed Soviet threat contributed to U.S. political supremacy. Subsequent changes in political, military, and economic factors have altered power relations among the Western nations, however.

The rapid growth of the national economies of continental Europe, along with the atmosphere of *détente* between East and West, have encouraged European countries to assert their independence from the United States in one matter after another. The establishment of the European Economic Community has further contributed to this trend. Thus, while the United States espoused the cause of European integration in the expectation that a united Europe would fit into the scheme of world-wide alliances under American leadership, the consequences of this policy have been rather different. Like Goethe's *Zauberlehrling*, the United States has come to confront an economically strong and politically ambitious Europe that—although only

[7] Speech at the National Conference of Young Conservatives on February 13, 1965, cited in Noel Salter, "Is Defense the Entry Ticket?" *Journal of Common Market Studies,* July 1965, p. 264.

partially integrated—appears less and less willing to accept guidance from the other side of the Atlantic.

In response to this situation came the "Declaration of Interdependence" and the emphasis on maintaining and strengthening the cohesion of the Atlantic alliance through a partnership between the United States and Western Europe. This objective found expression in President Kennedy's speech in Philadelphia on July 4, 1962: "The United States will be ready for a Declaration of Interdependence, that we will be prepared to discuss with a united Europe the ways and means of forming a concrete Atlantic partnership—a mutually beneficial partnership between the new union now emerging in Europe and the old American Union founded here a century and three quarters ago." But Kennedy appeared to be speaking of a distant goal, while several of the actions of the U.S. Administration created suspicion in the eyes of many Europeans that the proposed partnership would become a cover for American hegemony in a different form.

For one thing, a key provision of the Trade Expansion Act, calling for the elimination of all tariffs on commodities of which the United States and the Common Market, taken together, supply at least 80 per cent of world exports outside the Sino-Soviet area, appears to have been based on a miscalculation. The U.S. Administration reportedly held the view that the Common Market countries would welcome this proposal as a sign of the United States' determination to follow a liberal trade policy. It was further assumed that the 80 per cent rule would provide an inducement for admitting the United Kingdom into the Common Market since, without British participation, only a few products (such as margarine and aircraft) would qualify under this clause.

But while generally welcoming the American initiative to reduce tariff barriers and to limit the application of escape clauses, many Europeans looked askance at the proposal for eliminating duties on commodities that would have come under the 80 per cent rule in the event that Britain entered the Common Market. These commodities (chiefly machinery, railway equipment, automobiles, and organic chemicals) are the technically most advanced products entering world trade, and it was widely assumed that the United States was in an advantageous position in their manufacture. European newspapers quoted President Kennedy's January 25, 1962, message to Congress, according to which, "to a considerable extent, these are the goods where our capacity to compete is demonstrated by the fact that our exports greatly exceed our imports." Indeed, according to *The Economist* (March 24, 1962, p. 1094), the application of the 80 per cent clause would have entailed removing tariffs on $2.1 billion of U.S. exports to the enlarged Community and on $1.2 billion of U.S. imports.

At the EEC Commission, and in some of the Common Market countries, the continuation of tariff protection for technologically advanced products was considered necessary to exploit the advantages of large markets in the newly established Community through specialization and standardization. It was also claimed that the elimination of duties would weaken the bonds holding together the countries of the Common Market, of which the common tariff is the principal outward manifestation. Moreover, several commentators suggested that the United States' proposals were reminiscent of those made by Britain at the time the United Kingdom wanted to dilute the EEC through the establishment of an all-European Free Trade Area.

Although some of these objections appear to have been exaggerated, they give indication of the reaction of many Europeans to the American proposal for eliminating tariffs under the 80 per cent rule. In the defense field, complaints were voiced about the concentration of decision-making power in Washington. The allies were apparently not consulted on the adoption of the strategy of "flexible response" announced by Secretary of Defense Robert McNamara in June 1962. The new strategy meant a change in the role assigned to nuclear forces; these were no longer regarded as a preventive deterrent but as a means of ultimate defense. In the name of greater efficiency, McNamara also emphasized the need for a unified chain of command and proposed a division of labor by which the United States would supply nuclear weapons and retain the power of decision over their employment, while European countries would strengthen their conventional forces. To meet the objections directed against this proposal, at the Nassau meetings in December 1962 President Kennedy suggested the establishment of a multilateral nuclear force (MLF). But the multilateral force, too, came under criticism in Western Europe.

In opposition to the MLF proposal, it was argued that a multilateral force representing only 5 per cent of American nuclear power would be wasteful, while the participation of European countries in decision-making concerning its employment would be little more than a formality. In addition to the European members of the proposed directorate, the United States, too, would have retained a veto over the use of the MLF arsenal while remaining in exclusive control of atomic weapons outside the multilateral force. Since Britain and France would have given up the right of decision over much of their nuclear arsenal, the dependence of European countries on the United States in matters of nuclear defense would have increased under the scheme although these countries would have borne a larger share of the cost of nuclear armament.[8]

If we also consider that the U.S. Administration reacted rather impatiently to European criticism of its policy in the Dominican Republic and in Vietnam, it would appear that the change in American thinking with regard to U.S.–European relationships has been less than references to "partnership" and "interdependence" would indicate. One may also agree with Henry Kissinger that "many American schemes for strengthening NATO have taken the form of making our predominant position psychologically more acceptable; we try to create a structure which physically prevents any ally (except the United States) from acting autonomously. This tends to turn our Allies into advisers in an American decision-making process." [9]

Correspondingly, proposals made for developing an Atlantic partnership and increasing cohesion within the alliance have often appeared as an effort to "keep the allies in line" and to persuade the recalcitrant ones to return to the fold. But while this might have been an appropriate objective at the time a Stalinist Russia appeared to threaten Western Europe and dissension among the allies would have undermined the West's defense, the situation has since changed to a considerable extent. With the lessening of the threat of an armed conflict, the scope for differences of opinion has increased and Euro-

[8] In Stanley Hoffmann's view, "the plan for a multilateral force appears to be partly a formal concession (the strategic usefulness of which is recognized to be mediocre), partly a means to make the Europeans assume a greater share of the financial burdens of the common defense, and partly a clever way of controlling their future military and political course." Stanley Hoffmann, "De Gaulle, Europe, and the Atlantic Alliance," *International Organization*, Winter 1964, p. 23.

[9] Henry A. Kissinger, *The Troubled Partnership* (New York: McGraw-Hill, 1965), p. 228. Ronald Steel goes even further in arguing that "We would like Europe to be united but still under American direction; we would like it to be militarily strong, but to permit us a monopoly of the West's nuclear power. We speak of 'interdependence' but by it we mean that the United States should be independent of Europe, while our allies should be dependent on us." Ronald Steel, *The End of Alliance* (New York: Viking, 1964), p. 66.

peans, who accepted a relationship based on inequality in the immediate postwar years as a matter of course, are increasingly reluctant to do so.

It would be a mistake to assume that the desire to alter existing relationships within the Atlantic alliance is limited to General de Gaulle and his followers. For one thing, as far as relationships with the United States are concerned, one should not draw too sharp a contrast between the Gaullist position and that of the Center-Left opposition in France. While opposition leaders have strongly criticized De Gaulle for his rejection of the principle of supranationality in the Common Market, they too have demanded the transformation of the present system of alliance. In the defense field, Maurice Faure, the leader of the Radical Party, proposed the establishment of a European nuclear force instead of the MLF.[10] In turn, the influential Club Jean Moulin, while opposing the development of the French *force de frappe,* took a position in favor of a unified Atlantic nuclear force, managed jointly by the United States and an integrated Europe.[11] In the economic sphere, André Philip, a leading socialist spokesman, suggested postponing the Kennedy Round of tariff negotiations until Europe was economically and politically unified.[12] Finally, the former Socialist candidate for the French presidency, Gaston Defferre, claimed that the Gaullist policy on foreign investments might lead to the colonization of France by American interests. Defferre expressed the view that only through the establishment of a unified Europe would it be possible to assure the independence of France in the face of the Soviet Union and the United States.[13]

Indications are that British policy will also tend to be more independent of the United States, whether a Labour or a Conservative government is in power. Demands for reducing the present asymmetry in power relations within the alliance have been put forward with increased frequency in Germany as well. Willy Brandt, the leader of the Social Democratic party, repeatedly stated that Germany—a "giant" in economic relations—cannot remain a "dwarf" in the political sphere. Moreover, the controversy concerning atomic weapons at the time of the 1965 elections indicated the German desire to participate in decisions about the employment of nuclear forces.

10 *Le Monde hebdomadaire,* February 20–26, 1964.
11 *Le Monde hebdomadaire,* April 9–15, 1964.
12 *Le Monde,* October 28, 1964.
13 *Le Provençal,* April 29, 1964.

The Objectives of Atlantic Partnership

It appears, then, that the Atlantic alliance, based on American supremacy, is an outdated concept and can no longer provide a basis for U.S. policy-making. Instead, cohesion or partnership should be interpreted to mean concerted action with regard to common interests when the determination of the objectives, as well as the choice of the measures employed, is undertaken jointly by the partner countries. Sharing in the decision-making powers is of fundamental importance since the continuation of U.S. policy based on the assumption that Europeans will accept the objectives and strategy formulated in Washington is bound to increase dissension within the alliance.[14] Rather than reluctantly giving concessions in matters in which the cooperation of Western Europe is absolutely necessary, such as international monetary arrangements, an imaginative effort is needed whereby the United States would invite European participation in areas that have so far been considered exclusive American domain.

But what is the meaning of a partnership between independent political units with partly conflicting goals? And is cohesion within the Atlantic area a goal *per se,* relating solely or principally to internal matters, or is it a means to serve external objectives? While internal objectives such as the safeguarding of democratic institutions in European countries and the avoidance of future military conflicts between France and Germany were of considerable importance in the early postwar period, it would appear that the principal political objectives of the countries of the Atlantic area are to be found in their relationship with the outside world. These objectives include defense, the furthering of democratic institutions throughout the world, and the raising of living standards in less developed countries. In turn, among internal objectives the harmonious economic development of the countries of the Atlantic area occupies central place.[15]

So long as the possibility of an armed conflict between East and

[14] A statement in *The Economist* (December 12, 1964, p. 1219) may be instructive in this regard: "Unless it is feasible to hold out to the Europeans the possibility of one day standing on equal and independent terms with America in the things that really matter (which means economic power, and probably nuclear power as well), a majority of them will sooner or later decide that General de Gaulle was right after all, and the alliance will collapse from the dry rot of European resentment."

[15] It should be added that, for the United States, economic growth in the other industrial countries is also a political objective; the United States is espe-

West exists, the defense of the countries of the Atlantic area necessitates cooperation in political and military matters between the United States and Western Europe. But, since internal changes underway in the Sino-Soviet Area permit considerable flexibility, the character of this cooperation is changing and future developments are difficult to foresee. Nevertheless, whatever form military cooperation may take, it is likely to require some form of European participation in decision-making on the employment of nuclear forces or, failing this, the creation of an independent European deterrent.

As regards policies toward less developed countries, the military "payoff" of granting foreign aid has often been emphasized.[16] Yet, with the availability of intercontinental and submarine-based missiles, the importance of military bases in these countries is on the decline. Nor do these bases have much significance for the deployment of conventional forces. From the point of view of the United States—or the Soviet Union—it makes little difference whether American missiles are placed in Turkey, for example, and defense considerations alone may not justify the large-scale dispensation of foreign aid to the countries of Southeast Asia.

Rather than military considerations, the main issue for both East and West in their relationships with developing countries appears to be power and prestige. It is customary to speak of a struggle between ideologies when the choice of the form of government in less developed areas is taken as a measure of success or failure. But more important is the desire to gain the support—or at least to avoid the hostility—of developing countries in the political arena. On the one hand, attention is given to the position taken by the most prestigious of these countries, the utterances of whose leaders are often assumed to reflect world public opinion; on the other, efforts are made to win votes on controversial issues, such as the admission of Communist China into the United Nations. By concentrating aid in a few nations, the Soviet Union appears to attach special importance to winning friends among key countries while the United States often seems to be "counting heads" in an attempt to increase the number of favorable votes in the United Nations Assembly.

---

cially interested in an improvement in the economic performance of the United Kingdom.

[16] For a detailed discussion of related issues, see John Pincus, *Trade, Aid and Development: The Rich and Poor Nations* (New York: McGraw-Hill, 1967).

Some attempt instead to justify foreign aid on the basis of economic self-interest by arguing that the increased demand for imports on the part of less developed countries would contribute to full employment in industrial economies.[17] But the assumption underlying this argument, according to which domestic economic policies in industrial countries are not sufficient to maintain full employment, is hardly warranted. Thus the export surplus financed by foreign aid is likely to represent a redistribution of income rather than an addition to it.

A redistribution of incomes between nations can be rationalized on moral grounds. However, such a redistribution appears to be also in the self-interest of the developed countries. With gross domestic products rising at a rate higher in developed than in less developed economies, and continuing rapid population growth in the latter, absolute as well as relative differences in living standards would widen to a considerable extent. Sooner or later this situation is bound to have unfavorable political repercussions and might increase the strength of forces hostile to the West.

Similar considerations apply to the trade relations of the industrial economies with developing countries. Trade is a partial substitute for aid, and trade arrangements among the industrial nations have a bearing on economic growth and on improvements in living standards in less developed areas. Accordingly, in evaluating alternative methods of trade liberalization, special attention should be given to the interests of the developing countries. The implications of this conclusion on the choice among alternative trade arrangements will be examined in the final chapter of this study.

Conflicts between National and International Objectives

It has been indicated that the countries of the West have common external objectives in their relationships with the Communist countries and the less developed nations. More generally, these countries have a vested interest in a world order in which basic freedoms are respected; and the similarity of their cultural patterns and social values, as well as their economic interdependence, provide further incentives for Atlantic cooperation. But while the countries of the Atlantic area

17 On this point, see, e.g., the international reserve plan presented by Albert Hart, Nicholas Kaldor, and Jan Tinbergen (UN Conference on Trade and Development, background document E/conf. 46/P/7. Geneva, 1964).

may agree on these goals, there are other political objectives, national as well as international, that may come into conflict. These include the creation of an "identity" for the Common Market, the idea of European unity, as well as the endeavor of individual countries to maintain their independence and to increase their prestige and power.

Aside from the common agricultural policy, the external tariff is presently the principal manifestation of the identity of the European Economic Community; an inducement is hence provided against the elimination of this tariff. Also, since the establishment of the Common Market has entailed a compromise of national interests, some of the member countries may be reluctant to agree to modifications in certain fields lest these lead to changes in others. It has been argued in France, for example, that in case of a substantial reduction in the common external tariff, the Germans and the Belgians may be reluctant to keep other parts of the bargain, such as the purchase of much of their food requirements from France.

The idea of European unity has appeared in various forms in the individual countries of Western Europe and among persons of different political persuasions. This idea is especially strong in the Netherlands and Germany although public opinion polls indicate support by a great majority in Italy, Belgium, and France as well. According to a Gallup poll conducted in 1961, in none of these countries does the number of the opponents of European integration reach one-tenth of the total.[18]

There is little concern about European unity in the Scandinavian countries, however, although some differences in opinion exist among them. A sense of identification with Europe as a political entity is not entirely missing in Denmark, but many Norwegians would prefer political arrangements with the United States and the United Kingdom to being submerged in a union led by Germany and France. Ethnic ties with the United States and the juxtaposition of the long-established democracies of North America and northwestern Europe with the politically less stable regimes of much of continental Europe are often mentioned as factors bearing on this view. In turn, the long-standing neutrality and peculiar federal structure of Switzerland make it difficult for that country to take part in a European union.

While considerations of national power and prestige seem to have little importance for the countries of Scandinavia and Switzerland, they have considerable influence on foreign economic policy in

[18] "L'opinion publique et l'Europe des Six," *Sondages,* 1963 (1), p. 46.

France or Britain. In general, it would appear that the relative importance of political objectives for decision-making on foreign economic policy is related to the size of the country; whereas a small country is conscious of the fact that it cannot play an important role in world affairs, large countries are bent on improving, or at least maintaining, their power position.

Considerations of political power may have influenced De Gaulle's decision to veto the British application for entry into the Common Market, since Britain could have presented a threat to French leadership. With the increasing economic power and political ambitions of Germany, the situation may change, however; instead of a challenger for leadership, Britain may ultimately become a balancing force. This is reported to be the view of Michel Debré, the present Minister of Economic Affairs, for example. Finally, considerations of power balance within the EEC may have helped to persuade the French opposition parties to favor Britain's entry into the Common Market.

Changes in the British attitude toward participation in European integration projects, too, seem to have been in great part politically motivated. After World War II, when the idea of Britain taking part in the three interlocking circles represented by the Commonwealth, the North Atlantic area, and Western Europe was at its high point, a commitment to Europe appeared "unthinkable." [19] According to Churchill's famous words to De Gaulle, in case of a choice, the United Kingdom would have preferred maintaining ties with the United States to an arrangement with the countries of the European continent.

The Suez crisis made it clear, however, that Britain's special relationship with the United States was weakening while the emergence of a continental power center in the form of the European Economic Community provided a challenge to Britain's European policy. The first reaction on the part of the United Kingdom was to propose the creation of an all-European Free Trade Area that would have left intact Britain's relationships with the Commonwealth as well as her freedom in conducting commercial policy. Following the breakdown of the free trade area negotiations, the establishment of the European

[19] This is the expression Macmillan is reported to have used in a conversation with De Gaulle on April 5, 1960, in response to the latter's question whether the British government would contemplate joining the Common Market. Cited in Robert Kleiman, *Atlantic Crisis* (New York: Norton, 1964), p. 63.

Free Trade Association appeared as a stopgap measure. In turn, after early efforts to reach an accommodation between the EEC and EFTA came to nought and the successful operation of the Common Market contributed to the decline in the power position of the United Kingdom, Britain decided to apply for membership in the EEC.[20]

The failure of the protracted negotiations on entry into the Common Market gave rise to a disenchantment with European integration in the United Kingdom and led to proposals to strengthen EFTA, to establish a free trade area with the United States and Canada, or to turn again toward the Commonwealth. The latter alternative appeared to be foremost in the plans of the Labour party prior to the 1964 general elections, but the Labourites have subsequently come to realize the impossibility of transforming the Commonwealth into a tighter political or economic unit. At the same time, the Labour party's formerly hostile attitude toward participation in the Common Market has given place to a search for ways and means of assuring entry into the EEC.

While the desire to enter into the Common Market is evident in the United Kingdom, recent events on the continent have helped to improve the climate for a second British application. For one thing, the Five (Belgium, Germany, Italy, Luxembourg, The Netherlands) have often taken common positions in disputes with France; for another, the results of the French Presidential elections of December 1965, and the subsequent compromise solution of contentious issues that had caused a seven-month deadlock in the EEC, point to a softening in French attitudes. Nevertheless, as long as General de Gaulle is at the head of the French government, the prospects for British membership remain uncertain. Thus, rather than attempt a prognosis concerning Britain's chances for entry, I shall turn to the question of the relationship between European and Atlantic integration.

It has often been argued that there is no conflict between European

[20] The deterioration of the United Kingdom's power position has been vividly described in *The Economist* (May 18, 1963, p. 633) following the breakdown of the Brussels negotiations for Britain's entry into the EEC:

> The grandest victim of the common market's cold douche has been the illusion that Britain was still a world power, an illusion fostered by a heroic war record and by a touching faith in the welfare state. . . . The beginning of the free trade area negotiations coincided with the Suez fiasco; the disastrous end of the Brussels talks coincided with the discovery that Britain's strategic nuclear force could expect, in the future, to be "independent" only on American sufferance.

integration and increasing ties within the Atlantic area. Thus, in the opinion of the founder of the European Coal and Steel Community, Robert Schuman, "between the Atlantic idea and that of unified Europe there is neither antagonism nor confusion. Europeans . . . must reaffirm their Atlantic convictions at a time when the tasks confronting Europe are greater than ever before." [21] Most Europeans believe, however, that the two objectives cannot be pursued simultaneously, and that European integration should have precedence over Atlantic arrangements. Christian Herter, one of the most vocal supporters of Atlantic integration, noted that "Talks with European political leaders and others who have studied the problem of how to achieve greater unity [in the Atlantic area] have shown me that the great majority feel that Europe must settle its own integration before discussing with Canada and the United States the specific constitutional character of any greater Atlantic Community." [22]

But will European integration be conducive to Atlantic arrangements? The presumption to the affirmative underlay U.S. policy in the postwar period and led to American pressure first for integration in Western Europe and later for Britain's entry into the Common Market. Also, it is usually assumed that the opponents of De Gaulle's scheme for establishing a loose confederation rather than a federation in Western Europe are necessarily supporting wider Atlantic arrangements. The distinction made by John Pinder is symptomatic of this type of thinking. In his *Europe Against de Gaulle,* Pinder contrasts "Gaullists" and "Monnetists": the former are said to be opposed to European federation *and* integration in the Atlantic area while the latter appear as resolute champions of both.[23]

The reality is less simple. The opponents of De Gaulle's European policy often emphasize that independence from the United States presupposes the unification of Europe, since France alone can play only a secondary role on the world scene. Similar opinions have been expressed with increasing frequency in the United Kingdom. It has been noted that Britain's foreign policy could become more independent of the United States if European unity materialized; Britain might

[21] Robert Schuman, "The Atlantic Community and Europe," *Orbis,* Winter 1958, p. 409, cited in Frank Munk, *Atlantic Dilemma* (Dobbs Ferry, N.Y.: Oceana, 1964), p. 48.

[22] Christian A. Herter, "Atlantica," *Foreign Affairs,* January 1963, p. 300.

[23] John Pinder, *Europe against de Gaulle* (New York: Praeger, 1963).

have avoided, for example, making certain political commitments in the sterling crisis of the years 1964–65.[24]

Realism requires therefore that the United States be prepared for the eventuality that an integrated Europe will increasingly assert its independence. Still, one can hardly recommend following a policy of establishing closer relationships with some European countries, such as the United Kingdom and Continental EFTA, at the expense of others. Such a policy is likely to be regarded as an application of the principle of *divide et impera* and it would not fail to create resentment among the supporters of European unity. Correspondingly, whatever gain the United States might derive from closer relationships with some of the countries of Western Europe, she would have to pay the price of alienating other nations in the area.

But neither would such an alternative be in the interest of the United Kingdom. Given the asymmetry in power relations, an arrangement between the United States and Britain with the exclusion of the Common Market is not conceivable on the footing of equality and it would reduce rather than increase British influence in world affairs. On the other hand, the United Kingdom could play an important role within the Common Market, and may exert more influence on United States policy as a member of the EEC than as a participant of a U.S.-led group.[25]

[24] One may also recall a statement made in a different context by Reginald Maudling, the Conservative Shadow Chancellor, before the European Consultative Assembly in 1959:

> There must be one solution, and it must be a European solution, in the sense that it is a system for Europe whereby we do not discriminate against one another but we discriminate against the rest of the world; we treat one another, as Europeans, differently from the way we treat other countries, but we treat one another as Europeans in the same way as we treat all other Europeans.
>
> There are some people who say the opposite of that. They say that the [European Economic] Community must find its place in the world as a whole and not merely in Europe. They say that while it is true that the Community has problems in its relations with Scandinavia and Switzerland, it equally has problems of relations with the United States, Japan, and Costa Rica. I do not accept that point of view and I do not think that any of us who support the ideal of Europe as a unity can support that idea.

Cited in Miriam Camps, *Britain and the European Community, 1955–1963* (Princeton, N.J.: Princeton University Press, 1963), p. 191.

[25] In discussing "the weight of British influence in Washington," U. W. Kitzinger writes: "If one believes that even today Britain has a unique contribution to make in foreign policy, then one may well wonder whether, by giving up

Clearly, by pursuing a solution based on partnership with Western Europe, the United States takes the risk that a new European power center will follow its own objectives. But is this risk not worth taking if the alternative is likely to be increasing dissatisfaction on the part of Europeans with the continuation of present relationships within the alliance? The common interests that the United States and countries of Western Europe have with regard to Communist countries and developing nations, as well as in preserving Western cultural and social values, suggest an affirmative answer. The United States needs Western Europe and Western Europe needs the United States to strengthen their position toward the Soviet Union. The United States would be weakened considerably if she remained alone; in turn, the bargaining power of Western Europe vis-à-vis the East would decline without the support of the United States. Cohesion within the Atlantic Alliance tends to discourage the Communist countries to follow a "hard line," and there is little doubt that the Soviet Union will be more amenable to solving outstanding problems in the European area if she were not discussing these with the countries of Western Europe alone.

Common interests do not mean that the United States and Western Europe would take identical positions on all major issues of international politics, however. Differences in opinion exist in regard to Vietnam or Communist China, for example. In fact, attempts to attain uniformity are likely to be more harmful than useful since they tend to increase dissension within the alliance. Rather, it should be recognized that, in the present world situation, there is no need for agreement on all issues on the part of the United States and Western Europe. As Henry Kissinger has noted, "If we face the fact that the interests of Europe and the United States are not identical everywhere, it may be possible to agree on a permissible range of divergence [and] each partner will regain a measure of flexibility." [26]

Conclusion

The political objectives of trade liberalization and the political implications of alternative trade arrangements have been the subject of

---

what in twenty or thirty years' time may look a rather spurious independence of action, Britain would not . . . gain in effective influence if she were to enter the Community." *The Politics and Economics of European Integration* (New York: Praeger, 1963), pp. 153–54.

[26] Kissinger, *The Troubled Partnership*, cited, p. 233.

this chapter. I have argued that, in the postwar period, United States support for integration in Western Europe in general, and for the European Common Market in particular, was based largely on political considerations. This policy has had some unforeseen consequences: the bargaining strength of the Common Market countries has greatly increased and—in conjunction with the lessening of the chances of an armed conflict with the Soviet Union and the increased power and ambition of several European countries—there has been a tendency to reassert the independence of Western Europe from the United States.

In response to this situation came the emphasis on partnership and increased cohesion on the part of the United States. I have suggested that "cohesion" and "partnership" in the Atlantic area can serve a useful function by contributing to the attainment of the common objectives of the Western nations in their relationships with the Communist countries and less developed areas. This involves an understanding on basic principles in dealing with internal and external problems and the minimization of conflicts. Correspondingly, trade arrangements in the Atlantic area should aim at furthering cohesion through harmonious economic development within the area and lessening the possibility of conflicts when attention should be paid to the repercussions of alternative arrangements for developing countries.

At the same time, these objectives would not be appropriately served if the United States sponsored arrangements that would accentuate the imbalance in power relations on the two sides of the Atlantic. And while the emergence of a strong European power bloc would create possibilities for a divergence in policies between the United States and Western Europe, this should not cause undue concern. The basic interests of the two areas continue to be by and large the same and, at any rate, the world political situation permits a divergence of views on a wide variety of matters.

Political considerations, then, point to the conclusion that the United States should refrain from taking measures that would reduce the chances of integration in Western Europe. But U.S. actions relating to European integration have often been interpreted in the past as a manifestation of her desire for continuing hegemony. It may appear desirable, therefore, that the United States follow a policy of nonintervention in European affairs rather than attempt to "mold" the future destiny of Western Europe.

CHAPTER THREE

The System of Protection in the Industrial Countries

Trade Negotiations and The "Height" of National Tariff Levels

As an introduction to the inquiry into the economic effects of trade liberalization, this chapter will examine the measures used by industrial nations to restrict imports and protect domestic industry. The discussion will focus on tariffs that are the principal means of protection in the case of industrial materials and manufactured goods. Efforts made to measure the "height" of national tariff levels will be dealt with and attention will be given to questions relating to the structure of these tariffs. The chapter will close with a short discussion of nontariff barriers and their restrictive effects on trade in industrial products.

Traditionally, the international comparison of tariffs has been approached on the implicit assumption that the restrictiveness of duties [1] is proportional to their height and is the same for all countries and for all commodities. Obviously, these assumptions are not realistic since the responsiveness of import demand to changes in tariffs will depend on a variety of factors—the reaction of producers and consumers to price changes, the share of imports in domestic consumption and production, the substitutability of imports for domestic products, and so on—and it will differ from country to country as well as from commodity to commodity. Nevertheless, these

[1] The restrictive effect of the tariff refers to the reduction in imports brought about by the imposition of duties. The imposition of duties will usually lead to lower imports as a result of a fall in the domestic consumption and an increase in the home production of the protected commodities, of which the latter is referred to as the protective effect of the tariff.

assumptions have customarily been made, in part because of our ignorance regarding the various factors that influence the responsiveness of import demand, and in part because they permitted simple and straightforward comparisons of individual tariffs and of national tariff levels. I shall provisionally accept these assumptions so as to judge the efforts made to measure the "height" of national tariff levels on their own grounds, and shall remove them at a later point.

Attempts to compare the height of national tariff levels have been made since the turn of the century,[2] and these inquiries have been given added impetus by the establishment of the European Common Market and by the Kennedy Round of tariff negotiations. In international comparisons of tariff levels, two procedures have been generally employed: the calculation of weighted and unweighted averages of duties. Under the first alternative, tariffs on individual commodities are usually weighted by the imports of the country in question, which is equivalent to expressing the amount of duty paid in a given year as a percentage of the value of total imports. In turn, the second procedure entails calculating a simple (unweighted) average of duties from national tariff schedules.

There are numerous instances of calculating tariff averages by weighting duties with the country's own imports. This method has been used, for example, in a report of the Joint Economic Committee of the U.S. Congress to compare the restrictiveness of tariffs in developed countries.[3] But the use of the country's own imports as weights in averaging tariffs provides distorted results and cannot properly be used in making international comparisons. Under this procedure, low duties associated with high levels of imports are given large weight whereas high duties that restrict trade have small weight, and prohibitive duties do not figure in the calculation at all. Thus, while in the mid-fifties French tariffs exceeded duties in other Common Market countries in most categories of products, on the basis of tariff averages weighted by her own imports France would have been classified a low-tariff country. This result has been mainly due to the fact that highly protected manufactured goods had a small share and materials

[2] The earliest efforts were U.K. Board of Trade, Second Series Cd 2337, 1905, League of Nations, *Tariff Level Indices* (Geneva 1927), and J. G. Crawford, "Tariff Level Indices," *Economic Record,* December 1934, pp. 213–21.

[3] U.S. Joint Economic Committee, *Trade Restraints in the Western Community*, Report of Subcommittee on Foreign Economic Policy, 87th Congress, 1st Session (Washington: GPO, 1961).

bearing low duties a large share in imports into France.[4] Moreover, as the data of Table 3.1 indicate, tariff averages weighted by own imports tend to give a lower result than any other measure.

Table 3.1 also provides estimates of unweighted tariff averages for the United States and the European Common Market, prepared by the Committee for Economic Development in the United States and the Commission of the European Economic Community. The two sets of estimates differ to a considerable extent: while in the CED report the simple average of U.S. duties on nonagricultural commodities is given as 15.2 per cent and that of Common Market tariffs as 13.2 per cent, the results of the Commission's study are higher for the United States (17.8 per cent) and lower for the Common Market (11.7 per cent). The differences reflect the influence of various factors.

To begin with, in cases where the U.S. tariff classification gives a range rather than a single figure for a heading of the Brussels Tariff Nomenclature (BTN), the lower and upper limits of the range have been taken separately in the Commission's study and the BTN heading in question has been assigned double weight. Since U.S. tariffs are generally given in terms of a range for commodities with high duties, the tariff averages derived in this manner are subject to an upward bias. By contrast, estimates made by the Committee for Economic Development for the United States are biased downward because own imports have been used as weights in deriving tariff averages for the individual BTN headings. Finally, the discrepancies in the estimates relating to the Common Market are largely explained by the fact that while the CED used pre-Dillon Round duties in all cases, the Commission has adjusted the EEC tariffs for the reductions agreed upon in the course of the Dillon Round of tariff negotiations in 1961—although it has made no such adjustments in regard to U.S. duties.[5]

Aside from the differences shown in the cited estimates, the assumptions underlying the use of unweighted averages are open to criticism. This method of calculation assigns equal weights to all BTN headings under the supposition that the "law of large numbers" will lend meaning to the results. But the individual BTN headings differ in importance to a considerable extent. For example, in the

[4] Bela Balassa, *The Theory of Economic Integration* (Homewood, Ill.: Irwin, 1961), pp. 45–46.

[5] The reductions may have amounted to 5 to 10 per cent of the pre-Dillon Round level of tariffs.

TABLE 3.1 Alternative Estimates of Tariff Averages for the
United States and the European Common Market [a]
(per cent)

	United States			Common Market		
	All Goods	Agricultural Commodities	Nonagricultural Commodities	All Goods	Agricultural Commodities	Nonagricultural Commodities
Unweighted averages:						
EEC study	n.a.	n.a.	17.8	n.a.	n.a.	11.7 [b]
CED study	13.9	8.5	15.2	14.0	17.8	13.2
Weighted averages:						
Weighted by the country's own imports	7.6	6.7	7.8	8.3	14.3	5.6
Weighted by the combined imports of U.S. and EEC	8.1	7.0	8.5	10.2	19.9	6.5
Weighted by the other country's imports	12.1	25.6	7.7	8.3	7.4	8.8

Source: "The Height of the United States and EEC Tariffs," in Committee for Economic Development, *Trade Negotiations for a Better Free World Economy,* A Statement on National Policy by the Research and Policy Committee of the Committee for Economic Development (Washington, 1964), pp. 67–73; Marcel Mesnage, "Comparison statistique du Tarif Douanier Commun de la CEE, du Tarif des Etats-Unis d'Amérique et du Tarif de Royaume-Uni de Grande Bretagne et d'Irlande du Nord," Office Statistique des Communautés Européennes, *Informations Statistiques,* 1963 (3), pp. 101–23.

Notes: (a) The estimates have been derived from tariff rates relating to headings of the Brussels Tariff Nomenclature. The commodity composition applied is as follows: all goods (BTN 1–99), agricultural commodities (BTN 1–24), nonagricultural commodities (BTN 25–99).
  (b) Adjusted for tariff reductions in the Dillon Round.

Common Market countries, imports of automobiles (BTN 87.02) amounted to $667.6 million in 1962 as against imports of zinc articles for construction (BTN 79.05) of $14,000.

To give expression to the relative importance of individual commodities in international exchange while avoiding the distortions due to the use of own imports as weights, an appropriate solution would be to weight tariffs by the value of world trade.[6] A step in this direction has been taken by the Committee for Economic Development, which has calculated tariff averages for the United States and the European Common Market by using the combined imports of the two areas as weights (Table 3.1). But should we follow the CED in estimating an average of tariffs for *all* commodities entering international trade? Although calculations of this type have a long history, various considerations support the contention of the EEC Commission that tariff comparisons should properly be restricted to nonagricultural commodities.

The tariff is only one of several measures applied by the industrial countries to protect their domestic agriculture. It thus makes little sense to compare tariffs on agricultural products in the Common Market and the United States, when the EEC applies fixed as well as variable duties while the U.S. system of protection involves the use of price-support measures and quotas.[7] Neither would tariff comparisons be meaningful with the United Kingdom, which relies on subsidies for protecting domestic agriculture.

Accordingly, the usefulness of tariff comparisons is enhanced if the scope of the investigation is limited to commodities not subject to nontariff measures. But we face a further problem that has been largely disregarded in international tariff comparisons: the implications of duties on raw materials and intermediate products for the protection of goods at a higher level of fabrication.[8] It is easy to see

[6] Nevertheless, this method is not free of bias either, since the composition of world trade is affected by similarities in national tariff structures; e.g., trade in textiles is restricted by the high degree of all-round protection. (For further discussion, see my "Tariff Protection in the Industrial Countries: An Evaluation," *Journal of Political Economy,* December 1965, pp. 573–94.)

[7] The difficulties associated with the international comparison of duties on agricultural commodities are exemplified by a calculation made in the CED study. According to the latter, using U.S. imports as weights, the EEC tariff averages are 12.1 per cent if sugar is included and 9.6 per cent without sugar (same, p. 72).

[8] Several writers considered this problem in a national context, however. For references, see my "Tariff Protection in Industrial Countries: An Evaluation," cited.

that high duties on materials and intermediate products will raise the average level of tariffs but will reduce the degree of protection accorded to final goods by increasing the cost of material inputs.

We have therefore to distinguish between nominal and effective rates of protection; while nominal tariffs influence the consumer's choice between domestic and foreign goods, for the domestic producer the effective rate of tariff is relevant. In calculating the effective rate of protection, account is taken of duties levied on material inputs, and this measure will express the degree of protection of value added in the manufacturing process. For given world market prices, the effective rate of duty will indicate the excess in domestic value added, obtainable by reason of the imposition of tariffs, as a percentage of value added in a free trade situation.[9] The effective and the nominal rate of tariff will be identical if the weighted average of duties on material inputs is the same as the tariff on the final product; the effective tariff will be higher than the nominal rate of duty if the product bears a higher tariff than its inputs, and vice versa.

Assume, for example, that material inputs account for 60 per cent of the value of output of a given commodity in a free trade situation, and country A levies a 10 per cent duty on the materials and a 20 per cent duty on the product itself while B admits the materials duty-free and applies a 16 per cent tariff to the final product. According to the conventional analysis, the higher rate of duty in Country A would provide a greater degree of protection to the final product than does B's lower tariff, and the average of nominal rates of tariffs would also be higher in A. However, the rate of effective protection will be 40 per cent on the final product in country B as against 35 per cent in country A.[10] It follows that the protectiveness of national tariffs can-

[9] The effective rate of tariff (z) can be expressed by the use of a simple formula, where t and s refer to the nominal rates of duty on the final product and its material inputs, respectively, m stands for the material inputs coefficients and v for the proportion of value added to output in a free trade situation, all measured at world market prices. The application of this formula assumes given world market prices and the international immobility of labor and capital:

$$z = \frac{t - \Sigma\, ms}{1 - \Sigma\, m} = \frac{t - \Sigma\, ms}{v}$$

[10] The effective rate of protection can also be negative. Thus, in the above example, the effective duty will be -5 per cent if there is a 4 per cent tariff on the final product and 10 per cent on the material inputs. In such an event, the net effect of duties is an implicit tax on the domestic manufacture of the final commodity.

not be indicated by comparing nominal rates of duties or averages of these duties, weighted or unweighted.

Effective Duties in the Industrial Countries

I have concluded that, in international comparisons of the protectiveness of national tariffs, one should use effective rather than nominal rates of duties. In the present study, effective tariffs have been calculated for the principal industrial countries and country groupings —the United States, the European Common Market, the United Kingdom, Sweden, and Japan—which account for about 80 per cent of world exports and over 40 per cent of world imports of manufactured goods. The investigation has been limited to manufactured products; raw materials have been considered only as inputs. This solution has been chosen because the countries in question compete mainly in the field of manufactures that are protected largely by tariffs while quotas and subsidies predominate in agriculture.

Nominal and effective rates of duties for thirty-six manufacturing industries of the five countries (country groupings) under consideration are shown in Appendix Table 3.1.[11] In turn, Appendix Table 3.2 provides the country ranking of tariffs for each industry, the industry ranking of tariffs for each country, and unweighted averages of the latter rankings for the five countries (country groupings). In the same table, the thirty-six industries are also ranked according to the labor intensiveness of the manufacturing process, expressed in terms of labor input coefficients.[12]

With few exceptions, we find effective duties to be higher than nominal rates. This result is explained in part by the "graduation" of tariffs from lower to higher levels of fabrication and in part by the absence of tariffs on nonmaterial inputs (services) that do not enter international trade. The differences are especially pronounced (and effective rates are more than double nominal rates) in the case of textile fabrics and hosiery, leather, some chemical materials, steel ingots, and nonferrous metals. Since these commodities generally require little technological sophistication for their manufacture, they

[11] On the method of calculation, see the Appendix to this chapter. See pp. 178–184.

[12] Labor input coefficients have been calculated as the share of wages plus employer-financed social security payments in the value of output. Needless to say, these are aggregate figures and the labor intensiveness of individual products will vary within each of the thirty-six industries.

are actual or potential exports of the less developed countries. Correspondingly, the results provide evidence for the validity of complaints recently voiced by these countries concerning the protective effect of the tariff structure of industrial economies.[13]

Effective duties are lower than nominal tariffs in the case of printed matter and ships; in fact, in some of the countries, the protective effect of the low duties levied on these goods is more than offset by duties on their inputs, so that the effective rate of tariff is negative. Commodities admitted duty-free (for example, agricultural machinery in the United States and pig iron in Sweden) also have negative duties since at least some of their material inputs are subject to tariff. Finally, a comparison of the ranking of individual commodity categories according to nominal and effective rates of duties indicates that high tariffs on semimanufactures reduce the *relative* degree of protection in the case of most consumer goods (clothing and textile articles, shoes and other leather goods, sports goods, toys, jewelry) and investment goods (electrical and nonelectrical machinery, railway vehicles, airplanes).

The calculation of effective duties also affects the ranking of countries according to the degree of protection in individual industries. In terms of effective tariffs, the United States and Sweden appear more protective than nominal duties would indicate, while the opposite holds for the United Kingdom, the European Economic Community, and, especially, Japan. Thus, if comparisons are made by using effective rather than nominal rates of tariffs, the United States has a higher "rank" in regard to eight commodities and a lower rank with respect to three products; Sweden has a higher rank in thirteen cases and a lower rank in none. By contrast, in the case of the United Kingdom, upward adjustments are made in three instances and downward adjustments in nine; the relevant figures for the Common Market are five and ten, for Japan two and eleven. These changes in ranking are accounted for by the fact that the relatively low duties on materials in the United States and Sweden raise the protective effect of a given nominal duty in these countries.

In turn, the ranking of industries according to their effective duties is broadly similar among the industrial countries under consideration.

[13] Cf. United Nations Department for Economic and Social Affairs, *World Economic Survey, 1962*, Part I (New York, 1963), p. 79, and B. Balassa, *Trade Prospects for Developing Countries* (Homewood, Ill.: Irwin, 1964), p. 116.

Effective rates are generally high on textile fabrics and hosiery, clothing and shoes, steel ingots, and, with a few exceptions, on other textile articles (chiefly sacks, bags, and linen goods), sports goods, toys, and jewelry, as well as on automobiles, motorcycles, and bicycles. However, relatively low effective duties are shown for paper and printed matter, ships and airplanes, pig iron, rolling mill products, and nonferrous metals, and also for machinery and railway equipment.

The general tendency among industrial countries is to protect the domestic production of textile fabrics. The textile industry has long been the "sick man" of the manufacturing sector in many of these countries. At the same time, its footloose character, the relative simplicity of the technological process, and the labor intensiveness of its manufacture make the textile industry a candidate for becoming the first manufacturing export industry in many developing countries. Correspondingly, the main effect of the all-round protection of textile fabrics in developed nations is to retard the expansion of exports from less developed areas. Similar considerations apply to sacks and bags, toys and sports goods, and (among mechanical goods) to bicycles.

In most industrial countries effective duties are also high on consumer goods, including clothing and shoes, as well as on automobiles. A possible explanation is that in the case of these commodities cost differences are relatively small among industrial countries, while the possibilities of substituting foreign commodities for domestic merchandise are considerable and protectionist pressures are also strong. Whereas the opposing economic interests will influence—and moderate —tariffs on intermediate products and investments goods, there is no such countervailing force in regard to consumer goods, since the consumers rarely have a say in tariff-setting.

Effective duties are low on intermediate products, such as paper, nonferrous metals, and—with the exception of Japan—pig iron that utilize specific bulky inputs in their manufacture. Moderate levels of protection prevail in the case of machinery and railway equipment. These products are generally highly differentiated, and their international exchange contributes to lower manufacturing costs in all industrial countries. The low degree of protection for ships is largely illusory, however, since industrial countries generally provide subsidies to domestic shipbuilding; in turn, "buy national" provisions assist the domestic airplane manufacturers in some of the producing countries.

The question arises: Can these admittedly partial explanations of the structure of tariffs in the industrial countries be replaced or supplemented by the application of some general principle? One such principle is the labor intensiveness of the manufacturing process. It has been suggested that industrial countries, especially the United States, tend to protect labor-intensive industries.[14] Our results do not reveal such a tendency, however, and there appears to be no correlation between labor intensiveness and effective rates of duties in any of the industrial countries.[15]

It is suggested here that the explanation lies in the inadequacy of theoretical models of international specialization that rely on a single classifying principle such as the labor intensiveness of the production process. In appraising the structure of protection in the industrial countries, attention needs to be given to technological factors. It will then appear that these countries find it expedient to heavily protect industries where developing economies can easily compete, because labor-intensive production methods can be used *and* the technological process is rather simple. By contrast, low tariffs are levied on machinery and equipment, the manufacture of which is relatively labor-intensive but requires advanced technology and organizational know-how not available in less developed countries.

The next question concerns the similarities and differences in the protection of individual industries among the industrial countries. A

[14] Cf., e.g., Beatrice N. Vaccara, *Employment and Output in Protected Manufacturing Industries* (Washington, D.C.: The Brookings Institution, 1960), and William P. Travis, *The Theory of Trade and Protection* (Cambridge, Mass.: Harvard University Press, 1964), pp. 191–93.

[15] The rank correlation coefficients calculated between labor input coefficients and effective duties are between -0.08 and -0.14 in European countries and the United States, and -0.41 in Japan. With the exception of the Japanese case, the estimates are not significantly different from zero at the 5 per cent level of confidence, and the results are hardly affected if we calculate effective rates with regard to labor by assuming that capital is freely mobile between countries. For the United States, similar conclusions have been reached by Giorgio Basevi, who compared various measures of labor intensiveness on the one hand and effective duties calculated with respect to value added and to labor costs on the other. (Cf. his "The U.S. Tariff Structure: Estimates of Effective Rates of Protection of U.S. Industries and Industrial Labor," *Review of Economics and Statistics,* May 1966, pp. 147–60.)

comparison of the ranking of the commodity categories by effective tariffs indicates a large degree of correspondence in the structure of protection within Western Europe. Discrepancies are greater between the European countries, on the one hand, and the United States or Japan, on the other, and differences are the most pronounced between the United States and Japan, which are at the opposite end of the spectrum in terms of industrial development.[16]

Among individual products and product groups, synthetic and other chemical materials, as well as glass and nonmetallic mineral products, are high on the U.S. list of protected commodities. In the case of some synthetic and other chemical materials, the effective rate of duty is raised because the American selling price is used as a basis for levying duties on several of these products, while U.S. tariffs are notoriously high on glass and its manufactures. By contrast, agricultural machinery is admitted duty free in the United States and the degree of protection accorded to airplanes and automobiles is substantially lower in the United States than in the other industrial countries.

Agricultural machinery and airplanes are leading U.S. exports, whereas the observed disparities in tariffs on automobiles may be related to differences in the degree of substitutability of foreign for domestic cars in the United States as compared to European countries and Japan. Despite the inroads made by European producers in the American market, the possibilities for substitution between the large American and the small European cars appear rather limited. On the other hand, car manufacturers in European countries and Japan have to contend with the competing products of each other's industries, and governments use high tariffs to ensure safe outlets for domestic production in the home market. The consequences of a reduction in the degree of protection are evident in France and Italy, where the tariff cut following the establishment of the Common Market has led to an influx of foreign cars.

While a detailed examination of national tariff structures lies outside

16 Rank correlation coefficients, calculated for pairs of countries in regard to effective tariffs in thirty-six industries, are in the 0.65–0.85 range in intra-European comparisons, while the relevant coefficient is 0.40 between the rankings of effective duties in the United States and Japan. Finally, the rank correlation coefficient between effective tariffs in the various countries and country groupings on the one hand and an unweighted average of these rankings on the other is 0.732 in the case of Japan, 0.737 for the United States, 0.770 for the United Kingdom, 0.867 for Sweden, and 0.907 for the EEC.

the confines of this study, it may be added that effective duties are also high in the case of steel products and railway vehicles in Britain, miscellaneous textile articles (chiefly sacks and bags) and paper in the Common Market, metal castings in Sweden, and pig iron and rolling mill products in Japan. In turn, effective tariffs are relatively low on plastic and synthetic materials in the United Kingdom, on precision instruments in the Common Market and in Sweden, and on sacks and bags as well as on rubber products in Japan.

Effects of Tariffs on International Specialization

I come now to the question raised in the earlier part of this chapter regarding the "height" of national tariff levels. It will be recalled that estimates of the height of tariff levels are designed to indicate the restrictive effect of duties on imports. This in turn can be considered in two parts: the fall in consumption and the rise in domestic production of the protected commodities, when the nominal rate of tariff influences consumption decisions and the effective rate of duty is relevant for the domestic producer.

Let us first assume that import demand responds to changes in duties in the same way in every country and with respect to all commodities,[17] while exports are available at constant costs. Under these assumptions, the restrictive effect of national tariffs on imports would be proportional to the averages of nominal *and* effective duties, and an unambiguous conclusion in regard to the restrictiveness of tariffs in the individual countries could be reached as long as both the nominal and the effective tariff averages pointed in the same direction.

A comparison of tariff averages shown in Table 3.2 indicates that, among the five countries and country groups, the over-all average of nominal as well as that of effective duties is the highest in Japan, with the United Kingdom a close second and Sweden at the opposite end of the scale. The United States and the European Economic Community occupy the middle ground: the over-all average of nominal duties is slightly higher in the Common Market than in the United States, while the opposite holds true with regard to averages of effective tariffs.

Table 3.2 also provides information on averages of nominal and

[17] In other words, the price elasticities of import demand are assumed to be the same for every commodity and in all countries.

TABLE 3.2 Averages of Nominal and Effective Duties in the Industrial Countries, 1962
(per cent)

	United States		United Kingdom		Common Market		Sweden		Japan	
	Nominal	Effective	Nominal	Effective	Nominal	Effective	Nominal	Effective	Nominal	Effective
Intermediate products I	8.8	17.6	11.1	23.1	7.6	12.0	3.0	5.3	11.4	23.8
Intermediate products II	15.2	28.6	17.2	34.3	13.3	28.3	8.5	20.8	16.6	34.5
Consumer goods	17.5	25.9	23.8	40.4	17.8	30.9	12.4	23.9	27.5	50.5
Investment goods	10.3	13.9	17.0	23.0	11.7	15.0	8.5	12.1	17.1	22.0
All commodities	11.6	20.0	15.5	27.8	11.9	18.6	6.8	12.5	16.2	29.5

Source: Appendix Table 3.1 and United Nations, *Commodity Trade Statistics.*
Note: Tariff averages have been obtained by weighting with the combined imports of the five areas. For the composition of the four commodity groups, see n. 18 in text.

effective duties, calculated for two categories of intermediate products, for consumer goods, and for investment goods.[18] Semimanufactures whose main inputs are natural raw materials have been classified as intermediate products I, while all intermediate goods at higher levels of fabrication have been included in intermediate products II. Industries that produce intermediate as well as final goods have been classified according to the main uses of their products as determined from input-output tables.[19]

The results support my earlier conclusions regarding the general similarity of tariff structures in the main industrial countries. Thus the large share of products requiring specific and bulky resource inputs for their manufacture tends to reduce the average of effective duties for the first group of commodities in all the countries under consideration. Tariff averages are also uniformly higher for intermediate products at higher levels of fabrication and generally increase again in the case of consumer goods. However, a greater than average degree of protection of consumer goods is shown in Japan, and lower than average in the United States. Further, the EEC and the Swedish tariff structures appear to favor intermediate products at the lowest level of fabrication, while in the other industrial countries investment goods are the least protected.

Let us now remove the assumption that import demand responds to changes in tariffs in the same way in the case of every country and for all commodities. Tariff-induced changes in imports will then be affected by differences shown in regard to the responsiveness of domestic demand and supply to price changes, the ratio of domestic production and consumption to imports, and the structure of imports in the individual countries. For assumed values of these variables, I

[18] *Intermediate products I:* thread and yarn, wood products, paper and paper products, leather, synthetics, other chemical materials, nonmetallic mineral products, glass, pig iron, and nonferrous metals.

Intermediate products II: textile fabrics, rubber goods, plastic articles, miscellaneous chemical products, ingots and other primary forms of steel, rolling mill products, other steel products, metal castings, metal manufactures.

Consumer goods: hosiery, clothing, other textile articles, shoes, other leather goods, cleansing agents and perfumes, automobiles, bicycles and motorcycles, precision instruments, toys, sports foods, and jewelry.

Investment goods: agricultural machinery, electrical and nonelectrical machinery, railway vehicles and airplanes.

[19] I have not included printed matter and ships in any of these categories; the former has been omitted because of the special character of its trade, the latter because of the prevalence of subsidies.

have prepared illustrative estimates concerning the possible effects of the elimination of duties on imports into the individual countries.

To begin with, I have selected what may be considered "realistic" values of domestic demand and supply elasticities that express the percentage change in demand and supply in the individual countries in response to a 1 per cent change in price. It has further been assumed that these elasticities are the same within each of the four commodity categories and for all the industrial countries.[20] Still, the elasticities of import demand will differ from country to country by reason of the international differences shown in regard to the structure of imports and the proportion of imports in domestic production and consumption. Thus, for given domestic demand and supply elasticities, the larger the ratio of domestic production (consumption) to imports, the higher the elasticities of import demand.[21]

As explained in the Appendix to Chapter 4, I have assumed that the ratio of the consumption of competing goods to imports is 4 in the United States, 3 in the Common Market and Japan, 2.6 in the United Kingdom, and 2.2 in Sweden. For each country, production-import ratios have been taken to equal consumption-import ratios, and the same ratios have been applied to all four commodity groups.[22] Further, I have assumed that tariffs are removed simultaneously in the main industrial countries and that the parallel expansion of exports and imports does not affect the amount of imported inputs.

[20] The following domestic demand and supply elasticities have been assumed for the four commodity categories: Intermediate products I, $-.2$ and $.1$; Intermediate products II, $-.3$ and $.2$; Consumer goods, -1.0 and 0.8; and Investment goods, $-.3$ and $.3$. By comparison, Stern assumed demand and supply elasticities of $-.4$ and $.2$ for semimanufactures, $-.5$ and $.25$ for nondurable finished manufactures, and -1.0 and $.5$ for durable finished manufactures (Robert M. Stern, "The U.S. Tariff and the Efficiency of the U.S. Economy," *American Economic Review, Papers and Proceedings,* May 1964, pp. 459–79), while Floyd calculated a demand elasticity of $-.3$ and a supply elasticity of $.5$ for all commodities, taken together (John E. Floyd, "The Overvaluation of the Dollar: A Note on the International Price Mechanism," *American Economic Review,* March 1965), pp. 95–107.

[21] The relevant formula is $\eta_m = \eta(C/M) + \varepsilon(P/M)$, when C refers to domestic consumption, P to domestic production, and M to imports, while η and ε are the domestic elasticities of demand and supply and η_m the import demand elasticity.

[22] Consumption-import and production-import ratios have been assumed to be equal because most of the manufactured goods traded among the industrial countries are differentiated products that are imported as well as exported by the countries in question.

According to the results derived under these assumptions, the largest relative increase in imports would take place in Japan (39.9 per cent), followed by the United States (38.2 per cent), the United Kingdom (32.1 per cent), the European Common Market (28.2 per cent), and Sweden (15.4 per cent).[23] A comparison of these estimates with the tariff averages shown in Table 3.2 indicates that the small share of imports in domestic consumption (production) increases the restrictiveness of the American tariff to a considerable extent while the opposite conclusion applies to Britain and Sweden. Thus, while U.S. tariff averages are approximately equal to those of the EEC and are considerably lower than the averages of British duties, the United States is second only to Japan in terms of the restrictive effects of tariffs on imports.[24]

These results provide some indication of possible increases in the imports of manufactures in the industrial countries following an all-round reduction (elimination) of duties. In Chapter 4 I shall examine this problem in more detail and shall present estimates prepared on a commodity-by-commodity basis. I shall also consider there the implications that intercountry differences in export supply elasticities have for the effects of tariff reductions on trade flows.

The Tariff Disparity Issue

Aside from comparisons of tariff averages, in recent years much attention has been given to the dispersion of duties around the average. Raymond Bertrand first advanced the proposition that the protective-

[23] The following formula has been used in the calculations:

$$\frac{dM}{M} = \Sigma_k (\eta_k \frac{C_k}{M_k} \bar{t_k} + \varepsilon_k \frac{P_k}{M_k} \bar{z_k}) \frac{M_k}{M}$$

when subscript k refers to the individual commodity categories and barred values denote arithmetic averages of nominal and effective tariffs, respectively, calculated by using the combined imports of these countries as weights. For the derivation of this formula, see my "Tariff Protection in the Industrial Countries: An Evaluation," cited.

[24] The sensitiveness of the results to changes in the stated assumptions should also be noted. For example, the estimated percentage increase of imports into the United States would be 42.0 instead of 38.2 if the assumed values of domestic demand and supply elasticities were adjusted upward by one-tenth, or if the U.S. ratio of consumption to imports was 4.4 rather than 4.0.

ness of duties increases with their dispersion.[25] This argument has subsequently been taken up by the EEC Commission in the course of the Kennedy Round of tariff negotiations, and the proposition has been advanced that the greater dispersion of the tariff distribution in the United States, compared to the European Common Market, increases the restrictiveness of U.S. tariffs.

The dispersion of tariffs is indeed greater in the United States than in the Common Market, in part because the common external tariff of the EEC has been derived by averaging Benelux, French, German, and Italian duties. The data of Table 3.3 indicate that Common Market duties on nonagricultural commodities cluster in the 5 to 20 per cent range while in the United States a substantial number of tariffs fall outside this range. In particular, U.S. duties are below 5 per cent in 22.0 per cent of the cases and exceed 20 per cent for 28.1 per cent of the commodities considered; the corresponding percentages are 14.4 and 8.1 in the European Common Market.[26]

But is there a positive correlation between the dispersion of tariffs and their protective effect? Aside from the case when protection is excessive in the sense that a small reduction of tariffs would not stimulate imports at all, there is no *a priori* reason to assume that the protectiveness of tariffs would increase with their dispersion. There is no presumption, for example, that a 20 per cent duty on refrigerators and a 10 per cent tariff on washing machines would restrict imports more than a 15 per cent tariff on both.[27] At any rate, should the protectiveness of tariffs increase with their dispersion, a proportional

[25] Raymond Bertrand, "Comparaison du niveau des tarifs douaniers des pays du Marché commun," *Cahiers de l'Institut de Science Economique Appliquée,* Série R, No. 2, February 1958.

[26] The greater dispersion of U.S. duties is also indicated by the conventional statistical measures, although the differences are reduced if effective rather than nominal duties are considered. The standard deviation of the U.S. tariff distribution, derived from the data of Appendix Table 3.1, is 6.9 for nominal duties and 16.6 for effective tariffs. The relevant figures for the Common Market are 3.6 and 11.5.

[27] Harry G. Johnson notes that, in case of multilateral reductions in duties, the country with a greater dispersion of tariffs would experience a slightly larger increase in imports. (See his *The World Economy at the Crossroads* [Oxford: Clarendon Press, 1965], p. 61n.) The numerical importance of this difference is negligible, however, and can readily be disregarded for practical purposes. In the example cited above, the elimination of tariffs would lead to 39.7 per cent increase in the former case and 39.1 per cent in the latter if imports of the two products were of equal value and had an import demand elasticity of −3.0.

reduction in duties would lead to a larger increase in the imports of the country where the dispersion of the tariff structure was greater.

It appears, then, that the issue of tariff dispersion has economic significance only if tariff rates contain "water" and hence a small reduction in duties would not stimulate imports at all. Apparently this is what the EEC Commission had in mind when it shifted from the discussion of tariff dispersion to that of tariff disparities—the differences in the rates of duty on particular items. The Commission has

TABLE 3.3   The Distribution of Tariffs on
Nonagricultural Commodities, 1962
(per cent)

	United States	*Common Market*
No duty	10.4	8.1
(per cent)		
0.1– 0.9	4.0	1.9
1.0– 4.9	7.6	4.4
5.0– 9.9	13.2	15.1
10.0–14.9	24.5	29.0
15.0–19.9	12.2	33.4
20.0–24.9	9.3	7.3
25.0–29.9	7.6	0.6
30 and above	11.2	0.2
	100.0	100.0

Source: Committee for Economic Development, *Trade Negotiations for a Better Free World Economy* (Washington, 1964), p. 74.
Note: Tariff rates relating to BTN headings have been used in the calculations.

suggested that the question of tariff disparity should be dealt with by devising special rules for cases where one country's tariff on a given product is twice as high as that of another country *and* there is at least a 10 per cent spread between them. In such instances the country with the lower duty would reduce tariffs by one-half of the cut undertaken by its trading partner.

The disparity rule is directed chiefly against the United States, since a number of U.S. tariffs exceed the corresponding Common Market duty by 10 per cent or more. While, presumably for reasons of political expediency, the United States has apparently accepted the general proposition that tariff disparities should be reduced she has put forward two modifications to the rule proposed by the EEC. According to the first, it is presumed that no disparity exists if the high-tariff country imports substantial quantities of the product; secondly, the disparity rule is not to be applied if a country other than the United States is the principal supplier. In this way the scope of application of the disparity rule would be reduced from about one-fifth to one-tenth of U.S. exports, and the interests of third-country suppliers, too, would be taken into account.[28]

The question remains whether the U.S. tariff indeed provides excess protection so that reduction in duties would not lead to higher imports. Robert E. Baldwin convincingly argues that after the successive tariff reductions of the last two decades, "it is very unlikely that there is any appreciable degree of 'water' in the United States tariff structure." [29] Nevertheless, tariff reductions were selective, and hence excess protection might have been maintained on *some* commodities. The most likely candidates are the products on which the rate of duty on import value is raised through the use of the American selling price in levying tariffs. But this question can best be handled independently from the general problem of tariff reductions; it will be discussed in the following section devoted to nontariff barriers to trade.

Nontariff Barriers to Trade

In addition to tariffs, various kinds of government regulations and practices may interfere with the international exchange of commodities. For one thing, tax regulations often affect exports and imports differently than they do goods produced for domestic consumption; for another, governments use a variety of nontariff measures to restrict imports and, in a lesser degree, to promote exports. These measures will be briefly reviewed in the following section.

The first question relates to the effects of intercountry differences in the system of taxation on trade among the industrial countries. In-

[28] In the case of the application of the rules suggested by the Common Market, the Swiss watch industry would have been unfavorably affected, for example, since in view of the high U.S. tariffs, the EEC duty on watches would have been reduced by less than the average.

[29] R. E. Baldwin, "Tariff-cutting Techniques in the Kennedy Round," in Richard E. Caves, H. G. Johnson, and P. B. Kenen (eds.), *Trade, Growth, and the Balance of Payments*, Essays in Honor of Gottfried Haberler (Chicago: Rand McNally, 1965), p. 72.

direct taxes (sales tax, turnover tax, excise tax) are used to a considerable extent in Western Europe while the United States relies chiefly on direct taxes (personal and corporate income tax), although some items of current consumption and automobiles are subject to excise taxes in the U.S. In levying indirect taxes on products traded internationally, the so-called destination principle is applied: the exporting country's tax is rebated when the product crosses the frontier and the importing country's tax is imposed on it. But this procedure does not necessarily put the imported commodity on a competitive footing with the country's own products so far as taxes are concerned.

To begin with, an investigation conducted by the OECD has indicated that taxes paid at different stages of the production and distribution process are not fully rebated to the exporter, with the degree of undercompensation varying from industry to industry and even from corporation to corporation.[30] The competitive position of exported commodities is further influenced by the taxes they have to bear in the importing country. It is thought that imports are charged less than competing domestic commodities in Belgium, Germany, Italy, and the Netherlands, which levy taxes on transaction value at every stage of production and distribution. This is not the case in countries where taxes are calculated as a proportion of value added at the individual stages or levied in the final stage only. Correspondingly, while the undercompensation of taxes in the exporting countries is more or less offset in the case of products imported into the first group of countries, imports remain at some competitive disadvantage elsewhere.

Aside from the administrative problems of compensating general indirect taxes, trade may be affected by excise taxes levied on particular commodities. In France, for example, excises on whisky favor the consumption of domestically produced beverages, while the tax base as well as the high degree of progressivity in road taxes puts American cars at a disadvantage. In such instances, then, excise taxes will lead to the substitution of domestic goods for competing imports.

Unlike indirect taxes, direct taxes are not rebated on exports. But is the different treatment of the two types of taxes warranted? Traditionally it has been assumed that, while indirect taxes raise prices, direct taxes (in the present case the corporate income tax) have no

[30] Organisation for Economic Co-operation and Development, *Report on Border Tax Adjustments* (Paris, 1964), mimeographed.

such effect and hence do not need to be rebated on exported merchandise. In criticism of this proposition, the argument has been advanced that, in oligopolistic markets, at least part of the corporate income tax is shifted forward in the form of higher prices. While empirical investigations have given conflicting results,[31] it is of interest to consider the implications for trade of alternative assumptions made concerning the incidence of direct taxes. In this connection note may be taken of a calculation by Aliber and Stein on the possible effects on American exports of replacing the U.S. corporate income tax by an indirect tax.[32]

Aliber and Stein conclude that the rebating of indirect taxes on exports would lead to a decline of U.S. export prices by, at most, 5 per cent if the substitution of an indirect tax for the corporate income tax raised domestic prices by the full amount of the former. But the relative prices of U.S. exports would decrease by only 1 to 2 percent if other countries followed suit. Moreover, in the absence of an increase in the domestic price level, export prices would not change at all. It would appear, then, that the greater reliance on direct taxes in the United States, compared to European countries, does not discriminate against American exports to an appreciable extent.

I turn now to the nontariff measures used by national governments to restrict imports. Among these, quantitative restrictions prohibit the importation of particular commodities if certain conditions are not met or, alternatively, limit the amount imported. Prohibitive measures are not necessarily protective in intent, such as sanitary and health regulations or standards legislation, but they nevertheless interfere with international exchange. In turn, quotas—formal or informal—set limits to the importation of particular commodities, either in global terms or according to the country of origin.

While widely used in the immediate postwar period, quotas on nonagricultural commodities traded among the industrial countries have been progressively abolished in the framework of the OEEC (later OECD) and GATT. A major exception is coal, the importa-

---

[31] Results obtained by Krzyzaniak and Musgrave point to more than 100 per cent shifting; i.e., firms would raise their prices to more than compensate for an increase in corporate taxation, while Challis Hall's work suggests that no shifting occurs (M. Krzyzaniak and R. A. Musgrave, *The Shifting of the Corporation Income Tax* [Baltimore, Md.: Johns Hopkins University Press, 1963], and C. A. Hall, "Direct Shifting of the Corporation Income Tax in Manufacturing," *American Economic Review, Papers and Proceedings*, May 1964), pp. 258–271.

[32] R. Z. Aliber and H. Stein, "Price of U.S. Exports and the Mix of Direct and Indirect Taxes," *American Economic Review*, September 1964, pp. 703–10.

tion of which is prohibited in the United Kingdom and is regulated by quotas in some of the Common Market countries. Moreover, despite the liberalization measures undertaken in recent years, quantitative restrictions remain in effect on part of Japan's trade with the other industrial countries. In 1965, about one-tenth of Japanese imports of nonagricultural commodities were subject to quotas while a variety of labor-intensive goods originating in Japan (textiles, sewing machines, toys, radios, optical goods, pottery, and stainless steel flatware) come under formal or informal restrictions in the United States, Canada, and Western Europe.

State trading and government procurement can also be used to exclude or to restrict the imports of particular commodities. The relevant decisions may be of a discretionary character, or they may be specifically provided for in legislation and in executive orders. "Buy American" procedures are the best known examples. Under these, government purchases for use in the United States must be made from domestic producers unless their price exceeds the foreign bid price, inclusive of duty, by more than 6 per cent. An additional 6 per cent—a total of 12 per cent—applies if the commodity is produced in an area of substantial unemployment or by a small business firm. Finally, a 50 per cent differential margin pertains to defense procurement at home and abroad.

While specific "buy national" regulations are not in effect in the countries of Western Europe, purchase policies favoring domestic enterprises are often employed. A report prepared for the European Parliament has concluded, for example, that "in all Member States, almost all public work contracts have so far been assigned to national contractors since there is a universal tendency to keep public funds within the country." [33] There are also instances of discriminatory purchasing practices in the United Kingdom, where the Post Office often excludes foreign suppliers of equipment. Finally, a 10 per cent preferential margin is accorded domestic producers of defense equipment in Canada and domestic suppliers appear to enjoy advantages in government procurement of a variety of products in Japan.

Customs classification procedures, too, may have a restrictive effect on trade. In some instances, the tariff classification is detailed to the point that it discriminates among the foreign suppliers of a given commodity—as in the famous case of cows grazing at a certain altitude. More importantly, the uncertainties related to the classifica-

[33] Parlement Européen, *Documents de Séances*, 1965–66, Document 1, March 22, 1965, p. 3.

tion of imported commodities provide a disincentive to international trade. In particular, classification problems arise in the United States and Canada which, unlike other industrial countries, have not adopted the Brussels Tariff Nomenclature.

Similar considerations apply to customs valuation procedures. According to one study, "the United States is operating on a dual valuation system, with old, more ambiguous and more protective standards applicable to one group of commodities, and a modernized set of standards applicable to other dutiable imports." [34] But the most attention has been given to the American selling price issue. On U.S. imports of competitive benzenoid chemicals, rubber footwear, and canned clams, duties are levied on the basis of the price of comparable domestic products rather than import value. The use of the American selling price as a valuation base approximately doubles the tariff expressed as a proportion of import value in the case of benzenoid chemicals and triples it on rubber footwear and canned clams.

Among these products, benzenoid chemicals are the most important. In 1964 U.S. sales of these chemicals accounted for about 10 per cent of the total sales of the American chemical industry but they provided only 3.2 per cent of chemical imports. Aside from the restrictive effect of this valuation scheme, uncertainty is created since any benzenoid chemical automatically qualifies for the higher valuation base as soon as it is manufactured domestically. Moreover, so foreign producers argue, the high prices charged on domestic sales of coal tar chemicals permit U.S. companies to reduce the prices of other products and thereby improve their competitive position in domestic and in foreign markets.

The prevalence of oligopolies and the peculiarities of the accounting procedures applied also make the chemical industry one of the foremost candidates for dumping; other examples can be found in the case of steel, aluminum, and other metals. Dumping is defined by GATT as selling abroad at lower prices than domestically, which results in injury to the industry of the importing country. Dumping is not restrictive by itself but antidumping investigations may have such an effect. Thus, in the period 1958–1965, the Treasury Depart-

[34] Francis Masson and J. B. Whitely, *Barriers to Trade between Canada and the United States* (Montreal: Canadian-American Committee sponsored by the National Planning Association (U.S.A.) and the Private Planning Association of Canada 1960), p. 29. The products subject to the old valuation scheme account for about 10 per cent of U.S. dutiable imports.

ment initiated 194 investigations in the United States and although antidumping duties were imposed in only eight instances, foreign exporters incurred considerable costs in the process, appraisement was withheld, and uncertainties were created for the trader.

Mention should also be made of marking requirements in effect in the United States and in some European countries, which require that on imported articles the country of origin should be clearly indicated. While exemption is given whenever an article can be marked only at prohibitive expense, in some cases the cost of marking is quite high in comparison to the value of the item. It has also been charged that country-of-origin markings have limited the demand for certain foreign goods in the United States. It is possible, however, that in other instances the effect has been just the opposite.

I have considered so far various forms of nontariff barriers that have restrictive effects on imports. The converse of the issue is government assistance to exports. While export subsidies are prohibited under GATT, most countries apply various measures that benefit exports. These include export insurance, low-cost export credits, and, more recently, tied aid—the requirement that the recipient countries use the proceeds of loans and grants only in the aid-giving country. Since these measures differ from country to country, they will have an influence on the pattern of international trade.

Earlier in this chapter, estimates were provided on the restrictive effects of tariffs. Available information does not permit us to calculate the degree of under- or overcompensation in regard to taxes levied on commodities traded internationally. Neither is it possible to prepare estimates on the effects of nontariff measures on trade since, with the exception of U.S. and Canadian government procurement, the degree of discrimination against foreign goods cannot be expressed in numerical terms. At any rate, the uncertainty created by the potential application of nontariff measures is often more important than the direct effect of the measures themselves. In the face of this uncertainty, would-be exporters may not undertake the investments necessary to produce according to foreign specifications or to carry out the selling effort needed for entering foreign markets.

Conclusion

The purpose of this chapter has been to provide information on barriers to trade in nonagricultural commodities among the industrial countries. In this connection, a distinction was first made between nominal and effective duties; while nominal tariffs influence the consumer's choice between domestic and foreign goods, for the domestic producer the effective rate of protection is relevant. By taking account of nominal tariffs levied on the product itself and on its inputs, the latter measure expresses the degree of protection of value added in the manufacturing process.

With few exceptions, we find effective duties to be higher than nominal rates. This result is explained in large part by the "graduation" of tariffs from lower to higher levels of fabrication. The differences are especially pronounced—and effective rates are more than double nominal rates—in the case of textile products and hosiery, leather, chemical materials, steel ingots, and nonferrous metals. On the other hand, nominal as well as effective tariffs are low, and their differences relatively small, for machinery and equipment.

A comparison of national tariffs further indicates that, among the major industrial countries, the averages of nominal and effective duties are the highest in Japan, with the United Kingdom a close second and Sweden at the opposite end of the scale. The United States and the European Common Market occupy the middle ground: the average of nominal tariffs in the Common Market is slightly higher than in the United States, while the opposite holds for averages of effective duties. But a comparison of averages of tariffs does not indicate their restrictive effect; the latter will also depend on the share of imports in domestic consumption and production as well as on the responsiveness of demand and supply to price changes. Thus, the low share of imports in domestic consumption (production) increases the restrictiveness of the American tariff to a considerable extent while the opposite is true of Sweden and Japan.

It has further been indicated that, in addition to tariffs, trade is affected by a variety of government regulations and practices. Intercountry differences in fiscal and social regulations influence the pattern of international trade while nontariff measures, such as quantitative restrictions, government procurement and state trading, customs valuation and classification procedures, antidumping regulations, and marking requirements restrict imports. Finally, government-sponsored schemes of export insurance, low-cost export credit, and tied aid, benefit to a lesser or greater extent the exports of the various industrial countries.

CHAPTER FOUR

Trade Liberalization among Industrial Countries: The Static Effects

The Gains from Trade Liberalization

Why trade liberalization? What economic benefits can individual nations or groups of countries expect to derive from tariff reductions? These questions have frequently been raised in connection with the tariff negotiations of the last two decades, and the answers will condition the future progress of trade liberalization as well as the choice among alternative arrangements. In this chapter I shall examine several alternative approaches to the problem and present estimates of the static effects of tariff reductions undertaken by the industrial nations on trade in industrial materials and manufactured goods. The chapter will also consider the impact of trade liberalization on the industrial structure and on the balance of payments of the participating countries.

In public discussions attention has focused on the consequences of the lowering of tariff barriers for the balance of trade. Government spokesmen have sought to generate support for trade liberalization by extolling its presumed beneficial impact on the trade balance, which has often been taken to reflect the balance of economic advantages derived from tariff reductions.[1] Accordingly, increases in exports have been considered a "gain" and a rise in imports a "loss."

---

[1] This view has found expression, for example, in a statement by W. M. Roth, U.S. Deputy Special Representative for Trade Negotiations in the Kennedy Round. Roth declared that "we do not intend to give anything away. We do intend to bargain and bargain hard for the total benefit of the United States economy" (*The New York Times,* September 11, 1963). Giscard d'Estaing, former French finance minister, goes even further in asserting the necessity of attaining a trade balance with every large trading partner—especially the United States (*Le Monde,* July 2, 1964).

This approach reflects a certain resurgence of mercantilist thinking. Just as in the time of the mercantilists, the desire to improve the balance of payments appears the principal consideration,[2] although the motivation has been different in the two cases. Under present-day conditions of fixed exchange rates, balance of payments equilibrium provides a constraint to economic policy-making inasmuch as the national authorities have to take account of the implications of domestic policies for the external balance. Thus, the endeavor to obtain an improvement in the balance of trade is not irrational since this would permit pursuing domestic policies that would otherwise be constrained by the possibility of a balance of payments deficit. Different considerations apply, however, if we consider a group of countries rather than a single nation, because all countries lose if the fear of incurring a deficit causes them to limit reductions in tariffs. At any rate, as will be shown later, changes in the balance of payments of the more developed industrial countries are likely to be relatively small even if we assume that duties are completely eliminated. In turn, these changes can be remedied through modest adjustments in costs and prices.

But balance of payments considerations do not provide the only reason for placing imports on the negative side of the ledger. The argument has often been advanced that a decline of production and employment in competing domestic establishments associated with increases in imports has a political as well as an economic cost that needs to be weighed when embarking on a program of trade liberalization. The hesitation of the German government to accept a reduction in grain prices and the insistence of the French on establishing a common agricultural policy in the EEC can be explained in political terms, for example. In both cases, the agricultural population is an important bastion of the political party in power; a loss of peasant votes may spell defeat for the Christian Democrats in Germany, and the Gaullist majority in France likewise depends on farmer support. Protectionist influences also have been an important political force over the years in the United States.

---

[2] The balance of payments implications of trade liberalization have been emphasized, for example, by Richard N. Gardner, U.S. Deputy Assistant Secretary for International Organizations, who expressed the view that "the Kennedy Round can serve world economic interests . . . in helping to deal constructively with the U.S. balance-of-payments problem." *In Pursuit of World Order* (New York: Praeger, 1964), p. 145.

There is an apparent paradox here, since the majority of the population stands to benefit from trade liberalization—the consumers through lower prices and the exporters through higher sales. An explanation is that import-competing industries often have lower than average productivity and profits [3] and feel directly threatened by imports, while the gains to exporters and consumers are often not easily ascertainable. The situation changes, however, as exporters and consumers become more aware of the gains derived from multilateral tariff reductions. Trade liberalization enjoys firm majority support in the smaller European countries and the balance of power between protectionists and free traders has also shifted in the countries of the European Common Market. Thus, while France used to be regarded as a protectionist country *par excellence,* the French have increasingly come to appreciate the benefits of freer trade. In fact, the decline in De Gaulle's popularity at the time of the 1965 French presidential elections has in part been explained by the fear that his policies might ultimately lead to the isolation of France from the EEC.

It would further appear that the emphasis on the adverse economic effects of trade liberalization in particular industries reflects a certain myopia. Under full-employment conditions, any such effects are of a short-term character and will give place to economic benefits as resources are reallocated from import-competing to export industries. The case of German agriculture may serve as an example. Despite the decrease in the agricultural population in the postwar period, in 1964 about one-seventh of the German labor force was still engaged in agricultural occupations. Much of German agriculture is organized in small farms and, given the natural disadvantages of agriculture in Germany, these can hardly compete with foreign producers. At the same time, the German manufacturing industry faces an increasing labor scarcity that could be alleviated through the release of labor from agriculture. The ensuing reallocation of resources would entail an economic gain since the resource cost of food consumption is reduced if, instead of producing it domestically, food is obtained in exchange for industrial products.

While the popular view has been that increases in imports are undesirable, according to the critics of this approach it is the rise of

---

[3] This appears to be the case in the United States. Cf. Irving B. Kravis, "Wages and Foreign Trade," *Review of Economics and Statistics*, February 1956, pp. 14–30 and B. N. Vaccara, *Employment and Output in Protected Manufacturing Industries* (Washington, D.C.: The Brookings Institution, 1960).

imports itself that provides the principal benefits of trade liberalization: with a shift in purchases from high-cost domestic to low-cost foreign merchandise, the nation will be able to satisfy domestic needs at a lower cost.[4] The latter view appears in its simplest form in the writings of several authors on tariff protection in Australia and Canada. But in estimating the saving in costs that would result from the elimination of tariffs—the cost of protection—these authors have abstracted from the problem of what would happen to resources freed in the industries producing import substitutes.[5] This procedure may indeed be applicable to Australia and Canada since—aside from some agricultural products—they fit the textbook case of small countries who do not influence world market prices. Such countries can sell increasing quantities of their export products at the going price as reductions in tariffs lead to a reallocation of resources from import-competing to export industries. The situation is different in larger nations, however. In the event of unilateral tariff reductions, they will have to accept price reductions in order to increase sales abroad.

Accordingly, a country may benefit from trade liberalization with regard to its exports as well as its imports. On the export side, the gain consists in the opportunity to sell commodities at better terms than would have been possible in the absence of tariff reductions on the part of other countries. On the import side, the benefits of freer trade arise from the opportunity to consume low-cost imported goods in the place of more expensive domestically produced commodities, the purchase of which has been a result of the existence of tariffs. Countries have an interest, therefore, in obtaining tariff reductions from their trading partners and will prefer multilateral to unilateral tariff reductions.[6]

These are, then, the static benefits of freer trade that can be ob-

[4] In the colorful expression of Harry Johnson, "The mythology of tariff negotiation is very similar to that of seduction: in each case the benefit to be received is treated as a loss for purposes of negotiation; and in each case the consequence of this fiction is continual frustration and frequent nonconsummation." Harry G. Johnson, *The Canadian Quandary* (Toronto: McGraw-Hill, 1965), p. 30.

[5] J. B. Brigden, "The Australian Tariff and the Standard of Living," *Economic Record,* November 1925; W. M. Corden, "The Calculation of the Cost of Protection," *Economic Record,* April 1959; and John H. Young, *Canadian Commercial Policy* (Royal Commission on Canada's Economic Prospects, 1957).

[6] It will be apparent, however, that changes in the terms of trade cancel out on the world level, since one country's gain from an improvement in its terms of trade is another country's loss.

tained under the assumption of unchanged production methods. According to the traditional explanation, such gains result from the shift of resources from import-competing to export industries and entail a reduction in the activity of the former and an expansion in the latter. But while this explanation applies to agriculture and to the production of standardized goods in general, it represents an oversimplification as far as much of modern industry is concerned. National product differentiation is a characteristic feature of consumer goods industries and, by reducing the extent of discrimination against foreign goods, the lowering of duties will contribute to an increased exchange of these commodities. In turn, a multilateral cut in tariffs will permit a narrowing of product variety in the case of machinery and intermediate products at higher levels of fabrication where cost reductions can be obtained through the lengthening of production runs. Accordingly, as I shall argue in more detail below, the distinction between export- and import-competing industries becomes blurred and trade liberalization will tend to lead to changes in product composition rather than to a decline in the activity of particular industries.

However, reductions in costs due to the lengthening of production runs should be considered dynamic, rather than static, gains since these involve changes in methods of production. More generally, the dynamic benefits of tariff reductions refer to improvements in production methods that can be obtained by widening national markets through trade. These advantages of large markets consist of economies of scale on the plant, firm, or industry level, and the effects of intensified competition on the methods of production.

In the following, I will present some estimates of the static effects of trade liberalization: the expansion in exports and imports that would take place following multilateral reductions in duties under the assumption that production methods remained unchanged. While this restrictive assumption—the stock in trade of international economists —limits the usefulness of the results, it permits us to evaluate alternative trade arrangements in a static context and to separate static from dynamic considerations, which will be the subject of Chapter 5.

Estimates of the Effects of Alternative Arrangements on Trade Flows

To conform to the general purposes of the study, I have considered separately the effects on trade of (A) a free trade area among the industrial countries (in short, an Atlantic Free Trade Area), and (B) multilateral tariff reductions under the most-favored-nation clause. In the latter case it has been assumed that a 50 per cent across-the-board tariff cut would be undertaken by the industrial countries and extended to nonindustrial economies without corresponding concessions made by the latter. Moreover, I have attempted to indicate the possible implications of (C) a trade arrangement among industrial countries that excluded the European Common Market and (D) integration in Western Europe, although numerical estimates for these alternatives have not been prepared.

The year 1960 has been chosen as the base year for the estimates, on the assumption that the discriminatory effects of the European Common Market and the European Free Trade Association were not yet appreciable at that time. This choice has made it possible to consider the effects of trade liberalization in three parts: (1) the direct effects of tariff reductions; (2) the reduction of discrimination against nonmember countries in the EEC and EFTA; and (3) the indirect effects of trade liberalization operating through the "feedback" mechanism.

The direct effects of trade liberalization refer to changes in exports and imports that would take place following multilateral reductions in duties if no account were taken of the potential discriminatory effect of the Common Market and EFTA. The exports of nonmember countries would increase further as a result of the elimination of, or reduction in, EEC and EFTA discrimination through a lowering of duties. Finally, if tariff reductions were carried out under the most-favored-nation clause, imports from nonindustrial countries would also rise and there would be a feedback effect on the exports of industrial areas.

The scope of the investigation has been restricted to industrial materials (SITC classes 2 and 4 and unwrought metals) and manufactured goods (SITC classes 5 to 8, less unwrought metals). Estimates have been prepared for 107 commodity categories, corresponding to the three-digit groups of the Standard International Trade Classification, except for nonferrous metals where a more detailed breakdown has been used. Thirty-five of the commodity categories include industrial materials while seventy-two comprise manufactured goods.

The geographical breakdown of the estimates follows the classification used in Chapter 1; the industrial countries and country groups considered are the United States, Canada, the European Common Market, the United Kingdom, Continental EFTA, and Japan. Estimates on the effects of most-favored-nation-type tariff reductions have further been made for nonindustrial countries that have been classified into two groups: other developed economies [7] and less developed countries.[8] It has been assumed, however, that reductions in tariffs under the most-favored-nation clause would not be extended to Soviet-type economies.

The results are given in two variants. Variant I assumes that the expansion of the exports of manufactures would necessitate a rise in prices by one-third of the tariff reduction in Western Europe where tight labor-market conditions prevail, while Variant II is calculated with unchanged European export prices. In all other exporting areas, constant export prices have been assumed throughout and the same assumption has been made with regard to industrial materials, regardless of their origin.

DIRECT EFFECTS.   Table 4.1 shows the direct effects of the establishment of an Atlantic Free Trade Area on trade in industrial materials and manufactured goods. Trade among the industrial countries in these commodities has been estimated to rise by 18.7 and 21.2 per cent under Variants I and II, respectively. Much of the expansion would take place in manufactured goods where increases of 23.8 and 27.0 per cent have been projected under the two variants, while imports of industrial materials have been estimated to rise by only 2.2 per cent. This disparity between estimated increases of trade in the two commodity categories is explained by differences in tariff levels and in the responsiveness of import demand to changes in prices that result from a cut in tariffs.[9]

Tariffs are considerably higher on manufactured goods than on in-

[7] Australia, New Zealand, South Africa, and countries of Western Europe outside EEC and EFTA (Finland, Greece, Iceland, Ireland, Spain, Turkey, and Yugoslavia).

[8] The countries of Latin America, Africa (other than South Africa), the Middle East, and Asia (other than Japan and the Communist countries of Asia).

[9] If we assume that export prices are constant in the relevant range, increases in the imports of any commodity can be calculated by the use of the formula $\Delta M = \eta_m Mt/1 + t$ when M is the value of imports in the base year, t the rate of tariff, $t/1 + t$ the fall in import prices following the elimination of duties and η_m the import demand elasticity. For a detailed exposition of the methods of estimation, and of the underlying assumptions, see the Appendix to this chapter.

TABLE 4.1 Direct Effects of an Atlantic Free Trade Area and Tariff Levels in the Industrial Countries [a]

		Increase in Exports			Increase in Imports			Average Tariffs [b]	
		Industrial Materials	Manufactured Goods	Together	Industrial Materials	Manufactured Goods	Together	Industrial Materials *percent*	Manufactured Goods *percent*
		as a per cent of 1960 trade with industrial countries							
United States	I	1.7	26.3	19.1	3.0	31.2	24.8	2.6	13.2
	II	1.7	26.0	19.1	3.0	35.9	28.5		
Canada	I	2.0	10.3	5.7	0.7	20.2	18.4	1.6	14.6
	II	2.0	10.3	5.7	0.7	20.6	18.7		
Common Market	I	3.2	21.1	19.7	2.2	24.8	17.3	1.3	12.2
	II	3.2	26.9	25.1	2.2	28.3	19.7		
United Kingdom	I	2.0	18.7	16.7	2.3	26.4	18.8	3.3	16.5
	II	2.0	24.0	21.4	2.3	30.8	21.8		
Continental EFTA	I	3.3	25.6	19.4	0.7	13.7	12.3	1.0	9.1
	II	3.3	32.3	24.2	0.7	16.9	15.1		
Japan	I	3.7	48.5	44.9	1.9	34.2	17.7	4.2	17.1
	II	3.7	48.5	44.9	1.9	37.0	19.0		
Industrial countries	I	2.2	23.8	18.7	2.2	23.8	18.7		
	II	2.2	27.0	21.2	2.2	27.0	21.2		

Source: Trade—Appendix tables 4.1, 4.2, and 4.3   Tariffs—National tariff schedules and trade statistics.

[a] Explanation of symbols: I—Variant I, assumes (1) a rise in prices of manufactured goods exported from Western Europe equal to one-third of the tariff reduction and (2) no increase in any other export prices. II—Variant II, assumes that all export prices remain unchanged.

[b] Weighted by the combined imports of the countries in question.

dustrial materials. The industrial countries admit a number of crude materials duty-free, and the ratio of the average of tariffs on manufactured goods to that on industrial materials ranges from 4.1 in Japan to 9.2 in the European Common Market. Moreover, finished manufactures, which have the highest import demand elasticities assumed in the calculations, predominate within the manufactured-goods category, whereas the elasticities assumed for the semimanufactures and crude materials included in the industrial materials group are considerably lower.

Since about 97 per cent of the estimated expansion of trade would take place in manufactured goods, the discussion will center on this group of commodities. As regards the exports of manufactures, estimates prepared under the assumption of constant export prices (Variant II) show Japan at the upper and Canada at the lower end of the scale, with increases of 48.5 and 10.3 per cent respectively. The corresponding figures are in the 24 to 32 per cent range for European countries and the United States. Japan also leads in regard to imports, with an estimated increase of 37.0 per cent, followed by the United States (35.9 per cent), the United Kingdom (30.8 per cent), the European Common Market (28.3 per cent), Canada (20.6 per cent), and the Continental EFTA countries (16.9 per cent).

The results can be compared with those obtained in Chapter 3, where estimates have been made by utilizing nominal *and* effective tariffs, whereas in this chapter, the use of a more detailed commodity breakdown has necessitated calculating with nominal tariffs only.[10] The differences between the two sets of estimates are small and in no case exceed 10 per cent.[11] It appears, then, that the dissimilarities in the methods of estimation used in the two chapters do not substantially affect the over-all results as regards the effects of tariff reductions on trade among the industrial countries. The differences would be considerably larger for imports from developing countries, how-

[10] According to the estimates of Chapter 3, the elimination of tariffs would lead to increases in imports of 39.9 per cent in Japan, 38.2 per cent in the United States, 32.1 per cent in the United Kingdom, 28.2 per cent in the Common Market, and 15.4 per cent in Sweden.

[11] In the case of Continental EFTA, comparisons have been made with estimates for Sweden in Chapter 3 although the comparability of the results is reduced by reason of the fact that duties in Sweden are generally lower than the tariffs of the other Continental EFTA countries. This explains that in this case the estimates of Chapter 3 are lower than those of Chapter 4, while for most of the other countries the opposite is shown.

ever, since the disparities between effective and nominal duties applied to the manufactured exports of these countries are greater than the average.[12]

The assumed rise in European export prices would modify the results in the case of Variant I. Under this variant, the combined effects of higher prices and smaller export volume would reduce the increment in the value of exports of European countries estimated for Variant II by about one-fifth. In turn, differences in the estimated rise in imports between the two variants are influenced by the geographical composition of trade. Thus the increase in the imports of manufactures is only slightly smaller under Variant I than under Variant II in the case of Canada (−1.6 per cent) and Japan (−7.4 per cent), whose main trading partner is the United States, while the differences are larger for the other countries that purchase a large proportion of their imports in Western Europe: United States, −13.1 per cent; Common Market, −12.5 per cent; United Kingdom, −4.2 per cent; and Continental EFTA, −19.0 per cent. (Appendix Table 4.2.)

The estimated expansion of exports and imports is affected by the assumed elasticities of import demand and the level of tariffs in the individual countries under both variants. For finished manufactures, I have assumed that a 1 per cent fall in import prices resulting from reductions in duties would lead to an increase of imports by 4.1 per cent in the United States, 3.1 per cent in the Common Market and Japan, 2.7 per cent in the United Kingdom, 2.3 per cent in Continental EFTA, and 2.1 per cent in Canada.[13] On the other hand, the average of nominal duties on manufactured goods is the highest in Japan, followed by the United Kingdom, Canada, the United States, the European Common Market, and the continental member countries of the European Free Trade Association. (Table 4.1.)

But these averages conceal considerable differences in the tariff distribution among the industrial countries which influence the expansion of trade following reductions in duties. Thus Japan would greatly benefit from reductions in the high duties levied on textile products in the other industrial countries. On the other hand, her concentration on semifinished manufactured goods that bear low duties in foreign countries, as well as the partial loss of Commonwealth preference,

[12] See pp. 50–51 above.

[13] For the derivation of these figures, and price elasticities of import demand applied in the case of semimanufactures and crude materials, see the Appendix to this chapter, pp. 186–90.

would limit the expansion of exports from Canada. Finally, high tariffs in Japan and high import demand elasticities in the United States account for the relatively large estimated increases of imports into these two countries, whereas low tariffs and low import-demand elasticities, respectively, would have the opposite effect in Continental EFTA and Canada.

Changes in the balance of trade would also depend on the amount of exports and imports in the base year, 1960. In that year, the ratio of exports to imports for manufactured goods traded among the industrial countries was the highest in Japan (1.73), followed by the European Common Market (1.58), the United Kingdom (1.21), and the United States (1.19). In turn, the Continental EFTA countries (0.49) and Canada (0.39) had an import balance. (Appendix Table 4.1.) Differences in these ratios reflect the disparities in the commodity structure and the geographical composition of trade indicated in Chapter 1.

As a result of the combined effects of the trade pattern observed in 1960 and the estimated rate of expansion of exports and imports, the direct effects of the elimination of duties among the industrial countries would entail an improvement in the trade balance of the European Common Market, ($346 million under Variant I and $577 million under Variant II) and Japan ($353 and $333 million), as against a deterioration for Canada ($597 and $610 million), the United Kingdom ($92 and $52 million), and the Continental EFTA countries ($21 and $16 million). The United States balance of trade would show practically no change under Variant I and would deteriorate by $232 million under Variant II (Appendix Table 4.3).

DISCRIMINATORY EFFECTS. By reason of tariff reductions on intra-area trade, the establishment of the European Common Market and the European Free Trade Association has entailed discrimination against each other's members as well as against third countries. Eliminating tariffs in an Atlantic Free Trade Area would do away with discrimination among the industrial countries while multilateral tariff reductions under the most-favored-nation clause would diminish the extent of the discrimination against every outsider. The probable effects of elimination of, or a reduction in, EEC and EFTA discrimination can be estimated by measuring the potential impact of this discrimination on trade flows. Table 4.2 shows the estimated discriminatory effects of the EEC and EFTA on the imports of industrial materials and manufactured goods from nonmember countries. In

TABLE 4.2   Discriminatory Effects of the Common Market
and EFTA^a ($ million)

	Common Market	United Kingdom	Continental EFTA	Together
United States	311	42	36	389
Canada	11	19	1	31
Common Market	—	78	219	297
United Kingdom	198	—	—	198
Continental EFTA	275	—	—	275
Japan	19	2	5	26
Industrial countries combined	814	141	261	1216
Other developed countries	48	15	7	70
Less developed countries	47	9	4	60
Total	909	165	272	1346

Note: ^a The estimated decrease in imports of industrial materials and manufactured goods from 1960 levels due to the establishment of the European Common Market and the European Free Trade Association.

the case of the EFTA, the extent of discrimination against foreign producers in the markets of the United Kingdom and the continental member countries has been indicated separately.[14]

According to these estimates, the exports of nonmember countries to the Common Market would fall by $909 million from 1960 levels as a result of EEC discrimination; the decline in exports to the United Kingdom and Continental EFTA would be $165 and $272 million. Among the countries that are discriminated against, the exports of the United States would decrease by $389 million, while there would be little change in the exports of Canada and Japan. In turn, the fall in exports resulting from the discriminatory effects of the division of Western Europe into two trading blocs would be $297 million in the case of the Common Market countries (in EFTA markets), compared to $198 million for the United Kingdom and $275 for the Continental EFTA countries (in EEC markets).

The impact of the elimination of EEC and EFTA discrimination on trade flows and the direct effects of an Atlantic Free Trade Area are compared in Appendix Table 4.3. It appears that the removal of

[14] On the methods of estimation employed, see the Appendix to this chapter, pp. 193–95.

discrimination would augment the increase in the exports of the Continental EFTA countries as a result of the direct effects of an Atlantic Free Trade Area by about one-half; the corresponding magnitudes for the United Kingdom, the United States, and the European Common Market are 35 to 45 per cent, 25 per cent, and 15 to 20 per cent, respectively. Combining the direct and the discriminatory effects of an Atlantic Free Trade Area, an improvement in the U.S. trade balance is shown under both variants; on the other hand, the trade balance of the European Common Market would deteriorate under Variant I and improve under Variant II. Estimated changes in exports and imports are approximately equal in the United Kingdom and Continental EFTA, but a large incremental surplus is foreseen in the case of Japan and a large deficit for Canada.

In the event that the industrial nations were to cut tariffs by 50 per cent, their mutual trade would increase by about one-half of the amounts indicated for AFTA. However, under the assumption that tariff reductions are carried out under the most-favored-nation clause, imports from nonindustrial areas would also increase. According to the estimates shown in Appendix Table 4.4, imports would rise by $99 million from the group of other developed countries and by $262 million from the less developed countries. The reduction in EEC and EFTA discrimination accomplished through the lowering of tariffs would mean a further increase in imports of $35 million and $30 million, respectively, bringing the total export gain to $134 million for the other developed countries and to $292 million for the developing nations. The area distribution of the latter figure is Latin America, $75 million; Africa, $41 million; Middle East, $10 million; and Asia, $166 million.[15]

Under the assumption that industrial countries accumulate (decumulate) reserves [16] while nonindustrial economies spend all

[15] The method used in calculating increases in imports has been the same as under Variant II above. However, in regard to British imports from the Commonwealth countries, account has been taken of the lessening of preferential advantages in the way described in the case of Canada in the Appendix to this chapter. These adjustments account for the relatively small estimated increases in British imports of manufactured goods from nonindustrial countries.

[16] While this assumption appears realistic for most of the industrial countries, its application to Canada and Japan may be questioned. Should Canada reduce imports as a result of the decrease in her exports, the cumulative effect on U.S. exports may reach three-fourths of the cut in Canadian purchases abroad. On the other hand, in the case of Japan, nearly one-half the increase in imports would ultimately benefit the United States.

increases in their foreign-exchange earnings, the increased sales of the latter would provide a "feedback" in the form of higher imports from industrial countries. Taking account of the cumulative effect of purchases made by the nonindustrial economies, ultimately about 95 per cent of the increase in their foreign exchange receipts would return to the industrial countries while the remainder is assumed to "leak out" to the Communist countries. Accordingly, the extension of tariff reductions to nonindustrial economies would hardly affect the trade balance of the industrial nations taken together; neither would it make much difference for the balance of trade of individual countries.

The Static Effects of Trade Liberalization: An Evaluation

In order to evaluate the relative importance of estimated increases in trade following trade liberalization among the industrial countries, the results will now be compared to the total exports and imports and to the gross national products of these nations in the base year, 1960. As shown in Table 4.3, increases in the exports of industrial materials and manufactured goods in an Atlantic Free Trade Area would amount to 16 per cent of the 1960 exports of Japan, 14 to 16 per cent for the Continental EFTA countries, 10 per cent for the United States, 9 to 11 per cent for the European Common Market, 7 to 9 per cent for the United Kingdom, and 2 per cent for Canada. By contrast, Canada leads in regard to imports with an increase of 15 per cent, followed by the United States and Continental EFTA (11 to 13 per cent), European Common Market (11 to 12 per cent), Japan (7 to 8 per cent) and the United Kingdom (6 to 7 per cent).

The preponderance of manufactured goods in sales and of primary products in purchases in great part explains the large estimated increases in Japan's exports compared to the small rise in imports. The opposite holds true for Canada, where primary products (including industrial materials) predominate in exports and manufactured goods in imports. In turn, given the importance of her trade with the Commonwealth, tariff reductions undertaken in the framework of an Atlantic Free Trade Area would lead to relatively small increases in the total exports and imports of the United Kingdom, whereas the United States, the Common Market, and EFTA occupy the middle ground in both exports and imports.

The picture changes somewhat if the estimated expansion of trade is expressed as a percentage of the gross domestic products of the in-

TABLE 4.3   The Estimated Expansion of Trade in an Atlantic
Free Trade Area, Compared to Trade and
Gross Domestic Products in 1960

Expansion of Exports and Imports as a Percentage of

		Total Trade		Gross Domestic Products	
	Variants	*Exports*	*Imports*	*Exports*	*Imports*
United States	I	10.1	11.2	0.5	0.4
	II	10.1	12.9	0.5	0.5
Canada	I	4.0	14.8	0.8	2.7
	II	4.0	15.1	0.8	2.8
Common Market	I	8.9	11.1	1.0	1.1
	II	10.9	11.9	1.2	1.2
United Kingdom	I	7.3	6.6	0.9	1.0
	II	8.8	7.5	1.1	1.1
Continental EFTA	I	13.7	10.9	2.1	2.1
	II	15.9	12.6	2.4	2.4
Japan	I	15.8	7.1	2.5	1.0
	II	16.0	7.6	2.5	1.1
Industrial countries	I	9.5	10.4	0.8	0.8
	II	10.5	11.5	0.9	0.9

Sources: Estimated expansion of trade—Appendix Table 4.3.
Trade, 1960—United Nations, *Statistical Yearbook 1963* (data exclude intra-EEC
and intra-EFTA trade). Gross domestic products, 1960—Table 1.1.
Note: For explanation of variants, see Table 4.1, p. 76.

dustrial countries. Given the relative importance of trade in their national income, the Continental EFTA countries are now in the lead with increases in exports and in imports amounting to 2.1 to 2.4 per cent of their combined GDP. The corresponding figures are 0.8 per cent for exports and 2.7 per cent for imports in Canada, and 2.5 and 1.0 per cent in Japan. However, the relevant proportions hardly reach 1 per cent in the European Common Market and the United Kingdom and .5 per cent in the United States.

It appears, then, that increases in trade in an Atlantic Free Trade Area, estimated under static assumptions, would be a relatively small fraction of the gross domestic product of the industrial countries. Even smaller would be the gain in welfare resulting from the reduction in the cost of protection that is associated with the expansion of trade.[17] It should be added, however, that while the static gains of trade liberalization result in an once-for-all improvement in resource allocation, this improvement will be maintained over time and will be compounded as the economy grows.

The error possibilities of estimation should further be noted. To begin with, estimates of increases in trade flows following multilateral reductions in duties are subject to error because of our limited knowledge of the responsiveness of import demand to a decline in import prices. The relationship between the expansion of exports and changes in export prices, too, is subject to uncertainty. Nor is the averaging of tariff rates for the commodity categories utilized in this study free of error, and the results are affected by the use of nominal instead of effective tariffs in the calculations.[18]

Further, in making estimates, no account has been taken of the possible effects of the remaining quantitative restrictions on trade in industrial materials and manufactured goods. In trade among the industrial countries, these restrictions apply almost exclusively to the exports and imports of Japan, and introduce a considerable degree of uncertainty in estimates prepared for that country. At the same time, estimated increases in Japanese exports would be greatly reduced if exceptions were made to across-the-board tariff reductions. As indicated in Chapter 5, one of Japan's major export products, textiles, appears on the "exception lists" submitted by the United States and various European countries in the course of the Kennedy Round of tariff negotiations.

But the uncertainties are by far the greatest in regard to the impact of tariff reductions on imports from less developed countries. For one thing, quantitative restrictions limit the imports of a variety of manufactured goods from these countries; for another, increases in their exports to industrial nations have been underestimated by reason of

[17] Cf. the Appendix to this chapter, pp. 195–99.

[18] Some indication of the numerical importance of these error possibilities can be given if we consider that the use of "lower limit" or "upper limit" elasticities referred to in the Appendix to this chapter would lead to a downward or upward adjustment of 15 per cent in the estimated rise of imports into the individual countries and country groupings. In turn, differences between Variants I and II indicate the relative importance of modifying the price assumptions. Finally, as noted earlier, the use of nominal tariffs in the calculations affects chiefly the estimated increases in imports from the nonindustrial countries but it makes little difference for the over-all results as far as trade among the industrial nations is concerned.

the use of nominal tariffs in the calculations.[19] More importantly, calculations based on information pertaining to past periods can hardly indicate potential increases in the exports of manufactures from the developing countries over a longer time span. Once tariff barriers are lowered, an incentive is provided to producers in these countries for expanding the foreign sales of manufactured goods, when actual increases in exports will largely depend on the extent and the speed of transformation in their economic structure.

Given the error possibilities of estimation and the uncertainties relating to future developments, the discriminatory effects of an Atlantic Free Trade Area on imports from less developed areas have not been estimated. It is apparent, however, that while tariff reductions under the most-favored-nation clause would speed up the process of industrial transformation in developing countries, the discrimination associated with the establishment of an Atlantic Free Trade Area would retard this transformation. I will return to this question in Chapter 7, where the choice among alternative arrangements is discussed.

Neither have estimates been made for Alternatives C and D considered in this study: a trade arrangement among industrial countries that excluded the European Common Market (Alternative C) and integration in Western Europe with the exclusion of the United States, Canada, and Japan (Alternative D). Still, the calculations on the expansion of exports and imports in an Atlantic Free Trade Area permit us to indicate the interest of the individual countries in these arrangements.

Apparently it would make little difference to Canada and Japan whether barriers to trade with the EEC were removed: Common Market discrimination is not likely to have much effect on the exports of these countries and increases in their trade with the Community in an Atlantic Free Trade Area would be relatively small. For both countries, the United States is the most important trading partner. In the event that tariffs among industrial countries were eliminated, about 90 per cent of the increase in the exports of Canada, and 85 per cent of that of Japan, would find markets in the United States. Corresponding import figures are 85 and 65 per cent (Appendix Table 4.2).

Trade with the Common Market is of greater importance for the United States; nearly one-third of the estimated $1.7 billion increase

---

[19] In Chapter 3, I have noted that differences between effective and nominal tariff are the largest in the case of simple manufactures of interest to the developing countries.

of U.S. exports due to the direct effects of an Atlantic Free Trade Area would find markets in the Community, and the removal of EEC discrimination would provide a further export gain of $.3 billion. If we also consider that about 35 per cent of the projected rise in U.S. imports would originate in the Common Market, it is apparent that the United States has considerable interest in including the EEC in any Atlantic trade arrangement.

This conclusion applies with increased force to the United Kingdom and the countries of Continental EFTA. The estimated expansion of British exports and imports in trade with the Common Market exceeds that with all other industrial countries, taken together, and Britain also expects to derive a further export gain of $.2 billion from the elimination of EEC discrimination. The Common Market would also account for about 65 per cent of increases in exports and 85 per cent of the rise in imports of the Continental EFTA countries in an Atlantic Free Trade Area; in addition, the exports of Continental EFTA would increase by $.3 billion as a result of the removal of Common Market discrimination.

A consideration of the static effects of trade liberalization on trade flows thus suggests that, for the United Kingdom and the Continental EFTA countries, an accommodation with the Common Market would bring considerably larger benefits than an arrangement with the United States, Canada, and Japan. In turn, the interest of the Common Market in European integration is indicated by the fact that in an Atlantic Free Trade Area over one-half of the expansion of EEC trade would take place within Western Europe, and the Community would further benefit from the elimination of EFTA discrimination.

However, in the absence of multilateral tariff reductions, integration in Western Europe would increase the extent of discrimination against U.S. exports. Since European countries would also account for about 60 per cent of the expansion of U.S. exports and imports due to the direct effects of an Atlantic Free Trade Area, it is apparent that the United States has a considerable interest in trade arrangements encompassing all the industrial countries.

"Revealed" Comparative Advantage and Intraindustry Specialization

I have considered so far the possible effects of tariff reductions on trade flows under the assumption of unchanged production methods.

A further question relates to the eventual impact of trade liberaliza-tion on the industrial structure of the individual countries. Since the reallocation of resources depends on comparative advantage, we would have to ascertain where the comparative advantage of the industrial countries lies in their trade with each other. Efforts made to provide an explanation on the basis of prevailing theories of com-parative advantage have had little success; nor do manufacturing cen-sus and industry studies furnish sufficient data for this purpose. As an alternative solution, I have utilized information on "revealed" com-parative advantage in the present study.

Since the commodity pattern of trade will reflect relative costs as well as the influence of nonprice factors, such as goodwill, quality, and the availability of servicing and repair facilities, the "revealed" comparative advantage of the industrial countries can be indicated by their trade performance in respect to individual industries. For this purpose, I have derived indicators of relative export performance and export-import ratios for the United States, Canada, the European Common Market, the United Kingdom, Sweden, and Japan in regard to seventy-four categories of manufactured products. In evaluating the comparative advantage of these countries, greater weight has been given to export performance indices than to export-import ratios be-cause the latter are affected by differences in taste as well as by the idiosyncrasies of national protection.[20]

According to the results summarized in Table 4.4, the United States has relative advantages in manufacturing chemical materials and products, aircraft, wrought tin and nickel, followed by railway vehicles, metal-working machinery, and plastic materials. On the other hand, the United States is at a disadvantage in the production of woollen yarn and fabrics, cotton yarn, footwear, and pottery, as well as simple forms of steel (bars, rods, sections, and wire) and floor coverings. Cotton and woollen yarns, floor coverings, and pot-tery also appear on the list of products in which Canada has a com-parative disadvantage; additional commodities on this list are hoops and strips of iron and steel, wrought tin, synthetic dyes, and glass-ware. By contrast, Canadians possess relative advantages in the manufacturing of paper, organic chemicals, lead, copper, aluminum, pig iron, railway construction material, and fertilizers (Appendix Tables 4.6 and 4.7).

[20] For a detailed description of definitions and methodology, see the Appen-dix to this chapter, pp. 203–06.

TABLE 4.4   United States "Revealed" Comparative Advantage
in Selected Manufacturing Industries [a]

(Rankings for 74 commodity categories)

	Export Performance Indices	Export-import Ratios		Export Performance Indices	Export-import Ratios
Chemical			Woolen		
materials	2	5	yarn	74	72
Aircraft	1	13	Woolen		
Wrought tin	3	5	fabrics	73	73
Wrought			Cotton		
nickel	9	2	yarn	67	57
Railway			Footwear	71	71
vehicles	7	9	Pottery	72	74
Metal-working			Steel bars		
machinery	10	8	and rods	67	70
Plastic materials	18	4	Floor		
			coverings	64	66

Source: Appendix Tables 4.6 and 4.7.

Note: On methodology, see Appendix to this chapter.

In the case of the EEC, the interpretation of the results is made difficult by reason of the fact that the trade of these countries still reflects the comparative advantages of the individual member countries. Nevertheless, it is reasonably clear that the Common Market countries have relative advantages in manufacturing passenger cars, footwear, clothing, glass, and musical instruments, and disadvantages in producing paper, rubber goods, tractors, power generators, railway equipment, and aircraft. Tractors, buses and trucks, pigments and paints, and explosives are on the top of Britain's list, followed by woollen fabrics, bicycles, wrought tin, and copper, while Britain appears to be at a comparative disadvantage in the manufactures of fertilizers, jewelry, travel goods, paper, cotton and synthetic fabrics, and clothing.

Sweden has relative advantages in regard to railway-construction material, paper, ships, plumbing and heating fixtures, lead, copper, and rubber goods, and disadvantages in cotton and synthetic yarns, woollen fabrics, synthetic dyes, fertilizers, and photographic equipment. Finally, the Japanese lead in exporting footwear, cotton yarn and fabrics, clothing, pottery and—surprisingly—buses and trucks, while they appear to be at a disadvantage in the manufacture of aircraft, tractors, wrought nickel and zinc, essential oils, and chemical products.

The reader will note that, with few exceptions, the commodities at the two ends of the comparative scales are standardized products. This is hardly surprising since the international exchange of these products is determined largely by intercountry differences in relative costs. In the case of standardized goods, the traditional conclusions on the reallocation of resources from import-competing industries to export industries follow: reductions in tariffs lead to a contraction of activity in industries where the country in question is at a comparative disadvantage and to an expansion in industries where it has relative advantages.

But the majority of manufactured goods traded by the industrial countries are differentiated products whose international exchange is characterized by intraindustry rather than interindustry specialization. Thus, in the presence of national product differentiation, multilateral tariff reductions can lead to an increased exchange of consumer goods without requiring substantial changes in the structure of production. Further, the expansion of trade in machinery and in intermediate products at higher levels of fabrication may entail specialization in narrower ranges of products rather than a decline in the activity of national industries.

The experience of the Common Market indicates the importance of itraindustry specialization in the international exchange of manufactured goods. Thus we observe a tendency toward diversification rather than specialization in the export patterns of the EEC countries. Instead of increasingly specializing in industries where they had been leading exporters prior to the creation of the EEC, the individual member countries have lost ground in these industries and have reduced reliance on them in expanding their exports. These changes have, in turn, contributed to an increasing uniformity in the structure of exports of the EEC member countries.[21]

Another approach to the problem is to consider the relative magnitudes of the export (import) balances of the member countries for individual commodity categories. For this purpose, I have expressed,

[21] On the statistical tests applied, see my "Tariff Reductions and Trade in Manufactures among the Industrial Countries," *American Economic Review,* June 1966, pp. 466–73.

for every country, the absolute difference between exports and imports in each of ninety-one commodity categories as a ratio of the sum of exports and imports in the same category, and have calculated an unweighted average of these ratios.[22] Should interindustry specialization predominate, one would expect the resulting "representative ratios" to approach unity since a country would either export or import a commodity. In the case of intraindustry specialization, the ratios would approach zero because exports and imports would tend toward equality within each category.

In intra-EEC trade the relevant ratios were approximately in the 0.4 to 0.6 range in 1958 and 0.3 to 0.5 in 1963 (Table 4.5). While the figures shown for a given country and a particular year are difficult to interpret, information on changes in these ratios over time permits us to draw inferences regarding the effects of tariff reductions on specialization. With the "representative ratios" falling in every country following the Common Market's establishment, it can be concluded that reductions in duties have led to increasing intraindustry specialization in the EEC.

The results point to the importance of intraindustry specialization

TABLE 4.5   Representative Ratios
of Trade Balances in Intra-EEC Trade

	Representative Ratios of Trade Balances [a]	
	1958	1963
Belgium	.458	.401
France	.394	.323
Germany	.531	.433
Italy	.582	.521
Netherlands	.495	.431

Source: Office Statistique des Communautés Européennes, *Commerce Extérieur,* 1958 and 1963.

Note: (a) Calculated as unweighted averages of the ratio of the absolute difference of intra-EEC exports and imports to the sum of exports and imports in 91 industries by the use of the formula shown in footnote 22.

---

[22] The following formula has been used in the calculations:

$$\frac{1}{n} \sum \frac{X_i - M_i}{X_i + M_i}$$

when X_i and M_i refer to the intra-EEC exports and imports of commodity category i, and n is the number of commodity categories considered.

in the trade of manufactured goods among industrial countries and provide support to the hypothesis that trade liberalization would result in intraindustry rather than interindustry specialization in these countries. Accordingly, we have to revise the traditional conclusions on the welfare consequences of tariff reductions. While the gains due to the shift of resources from import-competing to export industries are relevant in the case of simple manufactures, economies of scale obtainable through specialization within commodity categories are likely to provide the main benefit of tariff reductions in the case of machinery, precision equipment, and intermediate products at higher levels of fabrication.[23] In turn, much of the benefit from the increased exchange of consumer products may take the form of improvements in consumer welfare resulting from a wider choice among goods that serve identical purposes but are different in form, appearance, or simply national origin.

It would also appear that the difficulties of adjustment to freer trade have generally been exaggerated. According to the traditional analysis, the reallocation of resources from import-competing to export industries would entail losses for entrepreneurs and workers engaged in import-competing sectors. But while these conclusions apply to the trade of standardized commodities, the process of adjustment is different in the case of differentiated products. For one thing, the increased exchange of consumer goods is compatible with unchanged production in every country; for another, changes in product composition can be accomplished relatively easily in the case of machine building, precision instruments, and a variety of intermediate products. This explains that the fears expressed in various member countries of the Common Market concerning the demise of particular industries have not been realized. There are no examples of declining manufacturing industries in any of these countries, nor have they experienced a wave of bankruptcies. Indeed, the number of bankruptcies has fallen since the Common Market's establishment, and there is little evidence of frictional unemployment.[24]

The American experience with trade liberalization may also be in-

[23] Economies of scale are understood here in a broader sense to include cost reductions obtained through the lengthening of production runs associated with the reduction of product variety in individual plants. Cf. pp. 98–104 below.

[24] According to national statistics on bankruptcies, after a temporary increase in the recession year 1958, the number of business failures in the EEC countries declined from slightly over 16,000 in 1956 and 1957 to 14,500 in the early sixties.

structive in this regard. The successive reductions in duties under-taken since the mid-thirties do not seem to have created serious disturbances in any American industry, and the application for relief in the form of escape clauses has generally been restricted to nar-rowly defined product categories, such as rosaries, woodscrews, safety pins, spring clothespins, and baseball gloves.[25] In regard to the majority of industrial products, further reductions in tariffs can be expected to have similar consequences, so that losses in narrow product groups can be remedied through changes in product composi-tion. At the same time—as I will argue in more detail at a later point —in cases where adverse short-term repercussions do exist, it is de-sirable to provide financial assistance for relocation and retraining that contribute to the reallocation of resources rather than to obstruct this reallocation by maintaining high tariffs.

Conclusion

This chapter has examined the static effects of trade liberalization: the changes in exports and imports that would occur following reduc-tions in duties by the industrial countries under the assumption of un-changed production methods. It has been shown that, in line with the pattern of existing trade, much of the increase in trade flows would take place within Western Europe on the one hand, and among the United States, Canada, and Japan on the other. However, for the United States, the expansion of trade with Western Europe would exceed that with Canada and Japan taken together, and the United States would further benefit from the lessening of EEC and EFTA discrimination through multilateral tariff reductions.

Trade liberalization would apparently have little effect on the bal-ance of payments of the more developed industrial countries, the United States, the European Common Market, the United Kingdom, and the Continental EFTA countries. In these areas, estimated changes in the balance of payments resulting from the establishment of an Atlantic Free Trade Area could be remedied by a less than 1 per cent change in the relative prices of manufactured goods.[26] And

[25] On problems relating to textiles and the steel industry, see the discussion below.

[26] The price changes necessary to offset the impact of the elimination of tar-iffs on the balance of payments can be calculated by the use of the formula $dp = dB/\eta_m T$, when dp is the required percentage change in the relative prices

while a 5 per cent reduction in prices would be necessary to offset the deterioration in the Canadian balance of payments estimated on the basis of 1960 data, a price change of appropriately this magnitude has been brought about as a result of the devaluation of the Canadian dollar undertaken in the early 1960s.

In turn, to counterbalance the estimated improvement of nearly $.4 billion in Japan's balance of payments in an Atlantic Free Trade Area, Japanese prices of manufactured goods would have to rise, relative to prices in the other industrial countries, by about 7 per cent. But, as noted above, the increase in exports estimated for Japan would be reduced to a considerable extent if exceptions were allowed in reducing tariffs. Furthermore, because of the existence of quantitative restrictions, the reliability of estimates on prospective changes in Japan's exports and imports is rather low.

As regards the impact of tariff reductions on resource allocation, the predominance of intraindustry, as against interindustry, specialization in manufactured goods traded among the industrial countries is the relevant consideration. With national product differentiation in consumer goods, machinery, and intermediate goods at higher levels of fabrication, trade liberalization does not entail massive shifts of resources from import-competing to export industries as presumed by the traditional textbook explanation, but leads instead to changes in the product composition of individual industries. Such changes can be accomplished relatively easily, and the example of the European Common Market indicates that the problems of short-term adjustments are considerably smaller than commonly assumed.

However, tariff reductions will result in interindustry shifts of resources in the case of standardized products where international exchange is determined largely by intercountry differences in relative costs. Cost differentials explain the rapid increase of U.S. steel imports in recent years, for example, and have importantly influenced the pattern of international trade in textiles. Imports of textiles from less developed areas have risen at a rapid rate and have led to the establishment of quotas in the United States and in the major countries of Western Europe.

---

of manufactured goods, dB the change in the balance of payments resulting from trade liberalization, T the sum of exports and imports of manufactured goods in trade among the industrial countries in 1960, and η_m the weighted average of import demand elasticities of the country in question and of its trading partners, the weights being the value of imports in their mutual trade.

Other standardized manufactures are likely to appear among the exports of developing countries in the future. With the decline in the share of primary products in world trade, the comparative advantage of these countries will increasingly lie in simple manufactures that are either labor-intensive or utilize domestic raw materials. Accordingly, the industrial nations will have to arrive at a decision in regard to the imports of standardized products from less developed areas, with a full understanding of the adjustment involved. The policy implications of this decision will be examined in Chapter 7.

CHAPTER FIVE

The Dynamic Effects of Trade Liberalization

Large-Scale Economies and Market Size

The preceding chapter dealt with the economic benefits of trade liberalization obtainable under the static assumptions of unchanged production methods. I shall now consider the dynamic effects of the widening of national markets through freer trade: cost reductions due to economies of scale and improvements in production methods resulting from intensified competition between domestic and foreign firms. These sources of gains have received relatively little attention in the trade literature, and static considerations also predominate in the traditional theory of customs unions. Economies of scale have apparently been regarded as an unimportant complication for customs union theory, and little consideration has been given to the impact of increased competition on the methods of production.[1] Further, several writers have expressed the view that a country the size of the United Kingdom could reap all possible large-scale economies, and hence the widening of its national market would bring few additional benefits.[2]

Empirical investigations provide evidence of the existence of large-scale economies in manufacturing activities, however. In a comparative study of fifty-one countries, H. B. Chenery has shown that output per head in manufacturing tends to increase with the size of national markets.[3] The countries considered by Chenery also include less de-

---

[1] Cf. R. G. Lipsey, "The Theory of Customs Unions: A General Survey," *Economic Journal*, September 1960, p. 496.

[2] Cf., e.g., Harry G. Johnson, "The European Common Market—Risk or Opportunity"? *Weltwirtschaftliches Archiv*, Vol. 79, No. 2 (1957), pp. 267–78.

[3] Hollis B. Chenery, "Patterns of Industrial Growth," *American Economic Review*, September 1960, pp. 624–54.

veloped economies; therefore, for present purposes, comparisons between the United States and other industrial countries are of greater interest. In such investigations, the relationship between intercountry differences in market size (output) and in productivity, or unit costs, has been examined on an industry-by-industry basis.[4]

In a study of twenty-two U.S. and Canadian industries, J. H. Young has found that the larger American output levels are as compared to Canadian, the greater is the U.S. productivity advantage over Canada. The results of his inquiry have led Young to conclude that market size is likely to be the most important single factor determining productivity differences between the two countries.[5] Similar results have been obtained in an OEEC study of forty-four American and British industries that shows a high degree of correlation between market size on the one hand, and productivity and unit costs on the other.[6] Among individual industries, differences in market size appear to be responsible for the U.S. cost advantage in the production of containers, transport equipment, and agricultural machinery, and for the British relative advantage in shipbuilding, grain mill products, and cement manufacturing.

These results conflict with the thesis that all possible sources of large-scale economies can be exploited in a developed industrial country with a population of 40 to 50 million. Indeed, there are indications that even a national economy of the size of that of the United

---

[4] While unit cost is the relevant variable for indicating the existence of large-scale economies, lack of statistical data has often necessitated the use of labor productivity as a "proxy" for costs per unit. The results of an OEEC study of U.S. and U.K. industries cited below indicate, however, that the error committed thereby may be relatively small (for a similar conclusion, see Marvin Frankel, *British and American Manufacturing Productivity* [Urbana: University of Illinois Bulletin, Bureau of Economic and Business Research, 1957], p. 45). A possible explanation is that the technologically advanced production methods used in industries which have relatively large markets are associated with low labor cost (high productivity) *and* low capital costs.

[5] John H. Young, "Some Aspects of Canadian Economic Development" (unpublished doctoral dissertation submitted to Cambridge University, England, 1955, p. 86). The rank correlation coefficient between output and productivity ratios is 0.76. It is statistically significant at the 1 percent level.

[6] The rank correlation coefficient between output and productivity ratios is 0.79, between output and unit cost ratios 0.71. Both are statistically significant at the 1 per cent level (D. Paige and G. Bombach, *A Comparison of National Output and Productivity of the United Kingdom and the United States* [Paris: Organization for European Economic Cooperation, 1959], p. 64).

States continues to reap large-scale economies. A. A. Walters has estimated that, in the first half of the century, a doubling of labor and capital inputs in the U.S. nonagricultural sector has been accompanied by an approximately 130 per cent increase in output due to economies of scale. Expressed differently, unit costs declined by 13 per cent as output doubled.[7]

The findings of these studies have immediate implications for trade liberalization, since tariff reductions will enlarge the market open to each producer and increase the number of firms he considers as his competitors. But what are the benefits of a widening of national markets through trade and what influences contribute to reductions in costs? To begin with, individual industries can realize economies of scale following an expansion of trade in manufactures by constructing larger plants or combinations of plants (economies of scale in the traditional sense), by reducing product variety in individual plants (horizontal specialization), and by manufacturing various parts, components, and accessories in separate establishments (vertical specialization). Tariff reductions also create possibilities for greater competition between domestic and foreign firms and so provide inducement for improving manufacturing efficiency and for advances in technology. And, whatever their cause, the resulting cost reductions tend to have a cumulative effect: improvements in particular industries are transmitted to other sectors through input-output relationships and through the effects of higher incomes on the demand for consumer goods.

As a result of the operation of these factors, trade liberalization is expected to have a favorable influence on the growth performance of the participating countries.[8] The opposite happened in the interwar period in Western Europe, where the narrowing of markets due to the imposition of trade restrictions hindered the economic growth of the individual countries. In a study of this period, Ingvar Svennilson concluded that "the arbitrary combinations of resources within smaller or larger national areas had a decisive influence on long-term growth in Europe as a whole. It is likely that the existence of this national

---

[7] A. A. Walters, "A Note on Economies of Scale," *Review of Economics and Statistics,* November 1963, pp. 425–27. In estimating the extent of large-scale economies, Walters has adjusted for the effects of autonomous technological improvements.

[8] For a detailed exposition, see Bela Balassa, *The Theory of Economic Integration* (Homewood, Ill.: Irwin, 1961), Part II.

structure slowed down not only the growth of some less favored countries but also the general development of Europe's own resources." [9]

In addition to trade barriers, the uncertainties related to the imposition of further restrictions had an unfavorable effect in Western Europe during the interwar period. Correspondingly, the widening of the market through trade liberalization will depend on the size of the tariff cut, as well as on the risk associated with the possibility that duties will be reimposed at some future date. While tariff reductions will enlarge the market open to individual producers, the inclusion of this risk factor in entrepreneurial calculations on production and investment will limit the expansion of international trade. Thus, the beneficial effects of trade liberalization will be enhanced if duties are "bound" in the sense that the trading partners undertake an obligation to refrain from raising tariffs unilaterally.[10]

Economies of Scale in Individual Industries

STANDARDIZED PRODUCTS.   Because of their preoccupation with one-product firms, economists have largely restricted their attention to economies of scale of the first type which permit reductions in costs as larger plants, or combinations of plants, are built. This is economies of scale in the traditional sense, and it pertains to the production of standardized commodities. The efficient operation of a single unit of equipment may require high output levels, for example; alternatively, the use of several interrelated units of equipment may be called for. In the latter case, it is necessary for maximum efficiency that the entire plant's capacity be equal to some multiple of the capacities of the individual units. The steel industry and aluminum production are often cited as examples.

Further, cost reductions per unit of output can be obtained in the use of containers, pipelines, and compressors, where capacity is related to volume while cost is a function of the surface area. From this principle, engineers have derived the so-called .6 rule, according to which a doubling of capacity would be accompanied by an approximately 60 per cent increase in total costs. Such relationships pertain to industries that utilize liquids as their principal input, such as petroleum refining, fertilizers, and various chemicals. In the manufacture of ammonia-based fertilizers, for example, a doubling of the output of ammonia entails a 40 per cent increase in labor costs and an 81 per cent rise in capital costs, whereas for ammonium nitrate and ammonium sulphate—the two most important types of fertilizers—the relevant figures are 27 and 68 per cent and 20 and 65 per cent, respectively.[11] In turn, in various branches of the petrochemical industry, labor costs have been shown to rise by 20 to 30 per cent and capital costs by 60 to 70 per cent as output doubles.[12]

Economies of scale can also be obtained in conjunction with various "nonproportional" activities such as design, production planning, channeling and collecting information, handling, shipping, and repair facilities.[13] As a rule, the unit cost of these activities tends to decline with the rise of output. Inventory holdings of materials, spare parts, and final products, too, need to increase less than proportionately as output expands.

The use of machinery embodying advanced techniques at higher output levels is another source of economies of scale. In this connection, a comparison of American and British experience can be of interest. In a study based on information provided by British subsidiaries of American firms, John H. Dunning noted several cases where high volume operation led to reductions in unit cost due to the application of automatic machinery. A producer of refrigerator components reported, for example, that higher productivity—and lower costs—in the U.S. parent factory is explained by the fact that the higher volume of output in the United States warrants using automatic machinery that is not profitable at smaller output levels. Thus, while 23.6 minutes per hundred units were necessary to manufacture a special component at low volume with relatively simple tooling, production time falls to 1.5 minutes per hundred and costs per unit by about one-half when larger volume justifies the more expensive tooling used by the parent company.

Similar instances have been observed in other industries, in manu-

[11] Thomas Vietorisz and A. S. Manne, "Chemical Processes, Plant Location and Economies of Scale," in *Studies in Process Analysis,* A. S. Manne and H. M. Markowitz, eds. (New York: Wiley, 1963), pp. 136–58.

[12] W. Isard and E. W. Schooler, *Location Factors in the Petrochemical Industry* (Washington, D.C.: U.S. Department of Commerce, 1959).

[13] Similar considerations apply to economies of scale in research that will be examined below.

facturing operations as well as in packaging.[14] Moreover, when automatic machinery has been installed in British plants, it is often operated for fewer hours or at lower speeds because of the smaller market for the product. Thus the use of more sophisticated machinery, along with the better utilization of this machinery, provides advantages for establishments located in the United States that serve a larger market. In fact, in all cases where sufficiently detailed information was available, Dunning found a direct correlation between differences in productivity and the size of the market served by U.S. as compared to British plants.[15]

I have considered here various sources of economies of scale that can be realized in manufacturing establishments producing a standardized commodity. There is evidence of economies of scale in a wide variety of manufacturing operations, although available information does not permit us to evaluate their relative importance in individual industries.[16] Still, a comparison of costs per unit of output in domestic and foreign plants of American firms can provide an indication of cost reductions obtainable at higher output levels.

The results shown in Table 5.1 reveal a close correspondence between relative plant size and unit costs. In cases where the foreign plant's output is less than 5 per cent of that of the U.S. plant, costs in foreign operations are, on the average, 31 per cent higher; for output ratios of 5 to 10 per cent, the ratio of foreign to domestic costs is 99; it falls to 96 in the case of output ratios of 10 to 25 per cent and to 86 for output ratios of 25 to 50 per cent. Finally, costs in foreign plants are, on the average, only 74 per cent of U.S. costs in cases where the output of the foreign plant exceeds one-half of that of the U.S. factory. Parallel with the changes in unit cost ratios, the number of firms that reported lower costs in foreign as compared to domestic

[14] A producer of a well-known brand of consumer goods has suggested that packaging provides "a classic example of far greater productivity per man-hour being attained in America because the heavy investment in the automatic machinery used in our U.S. factories would not pay off in England." John H. Dunning, *American Investment in British Manufacturing Industry* (London: George Allen & Unwin, Ltd., 1958), p. 134.

[15] Same, p. 149.

[16] For a detailed discussion of economies of scale in selected industries, see, e.g., J. S. Bain, *Barriers to New Competition* (Cambridge, Mass.: Harvard University Press, 1956), Chapter 3; Bela Balassa, *The Theory of Economic Integration*, Chapter 6; and John Haldi, *Economies of Scale in Economic Development* (Stanford University, 1960, mimeographed).

TABLE 5.1 Cost Ratios in Domestic and Foreign Plants
of American Companies, 1960

Foreign Output as a Percentage of Domestic Output

	Less than 5	5–9.9	10–24.9	25–49.9	50 and over
Average unit cost ratio	131	99	96	86	74
Percentage distribution of costs					
Lower than U.S.	16	40	47	58	85
Same as U.S.	12	12	26	12	—
Higher than U.S.	72	48	26	31	15
Total	100	100	100	100	100
Number of products	25	25	34	26	20

Source: Theodore R. Gates and Fabian Linden, *Costs and Competition* (New York: National Industrial Conference Board, 1961), p. 129.

Note: Data include information on foreign plants located in industrial countries only.

operations increased from 16 to 85 per cent between the first and the last category, while the number of those with higher costs abroad fell from 72 to 15 per cent.

HORIZONTAL SPECIALIZATION. These results provide powerful evidence of the existence of economies of scale on the plant level. But plant size and unit costs are not necessarily correlated in the case of multiproduct firms. In such instances cost reductions can be obtained by reducing product variety, which permits the lengthening of production runs for individual commodities (horizontal specialization). For a given product group, large markets will thus provide advantages to individual firms because the same assortment of commodities can be manufactured in specialized plants.

Higher productivity in U.S. as compared to Canadian textile plants has been explained by reference to the fact that, with the same assortment of commodities manufactured in the two countries, American firms can specialize in a single fabric while Canadian establishments often produce 5 to 100 types of fabric. Likewise, American firms generally supply the same range of products from a smaller number of plants in their British operations than in the United States. With reference to the benefits of horizontal specialization, some observers have even suggested that productivity differentials between the United

States and Western Europe are due more to differences in the length of the production run than to differences in plant size.[17]

The advantages of longer production runs derive from improvements in manufacturing efficiency along the "learning curve," the lowering of expenses involved in moving from one operation to another, and the use of special-purpose machinery. Improvements in manufacturing efficiency take place as the experience obtained in producing a particular commodity leads to better work performance and improved organization of work. Studies conducted in the United States during and after World War II have shown that, in several industries, labor productivity tends to increase by 18 to 20 per cent as accumulated output doubles. Improvements along the "learning curve" have been made, among others, in shipbuilding, aircraft production, and machine-tool manufacturing.[18] In the case of shipbuilding, the impact of the learning process on production costs has also been estimated. On the basis of an investigation of cost elements in several shipyards, Leonard Rapping concluded that during the Second World War each doubling of accumulated output was accompanied by a 10 to 27 per cent increase in the rate of output with given inputs.[19]

The unit costs of moving from one operation to another, too, decline with the lengthening of production runs. These costs include the expenses associated with the resetting of machines, the shifting of labor, and the reorganization of the work process. A machine-tool manufacturer has reported, for example, that the greater number of changeovers in the production of machine tools in its British plant involves a 14 per cent loss of production time as compared with production in the United States. Another firm has commented: "The fact that we, with an output of only one-twentieth of that of our U.S. associate, have to produce exactly the same range of products, means

[17] Cf. the statement by P. J. Verdoorn, reported in E. A. G. Robinson (ed.), *Economic Consequences of the Size of Nations,* Proceedings of a Conference held by the International Economic Association (London: Macmillan, 1960), p. 346. With regard to the Canadian and the British experience, see Young, cited, pp. 179–80 and Dunning, cited, p. 124.

[18] Cf. W. Z. Hirsch, "Manufacturing Progress Functions," *Review of Economics and Statistics,* May 1952, pp. 143–55, and Harold Asher, *Cost-Quantity Relationships in the Airframe Industry* (Santa Monica, Calif.: The Rand Corporation, 1956).

[19] Leonard Rapping, "Learning and World War II Production Functions," *Review of Economics and Statistics,* February 1965, pp. 81–86. Rapping also provides evidence of "traditional" economies of scale that depend on the volume of production rather than the amount of cumulated output.

that our setting-up to running costs in this country work out at 1:5, whilst in the United States the corresponding ratio is 1:30." [20]

American companies have also reported that the need to manufacture a large assortment of products in the United Kingdom forces them to use general-purpose machines in their British operations. In the absence of horizontal specialization, then, the cost reductions obtained by using special-purpose machinery cannot be realized. The industries in question include machine-tool building, light engineering, and food products.

VERTICAL SPECIALIZATION. The possibilities for subdividing the production process among individual establishments also depends on the size of the market. As the sales of the final product increase, parts, components, and accessories can be manufactured in separate plants, each of which may enjoy economies of scale. The production of automobiles is a frequently mentioned example. In conjunction with the growth of car output, electrical and ignition systems, radiators and heaters, steering wheels, transmission equipment, and a number of other components and accessories have come to be produced in separate plants in the United States. On the other hand, the degree of vertical specialization is generally lower in European automobile plants, where the annual output of cars is much smaller than in the United States.

The chemical industry, plastics, rubber, aircraft, and scientific instruments provide further examples of vertical specialization. With regard to these industries, C. F. Carter and B. R. Williams have observed that "the British market has not been big enough to encourage the growth of specialist producers of equipment—who themselves might have created new possibilities of progress." [21] Finally, British subsidiaries of U.S. firms operating in a wide variety of industries have reported that many of the materials and component parts that can be obtained in the United States are not available in the United Kingdom.[22]

The cost advantages derived from vertical specialization in the framework of large markets explain the apparent superiority of the United States in industries that use large quantities of intermediate products. According to a comparative study of the domestic and for-

[20] Dunning, cited, p. 143; also pp. 133–35.
[21] C. F. Carter and B. R. Williams, *Industry and Technical Progress* (London: Oxford University Press, 1957), p. 155.
[22] Dunning, cited, p. 115.

eign operations of U.S. companies, material costs are 10 to 25 per cent higher in Western Europe than in the United States. Within this category, cost differentials are the largest in the case of purchased components and fabricated inputs since, unlike their European counterparts, American producers can draw on a vast network of specialized suppliers who themselves enjoy economies of scale.[23]

It appears, then, that all three sources of economies of scale contribute to cost reductions in the event of increases in the size of national markets. Improvements will not continue, however, after an optimum size has been reached. Optimum size relates to the capacity of the plant in the case of one-product firms and to the size of the industry or that of the national economy in the case of horizontal and vertical specialization. But the output required for optimal operation will differ from industry to industry. Optimum plant size is lower in textile production than in paper manufacturing, for example, and the economies of specialization can be realized in a smaller market in the case of simple metal manufactures than in the case of automobiles.

In general, it would appear that the gain from economies of scale is inversely related to the size of national markets. In relative terms, the exploitation of economies of scale following the liberalization of trade would therefore provide the largest gains to small countries. Still, indications are that countries of the size of the United Kingdom can derive considerable benefits from economies of scale following the liberalization of international trade. Moreover, the optimum size of the economy tends to increase with the progress of technology. Thus, although in the United States economies of scale are likely to be fully exploited in traditional industries, an enlargement of the market through trade can lead to reductions in unit costs in some new, technically advanced branches of manufacturing sectors. Examples are high-speed electronic computers, large jet aircraft, and communications satellites.

Competition and Improvements in Production Methods

Trade liberalization will also create the conditions for more effective competition. For one thing, by increasing the number of firms each producer considers as his competitors, the opening of national

[23] T. R. Gates and Fabian Linden, *Costs and Competition: American Experience Abroad* (New York: National Industrial Conference Board, 1961), chap. 3.

frontiers will contribute to a loosening of monopolistic and oligopolistic market structures in the individual countries, and will reduce the risk of collusion among oligopolists. At the same time, there is no contradiction between gains from economies of scale and increased competition, since a wider market can sustain a greater number of efficient units.

Neither is there a contradiction between the decline of the small family firm and intensified competition following the liberalization of trade. As Tibor Scitovsky has aptly put it, competition should not be understood to mean a large number of producers coexisting in the market but rather the *ability* and the *willingness* of the individual firm to encroach upon the markets of others.[24] Small enterprises rarely have the financial means to encroach on other firms' markets, while a situation of domestic monopoly or quasi-monopoly often reduces the willingness of the firm to engage in competition abroad. Correspondingly, both the transformation of small-scale family firms into larger enterprises and the weakening of monopolistic and oligopolistic market positions will tend to intensify competitive pressures in domestic as well as in foreign markets.

Mention should also be made of the implications the availability of market information has for effective competition. Small firms are often handicapped by their limited knowledge of markets beyond the area they customarily supply and by their inability to use communications media on a large scale to provide product information. Furthermore, regardless of their size, obstacles to trade often discourage firms from supplying foreign markets with information on their products. The liberalization of trade would augment the flow of information on products and markets, in part through its effects on the size of the firm and in part by increasing the profitability of selling efforts abroad. In turn, the increased flow of information would make markets more transparent and thus contribute to greater competition.

Intensified competition may have beneficial effects on the national economies of the trading countries through "forced" improvements in manufacturing efficiency and through technological change. While the former has no place in traditional theory, which postulates the use of the most efficient production methods among those available to the firm, it may assume considerable importance in countries whose markets have been sheltered from foreign competition. Gains of this

[24] Tibor Scitovsky, *Economic Theory and Western European Integration* (Stanford University Press, 1958), p. 124.

sort received much attention in public discussions, especially on the occasion of Britain's application for entry into the Common Market in 1961. At the time, it was widely argued that the effects of foreign competition on business behavior would provide one of the principal if not *the* main, benefits, of joining the Common Market for the United Kingdom. Some regarded entry as a "cure-all," others as a "challenge" or a "salutary jolt" that would bring about a change in the outlook of business and provide an inducement for a transition from the "traditional ways of doing things" to the application of modern methods of production, organization, and marketing.

In criticism of this proposition, it was claimed that, rather than contributing to an improvement in the performance of the British economy, entry into the Common Market may put the United Kingdom at a disadvantage. In this connection, reference was made to the experience of Northern Ireland and Southern Italy; in both cases integration with more advanced regions had adverse consequences on the development of manufacturing industry and led to the emigration of capital and labor. This argument is based on a mistaken analogy, however, since the unfavorable experience of the two regions was largely due to deficiencies in their social and economic overhead capital, which is hardly the case in Britain. The United Kingdom possesses a highly developed industrial structure; hence, the relevant question is whether business firms would have sufficient incentive to carry out the transformation necessary to meet the challenge of foreign competition.

The reduction of tariff barriers—the stick of competition—provides a powerful inducement for such a transformation, but the outcome will also depend on the economic policies followed. The experience of the 1950s in the United Kingdom shows that producers may not utilize the opportunities provided by the liberalization of trade if recurring balance of payments crises lead to the application of "stop-and-go" policies which intermittently restrict domestic demand and put a brake on investment activity. Even industries oriented toward international markets, such as shipbuilding, have apparently been unfavorably affected by the sluggish pace of the British economy during the fifties.[25]

[25] J. R. Parkinson, *The Economics of Shipbuilding in the United Kingdom* (Cambridge: University Press, 1960), pp. 98–100. Partly as a result of the poor performance of the British shipbuilding industry, the share of the United Kingdom in the construction of ships outside the Communist countries declined from 38 per cent in 1950 to 13 per cent in 1960.

More generally, in the event of trade liberalization countries with high growth rates would have certain advantages over those that are growing at a relatively slow rate. The rapid expansion of domestic demand increases the mobility of resources and raises the return on—and lessens the risk of—new investments. These influences in turn contribute to the expansion of investment activity, when a high rate of investment permits the rapid application of new technology and reduces the average age of capital. By contrast, in slow-growing countries, low resource mobility and an unfavorable climate for investment create difficulties in exploiting the possibilities offered by the liberalization of trade. These considerations apply with special force to industries, such as steel and chemicals, which require large investment outlays; in such cases, the low rate of growth of domestic demand may not warrant the investment necessary for expanding exports.[26]

It follows that in countries that have had a poor growth performance, trade liberalization would have to be supplemented by policies aimed at raising the rate of investment and increasing resource mobility. Policies designed to facilitate the conversion of small family firms into larger enterprises and inducements provided to research activity may serve these objectives. But a major precondition appears to be a realistic exchange rate, since an overvalued rate would have the twin consequences of stifling the growth of exports and necessitating the application of a deflationary policy—as indeed happened in 1925 in the United Kingdom. At the same time, the experience of Germany, Italy, and Japan during the 1950s indicates that exports can play an important role in the growth process. In these countries, the expansion of exports contributed to an acceleration of economic growth through its effects on investment and technological change.[27] Thus, unlike unilateral tariff reductions, multilateral trade liberalization provides—in addition to the stick—the carrot of competition in the form of opportunities for increasing exports.

[26] These relationships have been examined in some detail by Zoran Hodjera in "Technological Progress, Growth, and Trade Liberalization," a background paper for this study.

[27] On "export-propelled" growth see Alexander Lamfalussy, *The United Kingdom and the Six* (Homewood, Ill.: Irwin, 1963); Wilfred Beckerman, "Projecting Europe's Growth," *Economic Journal,* December 1962, pp. 912–25; Bela Balassa, "Some Observations on Mr. Beckerman's Export-Propelled Growth Model," same, December 1963, pp. 781–85; and the controversy between Beckerman and Balassa in subsequent issues of the *Economic Journal.*

France is a good example of the transformation of a national economy in response to increased foreign competition. Following the reduction of protectionist barriers and the creation of the Common Market, the hitherto closed French economy has increasingly assumed an open character. The opening of the economy, along with the establishment of a realistic exchange rate and the policy of encouraging concentration, has produced considerable changes in business behavior. We witness the gradual disappearance of the "live and let live" attitude which impeded the introduction of modern production methods in the past. At the same time, the structure of individual industries is changing as larger, more viable, establishments take the place of the small family firm.

But competitive pressures in the Common Market are not confined to France. With reductions in tariff barriers and the increased flow of market information, there has been a widening of the horizon of national firms in the EEC countries, and business decisions increasingly reflect a realization of the fact that they have to compete on equal terms with the enterprises of the member countries. In conjunction with these developments, there is a general tendency of transforming small-scale enterprises into larger units which can compete more effectively in EEC markets. At the same time, thus far there are few signs that international cartels would be formed to restrain competition, as was feared by some observers prior to the establishment of the Common Market.

Aside from "forced" improvements in manufacturing efficiency, increased competition provides inducement for technological progress in the industrial countries. To begin with, changes in the structure of manufacturing industry following a cut in tariffs may make it possible to use production methods not available to the firm beforehand. Also, foreign competition tends to stimulate research activity aimed at developing new products and improving production methods. Increased trade may further contribute to the transmission of technical knowledge by increasing the familiarity of producers with new commodities and technological processes originating abroad.

Other things being equal, the gains from increased competition will depend on the size of the country and on the degree of protectionism existing prior to the liberalization of trade. If we assumed that trade policies were the same everywhere, the small countries would benefit most since their narrow national markets do not allow for the competition of efficient firms. Commercial policies followed by industrial countries differ to a considerable extent, however. While the Scandinavian countries and Switzerland long followed a liberal trade policy to compensate for the disadvantages of their small size, in Britain and France high tariffs sheltered much of manufacturing industry from foreign competition and reduced competitive pressures among domestic firms. Competitive pressures have increased to a considerable extent in France following the Common Market's establishment, but the incursion of the producers of the small EFTA countries in the British market has had only a limited impact on business behavior in the United Kingdom. Should Britain follow appropriate policies, she would therefore be one of the principal beneficiaries of greater competition in the event of trade liberalization among the industrial countries.

Reductions in their high tariffs would also benefit Canada and Japan. The gains from increased competition would be especially pronounced in the Canadian economy, the smaller of the two. It has been noted that, by limiting competition, the protection of manufacturing industries has retarded the growth of productivity in Canada.[28] But the effects of intensified competition would extend also to the Common Market and to the United States. In the United States the imports of foreign automobiles have prompted the introduction of compact cars in recent years, and competition from abroad has contributed to improvements in production methods in the textile industry and in bicycle manufacturing. The impact of increased competition is also apparent in the steel industry where price increases have been the smallest for products in the case of which the penetration of imports in domestic markets is the most pronounced.[29]

Comparative Advantage and "Exception Lists"

These conclusions on the beneficial effects of intensified competition have been based on the assumption that, as a result of the loosening of monopolistic and oligopolistic market structures *and* the transformation of small-scale firms into larger units, multilateral re-

[28] On this point see H. G. Johnson, *The Canadian Quandary* (Toronto: McGraw-Hill, 1963), passim.

[29] Cf. United States–Japan Trade Council, *Imports and Inflation* (Washington: 1966), p. 7. According to an earlier study, the effects of foreign competition were concentrated on non-integrated steel producers. (Walter Adams and J. B. Dirlam, "Steel Imports and Vertical Oligopoly Power," *American Economic Review*, September 1964, pp. 626–55.)

ductions in duties would make competition more effective. On the one hand, trade liberalization would serve as an antimonopoly device; on the other, the expected increase in the size of national firms would augment their ability to compete.

However, in discussions on the possible effects of tariff reductions in the framework of the Kennedy Round, it has been argued—especially in France—that the conditions of competition are falsified by reason of the advantages American firms have over their European competitors. In this connection, mention has been made of the alleged comparative advantages of the United States in fast-growing export industries, the larger size of American as compared to European firms, and the implications for technological progress of government spending on research and development in the United States.

An analysis of the seventy-eight commodity categories considered in Chapter 4 does not seem to bear out the first proposition. There is only a slight association between the "revealed" comparative advantage of the United States and the rate of growth of exports in the individual commodity groups. The degree of correlation is somewhat greater for Common Market exports, while a negative relationship is shown in the case of the United Kingdom and Japan. But the customary statistical tests do not permit us to derive any firm conclusions about these relationships since, with two exceptions, the results are not statistically significant.[30]

The ambiguity of the results is partly explained by the fact that, in addition to the industries dominated by new products, such as office machinery and plastic materials, trade has expanded rapidly in a number of traditional commodities, including footwear, fur clothing, travel goods, and musical instruments and phonographs. In the case of several of these commodity categories, the observed tendency toward an intensified exchange of consumer goods among industrial countries has contributed to the expansion of trade, and it has also made the delineation of comparative advantage more difficult.

---

[30] Rank correlation coefficients calculated between indices of the expansion of exports by the industrial countries in the period 1953–55 to 1960–62, on the one hand, and export-performance indices and export-import ratios, on the other, are the following: United States, 0.15 and 0.13; Canada, −0.02 and 0.02; Common Market, 0.18 and 0.25 *; United Kingdom, −0.11 and −0.23 *; Sweden, 0.03 and −0.08; and Japan, −0.04 and −0.16. The starred items are statistically significant at the 5 per cent level. (For sources, see Appendix Table 4.6.)

Were we to limit our attention to technologically advanced products, potential changes in the structure of domestic production rather than the immediate effect of tariff reductions on imports would be the relevant consideration. The elimination of duties may have little impact on the imports of commodities which have no close domestic substitutes but will influence the future development of domestic manufacturing. In this connection, the proposition has been advanced that a nation should maintain the protection of modern industries where it lags behind its trading partners in terms of technological development. This present-day version of the infant-industry argument has been utilized by several industrial countries in drawing up the list of commodities they wish to exempt from the Kennedy Round of tariff negotiations. The composition of these exception lists is of special interest since it provides some indication of the motivating forces of protection.[31]

The infant-industry argument dominates the exception list submitted by Japan, which is by far the longest: it reportedly covers about 40 to 50 per cent of Japanese imports of manufactures. The same argument has been used by the European Common Market with regard to certain kinds of electrical and other machinery, large aircraft, and nuclear reactors. The EEC list, comprising about 19 per cent of industrial imports into the member countries, is reported also to include several commodities in whose production the Common Market countries are at a comparative disadvantage (paper and newsprint, trucks, other commercial vehicles), as well as some standardized products where demand is sensitive to price changes (steel tubes, aluminum, magnesium).[32]

[31] Since the exception lists have not been made public, the following conclusions have been based on reports published in *The Economist, Journal of Commerce, Le Monde, The New York Times,* and the London *Times.* Whatever the inaccuracies of this compilation, it may have some usefulness in pointing to commodities that the consensus of informed observers places on the exception lists.

[32] It goes without saying that only some of the possible reasons for excepting commodities from tariff negotiations are considered here. A complete list is given in *Le Monde:* (1) military and strategic considerations; (2) security of source of supply; (3) high domestic material prices; (4) high domestic energy prices: (5) new specialized industries; (6) large dimension of foreign firms; (7) regional considerations; (8) overcapacity in foreign countries that may lead to dumping; (9) low levels of existing duties; (10) subsidies applied in foreign countries; (11) low wages in competing countries; (12) state trading in competing countries; (13) maintenance of a "harmony" in the tariff structure; (14)

Aside from plastic materials, new products do not appear on the British exception list. Rather, the United Kingdom apparently wants to protect certain declining industries (coal, cotton, textiles, and jute manufactures) as well as standardized commodities, such as lead and zinc metal. In turn, the U.S. exception list reportedly includes several labor-intensive commodities, some of which have been under considerable pressure in recent years (cotton, textiles, watches, optical instruments, and some machine tools). It should be added, however, that the U.S. and British exception lists—covering perhaps one-tenth of industrial imports into the two countries—are shorter than that of the EEC, while the Continental EFTA countries other than Portugal did not submit exception lists.

These considerations indicate a tendency in the large industrial countries to develop all branches of manufacturing and to resist the decline of industries where they are at a comparative disadvantage. It is easy to see that the policy of protecting declining industries is costly because it does not permit the movement of factors of production into the modern sectors of the economy where the possibilities for technological progress are often greater. On the other hand, one can hardly dismiss the infant-industry argument if the industries in question promise technological improvements that may importantly contribute to the growth of the national economy. I shall return to this question later in the chapter.

Firm Size and Research Expenditures

It has further been argued that, in the event of trade liberalization, their large size would provide advantages to American firms over European companies. If industrial corporations are ranked in terms of their 1964 sales,[33] we find that thirteen of the fifteen largest firms are American while the two giant British-Dutch companies, Royal Dutch–Shell and Unilever, occupy fourth and sixth place.[34] The

maintenance of preference accorded to associated territories (*Le Monde*, November 12, 1964). Given the wide variety of the reasons cited, one may be surprised that the EEC exception list is not much longer.

[33] *Fortune,* July and August 1965.

[34] Some observers have also pointed out that the sales of the largest manufacturing firm in the United States, General Motors, exceed the gross domestic product of the Netherlands (Pierre Drouin, "Les Américains ont-ils les dents trop longues?" *Le Monde,* May 13, 1965). But comparisons between the value

largest German firm, Volkswagen, is twenty-seventh, Italy's Fiat forty-first, and the French Rhône-Poulenc sixty-eighth on the list. In the same year, fifty-five American firms had annual sales exceeding one billion dollars, as against twelve companies from the Common Market countries, six from Britain, two from Japan, and one from Switzerland. Within the Common Market itself, eight German, two Dutch, one French, and one Italian company belong to this group.[35] American firms also predominate in the 500–1000 and 250–500 million categories although their proportion in the total is smaller here; by comparison, relatively more French and Japanese corporations are included (Table 5.2).

In European discussions of the advantages of large size, much

TABLE 5.2   Industrial Corporations Grouped According
to Their 1964 Sales
($ million)

	Over 2,000	1,000– 2,000	500–1,000	250–500	Together
United States	20	35	67	125	247
Total non-U.S.	5	16	66	80	167
Canada	—	—	5	5	10
Common Market	1	11	29	23	64
Belgium	—	—	2	1	3
France	—	1	11	9	21
Germany	—	8	10	10	28
Italy	—	1	5	2	8
Netherlands	1	1	1	1	4
EFTA	4	3	19	33	59
United Kingdom	4	2	15	28	49
Sweden	—	—	2	3	5
Switzerland	—	1	2	2	5
Japan	—	2	10	15	27
Other	—	—	3	4	7
	25	51	133	205	414

Source: Fortune, July and August 1965.

of sales and GDP are hardly meaningful since the former include—and the latter exclude—the value of purchased materials.

[35] The relatively poor showing of the French companies may partly explain the attention given to this question in France.

emphasis has been given to the financial superiority of American corporations that permits them to establish subsidiaries abroad. But these advantages relate to the problem of foreign investment rather than to competitiveness in export markets, which is our concern here.[36] On the other hand, the international competitiveness of firms of different size will be affected by economies of scale in production and in research. In the earlier part of this chapter I considered the former; some remarks concerning the latter are now in order.

There is a certain parallel between economies of scale obtained in the production of commodities and in the production of knowledge. To begin with, research activity involves a fixed outlay—varying in amount from industry to industry—in the form of equipment and laboratory facilities that is often beyond the means of a small firm.[37] Further, large enterprises can benefit from increased specialization in the production of knowledge: horizontal specialization as scientists concentrate in narrow fields of research, and vertical specialization as basic and applied research are separated.

Economies of scale in research may provide inducement to a more than proportional rise in research expenditures as the size of the firm increases. In fact, in 1962 company-financed research and development expenditures of U.S. manufacturing firms engaged in such activities averaged 2 per cent of sales revenue in cases where total employment exceeded 5,000; it was 1.5 per cent in companies with 1,000 to 5,000 employees, and 1.1 per cent in firms with fewer than 1,000 employees.[38] Within the first group, however, research activity does not appear to increase more than proportionately with the size of the

[36] Issues related to foreign investment will be discussed in the next chapter.

[37] In the European electronics industry, the following "threshold" development costs have been reported (in million dollars): radio communications receiver, 0.2–0.4; WHF transmitter, 0.7–1.0; laboratory oscilloscope, 0.8–1.2; marine radar set, 0.3 — 0.6; spectrum analyzer 0.3 — 0.6; machine-tool control equipment, 0.8–1.7; small scientific computer, 2.8—5.6; research satellite, 1.4—4.2; TV color camera, 4.4—8.4; small quasi-electronic telephone exchange, 5.6—11.2; large fully electronic telephone exchange, 15.8—25.2; ranger of electronic data processing computers, softwave and peripherals, 20.8—41.5; communications satellite, 28.0—112.0 (C. Freeman *et al.,* "Research and Development in Electronic Capital Goods," *National Institute Economic Review,* November 1965, p. 69).

[38] National Science Foundation, *Basic Research, Applied Research and Development in Industry, 1962* (Washington, D.C., 1965), pp. 107–22. It is also apparent that the number of firms engaged in research and development as a percentage of this total in each category increases with the size of the firm.

firm. Rather, the various indicators of research activity—expenditures on research, employment of research and development personnel, the number of patents, and the rate of innovating activity—generally show a less than proportionate increase with sales after a certain firm size has been reached.[39]

At the same time, the extent of research activity varies greatly from industry to industry. In the following discussion we will limit our attention to those branches of manufacturing where expenditures on research and development as a percentage of sales revenue exceed the average for manufacturing as a whole. In 1962, in the United States, this category included aircraft and missiles (23.0 per cent), communications equipment and electronic components (12.0 per cent), other electrical equipment (7.6 per cent), professional and scientific instruments (7.7 per cent), industrial chemicals (6.0 per cent), and drugs and medicines (4.3 per cent).[40] Similar results are shown for the United Kingdom, and the industries in question account for about three-fourths of industrial research and development expenditure in both countries.[41]

The importance of research in the chemical industry is indicated by the continuous development of new products that range from synthetic fibers, leather, and rubber to plastics and resins. Du Pont, the largest chemical manufacturer in the United States (and in the

[39] Cf. Edwin Mansfield, "Size of Firm, Market Structure, and Innovations," *Journal of Political Economy,* December 1963, pp. 556–76, and "Industrial Research and Development Expenditures: Determinants, Prospects, and Relation to Size of Firm and Inventive Output," same, August 1964, pp. 319–40; F. M. Scherer, "Size of Firm, Oligopoly, and Research: A Comment," *Canadian Journal of Economics and Political Science,* May 1965, pp. 256–66, and "Firm Size, Market Structure, Opportunity, and the Output of Patented Inventions," *American Economic Review,* December 1965, pp. 1097–1125. According to Scherer the "inflection point" was roughly around sales of $.5 billion in 1955.

[40] *Basic Research, Applied Research and Development in Industry, 1962,* p. 122. Data include company- as well as government-financed research. In 1962 the average ratio of expenditures on research and development to sales for all manufacturing industries taken together was 4.1 per cent.

[41] In 1962 in the United States, the relative proportions were: aircraft and missiles, 35.9 per cent; industrial chemicals, 6.7 per cent; drugs and medicines, 1.7 per cent; communications equipment and electronic components, 10.9 per cent; other electrical equipment, 11.2 per cent; and professional and scientific instruments, 3.9 per cent (same, p. 99). For data on the United Kingdom, see Organization for Economic Cooperation and Development, *Science, Economic Growth, and Government Policy,* a report by Christopher Freeman, M. Raymond Poignant and Ingvar Svennilson (Paris, 1963), pp. 80–81.

world), has long been in the forefront of innovating activity. But several European companies are comparable in size to the largest American firms in this industry: the combined sales of the three successor firms of the IG Farbenindustrie exceed sales by Du Pont, while British Imperial Chemical precedes any other American manufacturer, and the new Italian Montecatini-Edison group as well as the French Rhône-Poulenc are not far behind. At any rate, product innovations in the chemical industry can often be adopted relatively easily; other firms soon followed in the footsteps of Du Pont in manufacturing synthetic fibers, for example. Also, medium-size firms have often had a better growth record than larger enterprises, and there is little reason to assume that leading European chemical companies would be at a disadvantage compared to their American competitors.

Similar conclusions pertain to the production of electrical equipment (e.g., generators, turbines, and transformers) where the lower labor cost of British and German manufacturers apparently outweighs the technological advantages of American companies.[42] European firms do not have much to fear from the competition of U.S. producers of domestic electrical appliances or of professional and scientific instruments either. Finally, the technological lag between the U.S. and the European drug industry, resulting from developments during the Second World War, appears to be shortening.

The situation is different in regard to electronics. In the case of data processing equipment, for example, substantial cost reductions can be obtained by lengthening production runs, and the availability of a large, technically competent sales force provides a further advantage. Moreover, in an industry characterized by continuing changes in technology and a rapid rate of obsolescence, a long-term development program and large-scale research effort are required. These advantages of large size explain that, in the United States, only IBM has been consistently profitable, while in Western Europe several companies engaged in data processing—of which Bull Machines and Olivetti are well-known examples—have required a technical and financial "blood transfusion" from American firms.

The American computer industry has also benefited from government-financed research; the federal government supplied much of the

[42] It has been reported, for example, that in bids on power transformers and power-circuit breakers submitted to the Tennessee Valley Authority, foreign producers undercut American companies by a wide margin (*The Wall Street Journal,* April 22, 1966).

funds for research and development at the time the industry was in its infancy and still provides about one-half of the total. And while government purchases account for a decreasing proportion of total sales, defense and space orders are of importance in furthering the development of new, technically advanced computer systems. In particular, the computer requirements of U.S. air defense and space programs have contributed to the development of the third generation of computers which incorporate printed circuits.

Government financing of research and product development is of even greater importance in the newest fields of electronics, such as infrared, microwaves, lasers, and the miniaturization of electronic components. In all these cases, military and space programs stimulated research, and production began under government contracts. Industrial applications are being developed, however, and their experience in defense and space work, as well as the funds provided by the government for research and development, will provide a competitive advantage to American firms for some time to come.[43]

Economies of scale in production and research account in large part for the present superiority of the American aircraft industry. The wider domestic market for military and civilian airplanes has enabled producers to reduce costs in the United States, and U.S. producers have also benefited from large-scale research, about three-fourths of which is financed by the federal government. In addition, the efforts of the U.S. Department of Defense to increase military exports have contributed to the expansion of sales. By the use of long-term credits as well as sales pressure, the Defense Department has succeeded in increasing military exports from $200 million in 1960 to over $1.5 billion in 1963, with aircraft sales accounting for about two-thirds of the total.

Costs in aircraft manufacturing are higher in Western Europe, where production runs are shorter; high costs, in turn, restrict sales. This interaction of high costs and small sales led the U.K. government in 1965 to cancel military orders from British manufacturers for several types of aircraft, including two advanced vertical or near-vertical-take off planes, the TSR-2 bomber, and a freighter. In all in-

---

[43] Aside from the commercial applications of government-financed research and development, U.S. firms derive benefits from the contractual provision according to which they can spend 5 per cent of the value of government research contracts on their own research work (C. Freeman, *et al.*, "Research and Development in Electronic Capital Goods," cited, p. 72).

stances, American aircraft is purchased as a replacement. On the other hand, Buy American provisions do not permit the purchase of foreign military equipment by the U.S. Department of Defense unless the price differential between American and foreign products exceeds 50 per cent.

It appears, then, that government-financed research and large military orders have provided important advantages to American aircraft producers. With the increasing complexity of aircraft and the production of all-purpose planes with variable wings, these advantages are expected to increase further in the future and are likely to lead to a decline in the number of viable companies. Note, finally, that the government financing of 80 per cent of research and development expenditures on civilian supersonic aircraft in the United States contributes to the superiority of the American design over the British-French Concorde.

Policy Implications of International Differences in Regard to Technically Advanced Products

I have indicated the advantages American firms have in industries characterized by rapid technological development. These advantages result from the demand for technologically advanced products on the part of the U.S. government, the willingness of the government to finance a large proportion of research and development expenditures and, finally, from economies of scale in production and research. In the United States, the federal government finances over 55 per cent of research and development undertaken by the business sector, while this proportion is less than one-half in the United Kingdom, one-third in France, and 15 per cent in Belgium, Germany, and the Netherlands.[44]

It should be added that international differences in the benefits of government-financed research and development to the business sector are greater than comparisons of the relative proportions financed by national governments would indicate, since the United States devotes about 3 per cent of her gross national product to research and development as against 1 to 2 per cent in Western Europe.[45] At the same

[44] *Basic Research, Applied Research and Development in Industry*, p. 107, and C. Freeman and A. Young, *The Research and Development Effort* (Paris: Organization for Economic Cooperation and Development, 1965), p. 45.

[45] C. Freeman and A. Young, cited, p. 71.

time, large firms are the chief beneficiaries of government-financed research in the United States; in 1962, 59.3 per cent of research and development expenditure undertaken by firms with a total employment over 5,000 was financed from the federal funds while for firms with fewer than 5,000 employees the relevant proportion was 37.4 per cent.[46]

At the same time, in technologically progressive industries, research and product development, firm size, and technological change are largely interdependent. While government orders might have given the first impetus to a new product line, sooner or later civilian applications follow and the availability of markets permits the firm to expand production and increase spending on research. Firm size and technological progress continue to interact at later stages of development since large U.S. firms have the financial means to undertake research in new directions and possess a potential market for new products, with the government continuing to play a role both in financing research and in providing a sales outlet.

We can regard these government activities as a direct, or indirect, subsidy to business enterprise that provides a competitive advantage to American firms in certain research-intensive fields and has contributed to U.S. technological superiority in these industries.[47] To counter the effects of this subsidy and to reduce the technological lag, European governments may resort to various measures, such as the protection of domestic industry, support of research and development activities, and inducements to concentration.

Protection is a time-honored device for sheltering manufacturing activities in less advanced countries. It has generally been successful in regard to industries that have reached technological maturity, such as textiles and steel. In such instances, the production methods used by more developed industrial economies have been imitated in countries at a lower level of industrialization. It appears questionable, however, that tariff protection would be the best way to foster industries characterized by rapid technological progress. On the one hand, without an adequate research effort, an industry which requires

[46] *Basic Research, Applied Research and Development in Industry, 1962*, p. 107.

[47] It would be difficult to estimate the value of government-sponsored research and development to the business firm, however, since military and space products can rarely be sold for civilian uses without modifications, and in other instances the benefits are not easily ascertainable.

sophisticated technology may not get off the ground; on the other, tariff protection may reduce competitive pressures and hence the incentive to innovate.

But is there need for an original research effort, or can a country restrict itself to adopting foreign technology? In the postwar period, Japan progressed technologically by utilizing the results of American basic research and adapting U.S. innovations. Other nations have also made use of technological methods introduced in the United States, as witnessed by the positive balance of royalty payments and license fees.[48] Indeed, some have suggested that countries may be better off imitating American methods than incurring the expense of carrying out research on their own.

As far as the industrial countries are concerned, this appears to be a shortsighted view. While product innovations in the chemical industry are relatively easy to imitate, in several modern branches of manufacturing there is need for "creative adaptation," which is often difficult to distinguish from original research. Thus, according to a report of the British Federation of Industries, "evidence strongly suggests, that licensing arrangements are almost always supplementary to the firm's internal research effort and only very rarely a substitute for it." [49] These considerations also explain the rapid expansion of research activity in recent years in Japan and underlie the conclusions of the OECD report on research and development:

Complete "parasitism" in scientific and technical knowledge would probably be as inefficient as scientific "autarky" and neither is a practical policy. A country which tried to rely exclusively on imports of technical knowledge would always tend to be a decade or more behind in *every* industry; and while every country must expect to be behind sometimes in *some* industries, it could not afford to be constantly behind in all.[50]

[48] According to a direct communication received from the U.S. Department of Commerce, the U.S. net balance of technological payments, inclusive of management fees, with Western Europe increased from $219 million in 1960 to $388 million in 1964. Much of this increase, however, represents payments from U.S. subsidiaries in Western Europe and reflects the rapid expansion of American investments in that area.

[49] Federation of British Industries, *Industrial Research in Manufacturing Industry* (London, 1961), p. 50. This conclusion applies especially to electronic goods, in regard to which it has been shown that commercial success is not possible without independent development work (C. Freeman *et al.*, "Research and Development in Electronic Capital Goods," *National Institute Review*, November 1965, p. 63).

[50] *Science, Economic Growth, and Government Policy*, cited, p. 34.

The French Fifth Plan, as well as official pronouncements in other nations, provides evidence of the increased preoccupation of European governments with research and development. New investments in research facilities are expected to double during the period of the Fifth Plan (1966–70) and a substantial rise in spending is foreseen in other European countries too. But, aside from a few intergovernmental projects, such as the Concorde supersonic aircraft and the Europa communications satellite, national governments carry out their research policies independent of one another. Yet the optimal use of scientific manpower and the avoidance of duplication would require cooperation in research and development policies and, ultimately, a *politique de science* on the European level.[51] Further, the coordination of military spending programs would contribute to cost reductions by increasing the length of production runs in the manufacturing of individual products.

Inducements to concentration would also contribute to the exploitation of economies of scale in production and research in European firms. Interpreted in a wider sense, concentration can be understood to mean, in addition to mergers, concerted action by independent firms through specialization agreements and the establishment of joint subsidiaries, or export and research organizations. These forms of concentration influence research and technological change to different degrees: an outright merger can lead to technological improvements by increasing the size of the firm; joint research activities of individual enterprises or the establishment of common subsidiaries may permit the better utilization of the research efforts of individual firms; and a common export organization may be helpful in developing improved products for export and in marketing them abroad.

A tendency toward concentration is apparent in the Common Market countries as well as in some other European nations. There have been mergers and takeovers in a variety of industries, especially in steel, shipbuilding, electrical machinery, and household appliances. In several countries, automobile producers have set up joint subsidiaries for carrying out research, producing parts and components, and undertaking foreign sales, while in other industries specialization agreements have been concluded. But the movement toward concen-

---

[51] Steps in this direction were taken in the framework of the OECD, but the integration of Western Europe is likely to be a precondition of future progress.

tration has taken place largely in the framework of the individual national economies, and there are as yet few examples of mergers across national frontiers. In technologically progressive industries, however, such mergers may be necessary to improve the position of European firms in competition with American companies. This is the situation in the computer industry, for example, where national producers have been unable to stand up to U.S. firms.

Various measures would have to be taken to remove the obstacles that presently hinder mergers by firms across national borders in the EEC. Among other things, it would be necessary to integrate national capital markets, harmonize corporate tax rates, unify tax provisions on mergers, and standardize legislation on patents. Moreover, in order to ease the difficulties companies face in attempting to extend their operations across national frontiers, there appears to be need to provide a legal framework for a "European-type" company.[52] A proposal to this effect was made by the EEC Commission but it has run into opposition on the part of the French government.[53]

Conclusion

In this chapter I have considered the gains that can be derived from the widening of national markets through freer trade. It is apparent that these dynamic effects far outweigh in importance the static effects of trade liberalization. In Chapter 4 it was shown that, under the static assumption of unchanged production methods, the expansion of trade in an Atlantic Free Trade Area would amount to only a few percentage points of the industrial countries' gross domestic product and that the welfare gains would be a fraction of the increase in trade volume. On the other hand, the enlargement of national markets through a lowering of trade barriers will often lead to substantial reductions in manufacturing costs.

To begin with, the experience of U.S. companies at home and

[52] It has been reported that on the occasion of their merger in 1964 Belgium's Gevaert and Germany's Agfa found the creation of a single company a "fiscal and legal impossibility." Instead, they have transferred stock and have created two jointly owned companies, one Belgian and the other German (*Business Week*, February 26, 1966), p. 158. In other instances, fiscal and legal obstacles have prevented a merger.

[53] Cf. the five-point program of the Commission, reported in *European Community*, July 1965, p. 11. The proposal has also re-emphasized the need for precluding the abuse of dominant positions as provided for in the Rome Treaty.

abroad gives an indication of potential gains due to economies of scale on the plant level obtainable in foreign countries. It appears that, in cases where the output of the foreign plant is less than one-twentieth that of the U.S. plant, costs in foreign operations exceed domestic costs, on the average, by 31 per cent; but costs in foreign plants are 4 per cent lower for output ratios of 10 to 25 per cent and average 14 per cent lower in cases when the output ratios are between 25 and 50 per cent. Finally, in foreign plants whose output exceeds one-half of that of the U.S. factory, costs have been shown to be, on the average, 26 per cent lower than in comparable U.S. operations.

Lessening product variety (horizontal specialization) and the subdivision of the production process (vertical specialization) in a larger market would also contribute to cost reductions, while increased competition from foreign firms would create pressures for improving the methods of production. Accordingly, trade liberalization would supply the stick as well as the carrot of competition: the pressure of foreign competition would intensify following reductions in tariff barriers while tariff cuts by the partner countries would provide outlets for exports and permit the use of large-scale production methods.

However, large government orders, economies of scale in production and research, and the federal financing of research and product development provide advantages to American firms over their European counterparts in industries characterized by rapid technological progress. I have suggested that, in furthering the development of these industries in Western Europe, emphasis should be put on positive actions—inducements to research and encouragement of concentration—rather than on the negative measures of tariff protection. Protection involves a cost by raising the price of the product to the consumer and by reducing pressures for technological improvements. And, with the social productivity of research generally exceeding its private productivity,[54] the rate of return on the cost of protection is likely to be lower than the rate of return on research expenditure.

But the development of science-based industries is a time-consuming process which will often require some degree of protection during a transitional period. The exploitation of the potential benefits of the European Common Market will also take time and the early removal of tariffs may interfere with the process of structural trans-

---

[54] This result follows because research activity benefits a variety of enterprises through the application of basic research and the transmission of technical improvements.

formation within the EEC. Expressed differently, in the case of a full and immediate elimination of tariffs, the relative size of national markets would exert an influence on international specialization between the United States and Western Europe, and the advantages of American firms in technologically progressive industries might retard the development of these industries in European countries.

CHAPTER SIX

Trade Liberalization and Direct Foreign Investment

Tariff Reductions and Investing Abroad

This chapter examines the impact of trade liberalization on foreign investment and the reverse influence of investment decisions on international trade. The discussion is restricted to direct investments, the economic and political implications of which are more immediately relevant to the present inquiry than are those of portfolio investments.[1] The chapter deals chiefly with American investments in Western Europe, although some references will be made to investments in other industrial countries. Beyond the interrelationships of trade and capital flows, I shall consider the economic effects of direct investments and offer some suggestions for a policy of foreign investment among the industrial countries.

According to traditional trade theory, an increase in trade following reductions in tariffs would be accompanied by a decline in foreign investments, since one of the incentives for international capital flows—the existence of tariff barriers—would partially be removed. Moreover, to the extent that American investments have been attracted to the Common Market and the European Free Trade Association by tariff discrimination against U.S. exports, a lessening of this discrimination through multilateral tariff reductions would lead to a reverse flow of capital.

While these conclusions find application under the static assumptions of unchanged production methods and cost structures, they have

[1] Direct foreign investments, as defined by the U.S. Department of Commerce, include investments in foreign business enterprises (chiefly branches and subsidiaries of domestic firms) in which a U.S. resident or organization owns a 25 per cent interest. In turn, the purchase of foreign obligations excluded from the above category is classified as portfolio investment.

to be modified if account is taken of the dynamic effects of trade liberalization. In the preceding chapter I noted that trade liberalization will lead to changes in the structure of costs in countries whose domestic markets do not otherwise allow for the use of large-scale production methods. Accordingly, in the event of multilateral tariff reductions, the prospects of reducing costs by locating plants in these countries will provide an inducement for the inflow of capital. In fact, foreign investment will often be necessary to exploit the potential benefits offered by the widening of national markets through freer trade.

Trade liberalization may then lead to an expansion, rather than a contraction, of the flow of capital into hitherto protected national economies. Moreover, in the event that tariffs are eliminated and the chances for their reimposition is small, international firms will increasingly act as if they faced a single market. They will relocate plants in response to changes in market size and will take advantage of the opportunities provided by intraindustry specialization in setting up operations in the individual countries.

In applying these considerations to the case of an Atlantic Free Trade Area, or tariff reductions undertaken on an m.f.n. basis, one should first examine the effects of the EEC's establishment on American direct investments.[2] The Common Market has had the double effect of discriminating against American exports in favor of sales from plants located in the partner countries and enlarging the market for the individual producer. To varying degrees, both of these influences may have contributed to the rapid expansion of U.S. direct investments in the European Economic Community since 1957, when the Rome Treaty was signed.[3]

[2] I do not consider here American investments in EFTA, since the experience of the latter has been influenced by its assumed impermanence and the advantages offered by the Common Market over Britain as a location for American plants. For a discussion, see my "American Direct Investments in the Common Market," *Banca Nazionale del Lavoro Quarterly Review*, June 1966, pp. 121–46.

[3] The book value of American direct investments in the Common Market more than tripled between 1957 and 1964, while the share of the EEC in U.S. direct foreign investments in Western Europe increased from 40.4 to 44.7 per cent. In the same period, U.S. investments in Common Market manufacturing nearly quadrupled, raising thereby the EEC's share in American manufacturing investments in the European area from 37.9 to 47.3 per cent (U.S. Department of Commerce, *American Business Investments in Foreign Countries* [Washington, D.C., 1960], pp. 92–95, and Samuel Pizer and Frederick Cutler, "Foreign

The extent to which tariff discrimination has attracted American capital to the Common Market should not be exaggerated, however. To begin with, an inquiry conducted by the McGraw-Hill Company into the motivation of investment decisions by American companies in Western Europe failed to show the importance of tariff discrimination; rather, the principal inducement appeared to be the availability of large markets.[4] Furthermore, a statistical investigation carried out by the author showed no relationship between the degree of tariff discrimination in individual industries and changes in the industrial composition of U.S. investments following the EEC's establishment,[5] although one would have expected such a relationship to obtain if tariff discrimination had an important influence on the flow of foreign capital. Finally, the prospective decline of U.S. exports due to Common Market discrimination, estimated in Chapter 4 at $311 million,[6] would hardly have warranted a rise in the value of American investments in the manufacturing industries of the EEC countries by $2.3 million—from $.8 billion in 1957 to $3.1 billion in 1964.

The enlargement of national markets through integration appears to have been a more important inducement for U.S. investments than tariff discrimination. The widening of markets open to individual producers has created possibilities for exploiting economies of scale and reducing the cost of production in the EEC. Plants established in any of the member countries can now sell in the entire area, and producers may specialize in different varieties of a given commodity, or its parts, components, and accessories, in factories located in the various member countries.[7] An additional consideration is that the uncertainty associated with selling in the markets of the partner coun-

---

Investments, 1964–65," *Survey of Current Business,* September 1965, p. 24). Data refer to year-end values.

[4] McGraw-Hill Department of Economics, *Foreign Operations of U.S. Industrial Companies, 1960–1961* (New York: McGraw-Hill, 1960), p. 4.

[5] On the statistical tests applied, see my "American Investments in the Common Market," cited.

[6] Cf. Table 4.2.

[7] The largest Dutch company of electronic goods—Phillips—provides an example of product-by-plant specialization: it has begun to narrow down product variety in its plants located in the individual member countries and it expects to establish separate plants for the production of various components, parts, and accessories. Among American firms, IBM has reportedly decided to produce hybrid integrated circuits in France and cards to mount them on in Germany. Also, computer assembly has been restricted to one variety in France and to another two in Germany.

tries has decreased as a result of the assumed irreversibility of tariff reductions.

The establishment of an Atlantic Free Trade Area or substantial tariff reductions undertaken on an m.f.n. basis would further enlarge the market open to producers located in the EEC while tariff discrimination would be eliminated or, at least, reduced. At the same time, the importance of the widening of markets for foreign investment will be greater, the more likely it becomes that tariff reductions will not subsequently be reimposed.

Various considerations suggest that, rather than reversing the movement of American capital to Western Europe, the establishment of an Atlantic Free Trade Area is likely to accelerate this flow. To begin with, the adaptation of American firms to European operations is a cumulative process, within the firm as well as within the industry. Having overcome the real and assumed obstacles to establishing a plant in a European country, firms more easily venture into setting up another plant, and one firm's decision to start operations abroad often brings forth a response on the part of its competitors. Moreover, in industries where location near the consumer offers advantages, increases in exports tend to induce producers to set up plants abroad as soon as sales reach a level that warrants the establishment of a foreign plant.

The chemical industry exemplifies the process of expanding foreign sales and the subsequent shift from exports to producing abroad. The Dow Chemical Co., one of the largest chemical manufacturers in the United States, after having rapidly expanded sales in Western Europe in postwar years, has begun to produce certain chemicals abroad and expects to increasingly supply European markets from plants located in the area. *The Economist* (November 7, 1964; p. 631) reports that Dow's investments in European countries reached $100 million in 1964 and are planned to rise to $150 million in 1966 and to $250 million in another two or three years. Du Pont and several other American chemical companies are acting in a similar fashion. Correspondingly, the book value of investments by U.S. chemical producers in Western Europe increased fifteen times, from $74 million to $1,073 million between 1950 and 1964, and further increases are expected.[8]

Aside from the differential advantages of locating near the place of

[8] *Survey of Current Business,* September 1965, p. 27.

consumption [9] intercountry differences in the cost of production would often favor European locations in an Atlantic Free Trade Area. Despite rapid increases in wages in Western Europe during the post-war period, in 1964 wage costs (wages plus social security) in the manufacturing industries of the Common Market countries and the United Kingdom were still in the range of 30 to 40 per cent of that in U.S. manufacturing (Table 6.1).[10] At the same time, comparative studies have shown that differences in labor efficiency between the United States and Western Europe are small and are diminishing over time.[11] Hence, with identical capital equipment and organization in

TABLE 6.1   Hourly Wage Costs in Manufacturing Industries in the United States, the European Common Market, and the United Kingdom, 1964

	Wages ($)	Social Charges (per cent)	Social Charges ($)	Wage Costs ($)
United States	2.53	23.6	.60	3.13
Belgium	.72	30.1	.22	.94
France	.71	50.2	.36	1.07
Germany	.93	35.1	.33	1.26
Italy	.60	56.9	.34	.94
Netherlands	.71	33.1	.23	.94
United Kingdom	.98	13.9	.14	1.12

Sources: Wages—International Labor Office, *Yearbook of Labor Statistics, 1965* (Geneva, 1966).
   Social charges—G. L. Reid and D. S. Robertson, *Fringe Benefits, Labour Costs and Social Security* (London: Allen & Unwin, 1965), p. 99.

Note: Social charges are defined to include payments for hours not worked, obligatory and nonobligatory social security payments, as well as welfare benefits and other social contributions.

[9] These advantages include lower transport costs and the adaptation of the product to local needs as well as improved servicing and marketing.

[10] Note, however, that the data are subject to a considerable degree of error by reason of differences in the classification of workers and the difficulties of determining the magnitude of social charges.

[11] Utilizing answers to a questionnaire by American firms with international operations, Kreinin has concluded that, chiefly as a result of differences in training, skill, and incentives, labor efficiency is approximately one-sixth lower in Western Europe than in the United States (Mordechai E. Kreinin, "Comparative Labor Effectiveness and the Leontief Scarce-Factor Paradox," *American Economic Review*, March 1965, pp. 131–40). The results are by and large in

all industries, labor productivity in Western Europe would tend to approach the U.S. level.

Existing differences in the production methods applied are greatly affected by the size of national markets and the availability of capital. The reader will recall that, for the individual firm, the advantages of large markets consist of economies of scale in its own production and the availability of intermediate products, including parts, components, and accessories, at a low cost. If an Atlantic Free Trade Area is established, the advantages the large American market bestows on U.S. establishments would decline in importance, and differences in labor costs would have increasing influence on locational decisions. Assuming that the elimination of tariffs in AFTA would not be reversible, the risk of investing abroad and differences in the availability of capital would also decline.

But might not the rise of wages in Western Europe remove the European cost advantage as the inflow of American capital increased the demand for labor? And would the observed labor scarcity in Western Europe permit increased foreign investment? The answer to these questions will depend, among other things, on existing differences in the amount of capital per worker in the United States and Western Europe and on the size of American investment.

Since the amount of capital per worker in the manufacturing industries of the major European countries hardly exceeds one-third of the U.S. level,[12] there is need for a long process of transformation until American levels of productivity and wages are reached. This transformation is aided by the inflow of capital, but in 1964 spending by U.S. subsidiaries on plant and equipment hardly reached 5 per cent of total investment in European manufacturing.[13] Accordingly, the consequences for labor productivity in European manufacturing of, say,

---

conformity with the findings of a study by the National Industrial Conference Board that utilized information provided by American companies with manufacturing facilities abroad (Theodore R. Gates and Fabian Linder, *Costs and Competition: American Experience Abroad*) (New York: National Industrial Conference Board, 1961, p. 54).

[12] On U.S.–U.K. comparisons, see Deborah Paige and Gottfried Bombach, *A Comparison of National Output and Productivity of the United Kingdom and the United States* (Paris: Organization for European Economic Cooperation, 1959), p. 69.

[13] This ratio was approximately 4 per cent in the European Common Market, 13 per cent in the United Kingdom, and 3 per cent in the Continental EFTA countries (*Survey of Current Business,* September 1965, p. 29, and Organization for Economic Cooperation and Development, *National Accounts Statistics, 1955–1964* [Paris, 1966]).

a doubling in the share of U.S. investments would be relatively small. And if we also consider the underemployment still existing in European agriculture and commerce, it would appear that—for some time to come—U.S. firms will be able to make use of the cost advantage provided by the relatively low European wages when investing in new, efficient manufacturing facilities.

We may conclude that the establishment of an Atlantic Free Trade Area would accelerate the trend toward the internationalization of American firms. Decisions on the location of production facilities would increasingly respond to cost differences and would often favor European plants. American firms might thus move some of their operations to Western Europe, just as they have located in the South of the United States in the search of better profit opportunities. In the process of internationalization, the share of U.S. manufacturing subsidiaries in the total sales of U.S. companies abroad can be expected to rise further. Sales by U.S. manufacturing subsidiaries in Western Europe increased by 162 per cent between 1957 and 1964, while U.S. exports of manufactured goods to Western Europe grew by 125 per cent. By 1964 the sales of these subsidiaries had reached $16.5 billion, as compared to exports of $4.4 billion.[14]

The importation into the United States of commodities produced by the foreign subsidiaries of American companies is a related issue. For various reasons, these imports have hardly surpassed 1 per cent of the total sales of American manufacturing subsidiaries located in Western Europe. For one thing, transportation costs and duties tend to discourage importing from a foreign affiliate; for another, American firms tend to produce according to foreign specifications in their European plants and the commodities in question may not suit the U.S. market. Still, one may venture the guess that the sharing of markets between the American parent companies and their foreign subsidiaries has had a decisive influence in restricting this trade.

There are indications, however, that the policy of American firms regarding imports from their overseas subsidiaries is changing. Such imports nearly doubled between 1963 and 1964, with a large part of the increase taking place in the chemical industry.[15] Also, General

[14] *American Business Investments in Foreign Countries,* p. 112; Samuel Pizer and Frederick Cutler, "Financing and Sales of Foreign Affiliates of U.S. Firms," *Survey of Current Business,* November 1965, p. 19; and United Nations, *Commodity Trade Statistics,* 1957 and 1964.

[15] Pizer and Cutler, "Financing and Sales of Foreign Affiliates of U.S. Firms," cited, p. 19.

Motors, Ford, and Chrysler have apparently decided that, instead of producing small cars, they will import them from their European subsidiaries. These companies seem to have realized that cars produced by their European subsidiaries will compete more with other small cars imported from Western Europe than with domestic automobiles. Should U.S. tariffs be eliminated, similar developments may occur in other industries.

U.S. Investments in an Atlantic Free Trade Area: the Results of a Survey

To obtain further information on possible changes in U.S. investments in the event that an Atlantic Free Trade Area is created, a questionnaire was sent to all American firms with foreign manufacturing or marketing facilities to inquire about their possible reaction to the establishment of AFTA. One hundred ninety-one firms—nearly one-half of those producing abroad—replied to the questionnaire; 169 sent usable answers. The results are reported in considerable detail in M. E. Kreinin's chapter on the United States in *Studies in Trade Liberalization,* edited by the present author and published by the Johns Hopkins University Press. I will summarize only the main findings here.

Among those who gave usable replies, seventy-five respondents stated that the establishment of an Atlantic Free Trade Area would bring no change in their policy concerning foreign investments. A substantial proportion of these firms gave no reasons for their answer—perhaps because they did not take the prospect seriously enough. Others cited the resource intensiveness of their product, its perishability, and (in a number of instances) high transportation costs as reasons for maintaining present investment policies. In contrast, seven firms would expect a shift in the geographic composition of their foreign investment without a change in the total, while the remainder was fairly evenly divided between those who expect an expansion (forty-one) or a contraction (forty-six).

In explaining the motives underlying an expansion of foreign investment in an Atlantic Free Trade Area, much emphasis was given to differences in production costs. Several firms expressed the opinion that intensified competition in an Atlantic Free Trade Area would necessitate locating in low-cost areas in order to serve the host country's market as well as the markets of neighboring countries. As a producer of typesetting machines pointed out, "lower European production costs will require increased facilities abroad, both as a defensive measure, with respect to domestic market, and to permit expansion of foreign sales." Three of the respondents also indicated that they would expect to sell goods manufactured in their foreign plants to U.S. consumers.

Others noted that the widening of markets due to the all-round removal of duties would permit setting up large-scale, efficient plants in Western Europe to supply the entire area, thereby replacing American exports. Several respondents observed that while the initial effect of an all-round removal of trade barriers would be to increase exports from plants located in the United States, as the volume of sales increased it would become profitable to establish manufacturing facilities abroad. For example, according to a producer of floor-covering accessories and supplies, "an Atlantic Free Trade Area would give us considerable opportunity to further expand distribution in the areas concerned, by initially establishing warehousing and sales organizations. As these develop, consideration could be given to further plant expansion either of our present [European] plants, or in the areas wherein warehousing proved to be successful."

Among the geographical areas where expansion would be expected to occur the European Common Market occupies first place, followed by the countries of the European Free Trade Association and Japan. Only a few firms would plan to expand their Canadian operations, and Canada would be the main loser in the case of firms who would either contract their foreign investments or relocate their production facilities in an Atlantic Free Trade Area.

The reasons most frequently given to explain this treatment of Canadian investments are the relatively high cost of Canadian operations and the similarity of U.S. and Canadian tastes. While at present the Canadian cost disadvantage is often outweighed by the protective tariff, cost differences are said to become decisive in case tariffs are eliminated. At the same time, the similarity of tastes permits the distribution of the large majority of U.S. products in Canada. According to a manufacturer of electronic components, for example, "time, distance, shipping costs, etc., are no real problem in dealing with Canadian business. If duties were eliminated, we would deal with Canada on the same basis as a '51st state.' This would not be true in the EEC, EFTA, or Japan where we feel we would still have to maintain manufacturing facilities. . . ."

Different conclusions apply to American investments in European countries. Although some of the respondents indicated that they would contract operations in the Common Market if tariff discrimination were to disappear, the replies point to an expansion of American investments in Western Europe following the establishment of AFTA. Some increase in investment is envisaged also in Japan.[16]

The method of investigation applied is useful in providing information on the present expectations of large American firms with foreign subsidiaries concerning their investment decisions in an Atlantic Free Trade Area. However, the results are subject to various qualifications. To begin with, answers to a hypothetical question often record the impressions of the respondent and are not based on an extensive investigation of the problem at hand. Further, firms may give undue emphasis to existing capacity; several of the respondents envisaged contraction in foreign operations due to the consolidation of foreign plants, for example, without considering the need for expanding the more efficient plant in order to meet increased demand. There also appears to be a tendency to argue on the basis of current cost conditions without giving adequate consideration to the impact of the widening of national markets on production costs. Thus an investigation into the prospects of a U.S.–Canadian free trade area by Ronald and Paul Wonnacott has led to the conclusion that the present Canadian disadvantage in regard to productivity is largely due to differences in capital equipment, and it would disappear after the mutual elimination of tariffs, while the lower Canadian wages would attract the inflow of U.S. capital. It should be added that in an Atlantic Free Trade Area U.S. capital is more likely to move to Western Europe than to Canada since Canadian wage levels are only slightly below those in the United States, while differences in North America–Western Europe relationships are much larger.

A final point: I have examined here the case of an Atlantic Free Trade Area in the framework of which tariffs would be irreversibly eliminated. Tariff reductions of a more limited scope would not necessarily have proportionately smaller effects since there may be a threshold point regarding decisions for foreign investment. At the same time, the lack of a guarantee concerning future increases in tariffs would slow down the described process of transformation and limit the expansion of American direct foreign investment.

---

[16] The number of replies concerning Japan is rather small. At any rate, the answers relating to Japan have little practical importance, since there are severe restrictions on foreign investments in that country.

The Economic Effects of Foreign Investment

The textbook argument for foreign investment is based on a consideration of capital and labor endowments in individual countries. Under the assumption that the conditions of production are everywhere the same, it is profitable to invest in the country where the amount of capital per worker is smaller, and the flow of capital will lead to an improvement in the allocation of economic resources in the world as a whole. Indeed, both countries are assumed to benefit from foreign investment; the investor gains from obtaining a higher profit abroad while the recipient benefits from increases in labor productivity and wages.[17]

While profits remain the main consideration on the part of the investor,[18] improvements in productivity that take place under the assumption of unchanged technology provide only part of the benefit to the recipient country if the conditions of production differ between countries. In the case of Western Europe, the contribution of American capital in adapting productive facilities to larger markets, the effects of increased competition, and the "apport" of new technology and organizational knowledge are likely to be of much greater importance than the static benefits of foreign investment described by traditional theory. Finally, international agreements on the taxation of foreign income provide for the sharing of the profits of foreign subsidiaries between the investor and the recipient country.

It will be recalled that, given the existing differences in the amount of capital per worker in American and European manufacturing, a long process of transformation will be necessary until U.S. productivity levels are reached in Western Europe. This process can be speeded up by American investment, which increases the amount of capital available in Western Europe and raises the technological level of the European capital stock. On the one hand, the average age of capital is reduced; on the other, U.S. subsidiaries can draw on the experience

[17] In turn, wages would fall in the first country and profits decline in the second, but these changes would be numerically smaller than the beneficial ones and—if we abstract from income distributional considerations—both countries would derive a net benefit.

[18] Note, however, that the simplicity of the analysis is lost if we consider that foreign investments are undertaken chiefly by oligopolistic industries. On this point, see Stephen Hymer, "Direct Foreign Investment and International Oligopoly," November 1965 (mimeographed).

of their parent companies in introducing new products and applying modern technology and organizational methods.

The transfer of knowledge extends to blueprints and prototypes as well as to know-how pertaining to such diverse matters as machinery design and layout, waste utilization, and materials handling. Aside from raising productivity in American-owned plants, there may be an influence on the methods and the organization of production in national enterprises. The establishment of U.S. subsidiaries has increased competitive pressures in various European industries, for example, and has provided inducements for improvements in production methods.[19] U.S. firms can also have a direct impact on the production methods of their suppliers by furnishing them information on up-to-date manufacturing and managerial techniques used in the United States.[20]

European countries derive further benefits from U.S. investments because, in accordance with international tax treaties, they share in the profits of the local subsidiaries of American firms. Now, since the location of plants will respond to differences in after-tax profits, the social productivity of foreign investment for the investor country will be less than its private productivity—the difference being the tax levied by the country in which the investment takes place.[21] This tax will then provide a gain to the host country over and above the benefits derived from improvements in productivity.

[19] For a detailed discussion of productivity improvements associated with the implantation of U.S. firms in the United Kingdom, see John H. Dunning, *American Investment in British Manufacturing Industry* (London: Allen & Unwin, 1958), chaps. vi–ix. It has also been suggested that the French government sees the main benefit of the inflow of American capital in its impact on the transformation and the modernization of certain manufacturing industries.

[20] The establishment of a food processing subsidiary by Libby, McNeil & Libby in the lower Rhône region in France is an interesting example of the influence of an American firm on the production methods of its suppliers and on the structure of the industry. Libby has signed long-term contracts with the farmers of the region for supplying its processing plants with fruits and vegetables and, in turn, provides them with seed as well as with advice for improving their methods of cultivation. Besides benefiting the suppliers, the improvements obtained in quality and yield have induced several French firms to follow Libby's example and we witness the beginnings of a transformation of the processing of fruits and vegetables from inefficient, small-scale establishments into a modern industry in France. Libby has also contributed to the success of the French regional policy in the area (*Le Monde,* June 16, 1965).

[21] This is the usual outcome under international tax treaties, which provide for a reduction of the firm's domestic tax burden by the amount paid abroad.

In contrast to these benefits of American investments for Western Europe, several real or presumed drawbacks of the inflow of capital have received attention in recent years. Some have pointed to the losses suffered by national firms due to increased competition from American subsidiaries; others have objected to the alleged ruthlessness of the latter in the search of high profits. Thus, in commenting on the dismissal of several hundred workers in Remington's Caluire plant in France, Jacques Gervais, who is otherwise sympathetic to American investment, exclaims that "we are not in the U.S.A. where one hires or fires workers in response to business conditions. This way of action—although it may have its advantages for productivity—is not accepted in France." [22]

While these criticisms are largely a reflection of differences in attitudes toward efficiency and equity in the United States and in Western Europe, other objections relate to the role played by U.S. companies in the European economies. It has been argued that the interest of U.S. companies may come into conflict with the national interest and with the policies followed by European governments. In France, some have suggested that the investment and production policies of American subsidiaries may interfere with the national Plan, while in Britain references have been made to the difficulties the government may experience in carrying out countercyclical policies in an economy where the influence of foreign firms is strong.

But, with the loosening of the structure of planning that followed the opening of the French economy through the elimination of quantitative restrictions and entry into the Common Market,[23] the objections against foreign investments based on the presumed conflict between U.S. subsidiaries and the Plan have declined in importance. And while the possible political motivation of the decision taken by Ford's British subsidiary to adopt a four-day week following the introduction of deflationary measures by the Labour government received considerable attention, these suspicions do not appear to have been based on actual fact.[24] At the same time, there is no evidence that the activities of U.S. subsidiaries would have interfered with countercyclical policy in Canada, although Americans control

[22] Jacques Gervais, *La France face aux investissements étrangers* (Paris: Les Editions de l'entreprise moderne, 1963), p. 189.

[23] Cf. Bela Balassa, "Whither French Planning?" *Quarterly Journal of Economics,* November 1965, pp. 537–54.

[24] See *The Economist,* September 4, 1965, pp. 895–96.

over two-fifths of the manufacturing establishments in that country.[25] To all appearances, neither had the operation of American subsidiaries come into conflict with the Canadian national interest until the United States published guidelines for American corporations with the aim of reducing the U.S. balance of payments deficit.[26]

More generally, it has been argued that the inflow of U.S. capital leads to an *Überfremdung* of the industry of European countries and restricts their national sovereignty. The data on the share of American investment in European industries do not support his contention. As noted above, spending by U.S. subsidiaries on plant and equipment amounted to about 5 per cent of total investment in European manufacturing in 1963. Since U.S. subsidiaries have increased their share in new investment over the last decade, the relevant proportion is lower if the *stock* of capital outstanding rather than the *flow* of investment is considered.[27]

American Investments in Individual Industries

But would American capital gain commanding positions in certain key industries, particularly those characterized by rapid technological progress? It has been suggested that this may indeed be the case, since U.S. companies derive advantages from their large size in the form of financial power and the ability to engage in research and

25 Cf. John Lindeman and Donald Armstrong, *Policies and Practices of United States Subsidiaries in Canada* (Toronto: Canadian American Committee, 1961), pp. 17ff.

26 In turn, the Canadian government made public its own guidelines urging foreign affiliates to handle procurement, disposal of earnings, export policy, pricing, and processing of raw materials "with Canadian interests in mind" and requested a periodic report on operations and financing (*The New York Times,* April 1, 1966).

27 Estimates on the share of U.S. capital in the book value of European manufacturing industries are few and far between. In the case of Germany, the Deutsche Bundesbank has estimated that 8 per cent of the book value of German manufacturing corporations was in American ownership at the end of 1964, although this share is considerably smaller—perhaps between 4 and 5 per cent—if account is also taken of unincorporated enterprises (*Monatsberichte der Deutschen Bundesbank,* May 1965). In turn, according to G. Y. Bertin, in 1959, 3.5 per cent of French manufacturing industry was owned by foreigners, with Americans accounting for about one-half of the total (Gilles Y. Bertin, *L'investissement des firmes étrangères en France* [Paris: Presses Universitaires de France, 1963], p. 246). Finally, Dunning put the value of sales by U.S. subsidiaries at 4 per cent of total domestic sales of manufacturing producers in the United Kingdom in 1953 (Dunning, cited, p. 56).

product development. Considerations of this kind may underlie the position taken by Walther Hallstein, President of the EEC Commission, who has been quoted as saying that "we welcome a certain amount of long-term American investment, provided it benefits all sectors of the economy without excessive concentration in any single branch." [28]

The financial advantages of American firms relate to the availability and cost of investible funds from internal as well as from external sources. Trends in the availability of internal financing are indicated by changes in profit margins over time. Judging from labor cost and wholesale price indices, these margins have been widening in the United States and narrowing in Western Europe in recent years, thereby permitting increases in U.S. investments abroad. In fact, the share of foreign investments in total expenditures on plant and equipment by U.S. corporations has risen to a considerable extent; in industries producing rubber goods, transportation equipment, electrical machinery, nonelectrical machinery, and chemicals, this share averaged 21 to 32 per cent in 1964 for companies reporting to the U.S. Department of Commerce.[29] Also, most firms participating in a recent survey of the National Industrial Conference Board reported that their domestic capital needs did not limit investments abroad. The respondents frequently stated that "if a project is good, we find means to finance it." [30]

Aside from the availability of internal funds, American firms can rely on borrowing from the New York financial market; access to borrowed funds is more limited, and rates are higher, in Europe. Moreover, the introduction of the Interest Equalization Tax in July 1962 has virtually eliminated the sale of bonds by European firms in the United States, and it has disrupted the pattern characterized by the intermediation of the New York financial market between European lenders and borrowers. In the past, Europeans issued *and* purchased bonds in New York because of the relatively small margin between borrowing and lending rates due to the advantages of the large size—stability, low brokerage fees, and the ability to absorb large issues—of this market.[31]

[28] *The Wall Street Journal,* March 22, 1955.

[29] *Survey of Current Business,* September 1965, p. 30.

[30] Judd Polk *et al., U.S. Production Abroad and the Balance of Payments, A Survey of Corporate Investment Experience* (New York: National Industrial Conference Board, 1966), p. 63.

[31] Cf. Charles P. Kindleberger, "European Economic Integration and the Development of a Single Financial Center for Long-Term Capital," *Welt-*

The situation has been aggravated as a result of the so-called voluntary restraint program in the United States. For one thing, limitations have been placed on bank loans which served as a safety valve after the imposition of the Interest Equalization Tax on foreign bond issues; for another, U.S. affiliates have been induced increasingly to rely on European sources of finance. Alongside the shift of Japanese and Australian borrowing to Western Europe in response to the Interest Equalization Tax, sales of securities by U.S. subsidiaries have contributed to increased tightness and higher borrowing rates in European capital markets.[32] Accordingly, an asymmetry has been introduced regarding access to foreign funds for American and for European firms: the rates paid by the latter in the New York market are augmented by the Interest Equalization Tax, while the U.S. voluntary restraint program has reduced the availability of funds and has led to an increase of rates in Western Europe.

The research facilities of the parent company, too, often provide a competitive advantage to U.S. subsidiaries over national firms. However, the importance of research varies from industry to industry, and one should also take account of the benefits the host country derives from the research efforts of American companies in the form of the availability of new and improved products to processing industries and to the consumer, and the inducement given to competing national firms for technological improvements. It is therefore of interest to examine the experience of individual industries. Let us take first the case of the three industries that have been the main target of American investments in Western Europe: petroleum refining, chemicals, and automobiles.[33]

---

wirtschafliches Archiv, Vol. 90, No. 2 (1963), pp. 189–208, and Peter B. Kenen, "Towards an Atlantic Capital Market," *Lloyds Bank Review,* July 1963, pp. 15–30.

[32] *The Economist* (January 22, 1966, p. 348) reports that while bond issues by U.S. subsidiaries in European capital markets were practically nonexistent prior to the introduction of the voluntary restraint program, in the second half of 1965 bonds in the value of $365 million were floated in Western Europe, accounting for nearly one-half of all funds raised by international issues. Note further that, according to a McGraw-Hill survey, only 14 per cent of the companies have reduced their 1965–66 foreign investment programs in response to the voluntary restraint program, while 41 per cent of the firms have altered the methods of financing foreign investment, of which two-thirds expect to place greater reliance on long-term borrowing abroad (*Pulsebeat of Industry,* September 1965).

[33] Within the total of $6.5 billion invested in European manufacturing industries at the end of 1964, the value of American investments in transportation

During the interwar period, American companies assumed dominant positions in the Common Market countries in petroleum refining, chiefly because of the advantages of vertical integration from crude oil production to distribution. However, as a result of state action in setting up national firms, especially in France and Italy, the share of these companies in the sale of petroleum products in the EEC fell to one-half after World War II. State intervention in this area is likely to continue and to bring further changes in the future.

On the other hand, there is no evidence of American domination in the chemical industry. As indicated in the preceding chapter, the largest European firms are comparable in size to the leading American companies—even in terms of worldwide sales—and carry out research on a large scale. The U.S. share is greater in the European automobile industry, but even here we can hardly speak of U.S. domination. Volkswagen, Fiat, and BMC precede any U.S. subsidiaries in terms of production volume. The subsidiaries of American firms, taken together, account for less than one-third of the total production of automobiles in Western Europe, and in none of the European countries does their share reach two-fifths of domestic output. Still, there is little doubt that the financial power of the parent companies will assure the survival of the American subsidiaries in the expected reorganization of the European automobile industry which is bound to lead to the disappearance of some smaller national firms.

The dissimilar experience of the three European industries in which American investment is concentrated indicates the difficulties of generalizing as to the advantages of financial power and the availability of research facilities.[34] U.S. subsidiaries are usually part of a group of competing oligopolists in most other traditional industries. But American enterprises dominate the manufacturing of some new products, the prime examples being synthetic rubber and carbon black. Furthermore, fully or partly owned subsidiaries have assumed leading positions in the French and Italian computer industry.

Few objections have been raised against the monopoly position of American firms in manufacturing new products. Many agree with Raymond Aron, who expressed the view that, from the point of view of European countries, it is more desirable to purchase these com-

---

equipment (chiefly automobiles) was estimated at $1.8 billion and in chemicals $1.1 billion. In the same year, the value of investments in petroleum refining was reported to be $3.1 billion (Pizer and Cutler, cited, pp. 24–27).

[34] For a more detailed analysis of the situation in these three industries, see Christopher Layton, *Trans-Atlantic Investments* (Paris: The Atlantic Institute, 1966), Chapter III.

modities from American subsidiaries than to import them from the United States.[35] Too, as the example of synthetic fibers indicates, European companies may soon follow the lead of American firms in manufacturing competing products; in fact, several European firms have started or plan to begin the manufacture of synthetic rubber.

Different considerations apply to the computer industry, where American firms have assumed preeminence largely because of their ability to finance research and development on successive "generations" of computers. The case of Olivetti and the *affaire Bull* have created much commotion because they appear to have demonstrated that the financial power of French and Italian companies is not sufficient to withstand American competition in the computer field. Fears have also been expressed that in other research-intensive fields similar developments will take place. I shall return to this question in the concluding part of this chapter.

Direct Foreign Investment and the Balance of Payments

Much attention has been given on both sides of the Atlantic to the balance of payments effects of direct foreign investments. In the United States and the United Kingdom, both of which have experienced balance of payments difficulties in recent years, attention has focused on the short-term effects of the outflow of capital. By contrast, European observers have placed emphasis on the return flow in the form of royalties, fees, and dividends. Finally, one needs to consider the impact of foreign investments on trade flows.

If we abstract from the implications of foreign investment for international trade, the answer is simple: direct foreign investment will be "neutral" from the point of view of balance of payments if its rate of growth equals the rate of profit on investment abroad.[36] In the early 1960s this equality was approximately maintained in the case of U.S. investments in European manufacturing: direct investments grew at an annual rate of 15 to 16 per cent while earnings averaged 12 to 13 per cent of asset value, and royalties, license fees, and management fees amounted to 3 to 4 per cent. In 1964, for example, the flow of U.S. direct investments was $928 million, earnings $754

---

[35] *Figaro,* November 25, 1965.

[36] Profits are defined to include the earnings of these subsidiaries as well as the payment of royalties, license fees, and management fees to the parent company.

million, and royalties and fees $219 million, leaving a small net surplus of $45 million.[37]

But direct foreign investment will affect international trade in various ways: foreign subsidiaries of American firms purchase commodities from the parent company and from other enterprises located in the United States; they replace imports in the market of the host country, and contribute to the host country's export earnings. In the early sixties, the imports of U.S. manufacturing subsidiaries from the United States amounted to 15 to 16 per cent, and their exports to the United States to 3 to 3.5 per cent of asset value.[38] If we include new investments, earnings, and royalties in the calculations, the American balance of payments gain derived from investments in European manufacturing facilities will appear to be 12 to 14 per cent of the value of these investments.

To indicate the total impact of U.S. direct investments on trade and the balance of payments, consideration should further be given to the replacement of American exports by sales of U.S. subsidiaries in the host country and in other foreign markets. In the early sixties the domestic sales of U.S. manufacturing subsidiaries in Western Europe were about twice the book value of U.S. investments. Correspondingly, the U.S. surplus calculated at 12 to 14 per cent of asset value would disappear if only 6 or 7 per cent of sales by subsidiaries replaced exports from the United States.[39] Available evidence indicates that this figure is likely to be on the low side, however.

[37] In the same year U.S. firms invested $1,342 million in all sectors of the European economies, taken together, while their earnings were $1,112 million, and royalties and fees $306 million (Pizer and Cutler, cited, pp. 23–32).

[38] In 1964, imports amounted to $961 million, and exports to $208 million. The import figures do not include goods imported on a commission basis (*Survey of Current Business,* September and December 1965).

[39] The reader will note that these comparisons are based on the assumption that U.S. investments in European manufacturing will continue to rise at rates experienced in recent years. Should we wish to consider instead the annual balance of payments effects of a *given* investment, the relevant items are: repatriated earnings (about 7 to 8 per cent of the original investment), royalties and fees (3 to 4 per cent), exports to subsidiaries (15 to 16 per cent), and imports from subsidiaries (3 to 3.5 per cent). The annual reverse flow would therefore amount to 22 to 24 per cent of the original investment if no account were taken of the replacement of U.S exports by the sales of foreign subsidiaries and the reinvestment of part of the foreign earnings. (For a similar calculation, see L. B. Krause, "Private Foreign Investment," in Walter S. Salant *et al., The United States Balance of Payments in 1968* [Washington, D.C.: The Brookings Institution, 1963], p. 144.)

To begin with, the proportion of sales by U.S. subsidiaries that replaced exports from the United States may approach 100 per cent in the case of some new products. Gervais notes, for example, that the production of synthetic rubber and carbon black by American subsidiaries alone provides a $65 million annual saving of imports to France.[40] The cost advantage of the local subsidiaries over the parent company provides an incentive for import replacement in the case of traditional imports as well. Taking account of differences in production costs and the cost of transportation from the United States, Dunning reports that U.S. subsidiaries can provide the same commodities in Britain on the average 15 to 20 per cent cheaper than can the parent company.[41]

Accordingly, the net effect of direct foreign investment on the U.S. balance of payments will probably be negative even if we disregard the possibility that exports by foreign subsidiaries replace the foreign sales of the parent company in third countries. Exports by U.S. manufacturing subsidiaries in Western Europe amounted to $3.8 billion, 23 per cent of their total sales, in 1964.[42] In that year, subsidiaries accounted for 8 per cent of the exports of manufactures from European countries—about double the U.S. share in the value of total assets of European manufacturing.[43]

These figures indicate the export orientation of U.S. manufacturing subsidiaries, although it is difficult to judge to what extent their foreign sales would replace exports from the United States. While there is evidence of market-sharing agreements between the parent company and its foreign subsidiaries, this does not exclude the possibility of export replacement. Moreover, the subsidiaries compete with other American firms in the markets of third countries.

Conclusion

It has been shown that American direct investments benefit the European economy in various ways. U.S. manufacturing subsidiaries

[40] Gervais, cited, p. 177.

[41] Dunning, cited, pp. 151–52, 233, and 291. It should not be forgotten, however, that in some industries the commodities produced by U.S. subsidiaries are tailored to the needs of the European market: this is the case of passenger automobiles, which account for about one-fourth of sales by U.S. subsidiaries in Western Europe.

[42] Pizer and Cutler, cited, p. 19. Of this amount, $200 million went to the United States.

[43] Same, p. 19; United Nations, *Commodity Trade Statistics*, 1964 (New York, 1965), and notes 26 and 27, above.

contribute to technological and organizational improvements both directly and indirectly, through their influence on the methods used by domestic firms in Western Europe. Also, by augmenting the availability of capital and of technical and managerial know-how, investments by American companies facilitate the exploitation of economies of scale in European manufacturing industries and reduce the time needed for reaching the present U.S. level of productivity and living standards. The taxation of the profits of foreign subsidiaries provides a further benefit to the countries of Western Europe, while their balance of payments may improve as a result of U.S. direct investments.

Objections have been raised, however, against the foreign ownership of capital, and it has been argued that the ultimate result would be the *Überfremdung* of European industry. But current indications hardly support the contention that *Überfremdung* would be a danger in the foreseeable future, since not even a doubling of the share of U.S. subsidiaries in the annual expenditures on plant and equipment would bring American ownership in European manufacturing above 10 per cent. On the other hand, one cannot dismiss the argument that, in industries characterized by rapid technological progress, the disadvantages of European firms in regard to the availability and cost of financing and the ability to engage in research and development would adversely affect their competitiveness vis-à-vis the U.S. subsidiaries.

The exclusion of American capital from certain branches of manufacturing would hardly be an appropriate remedy, since the technological lag between the United States and Western Europe would tend to increase if the transfer of technical know-how and the inducement for improvements in production methods provided by the establishment of U.S. subsidiaries were to diminish. Instead of applying restrictive measures, it would appear desirable to create the conditions for effective competition on the part of European firms by encouraging concentration and research activity, improving the access of European firms to external financing, and remedying the distortions due to international differences in antitrust legislation. Problems relating to concentration and research were considered in the preceding chapter; I shall now deal with external financing and anti-trust legislation.

The integration of capital markets in Western Europe would improve the access of European firms to external financing. But it will take some time to overcome national sensibilities that hinder this integration and, at any rate, the transformation of national capital markets is a slow and arduous process. In the meantime, the conditions of borrowing by American and European firms in each other's capital markets could be equalized if the governments of the major European countries imposed a tax equivalent to the U.S. Interest Equalization Tax on the borrowing of U.S. subsidiaries in Western Europe.[44]

The antitrust legislation of the United States is a further source of asymmetry. Domestic legislation precludes U.S. corporations from establishing dominant positions through the purchase of their competitors at home, but these rules do not apply to the appropriation of foreign firms. To remove this incentive for expansion through the purchase of European enterprises and to impede the establishment of dominant positions by American firms in Western Europe, an appropriate remedy would be to institute an antitrust policy on the European level. Such legislation would also reinforce the provisions of the Rome Treaty that aim at precluding the domination of particular industries by domestic firms.

But what position should the United States take in regard to direct investments in Western Europe? The answer depends to a considerable extent on the political objectives pursued. The United States cannot neglect the political implications of the aversion of many Europeans to foreign ownership; moreover, it is necessary to take account of the interests of the developing countries. These countries have experienced a slowing down in U.S. direct investments, in part because of the increased opportunities for investment offered by European economies.[45]

These considerations point to the desirability of a shift of U.S. investments from Western Europe to the developing countries. The United States balance of payments would also benefit from such a change. For one thing, investments in less developed countries are accompanied by larger imports of intermediate products and machinery from the United States than are investments in Western Europe. For another, developing countries customarily spend all their foreign-

[44] In turn Pierre Uri proposed (*Le Monde,* February 27, 1965) that a tax should be levied on *all* American direct investment in Western Europe.

[45] The book value of American investments in Western Europe nearly tripled in the period 1957–64 as compared to a rise by less than one-third in less developed countries while, in the preceding seven years, the value of U.S. investment in the two areas increased by 139 and 87 per cent, respectively (for sources see note 3).

exchange receipts, while this is not the case in European nations.[46]

But this conclusion should not be interpreted as advocating direct controls on foreign investment. Direct controls are notoriously inefficient and invite evasion. Rather, use should be made of the price mechanism and the measures to be taken should be designed to remedy existing distortions in U.S.–European relationships as well as to counteract the disincentives that stem from the lack of social and economic overhead capital and the political uncertainties for foreign investment in less developed countries. One such measure would be to equalize the tax treatment accorded to direct and to portfolio investments in Western Europe. This would have the double effect of removing the preferential treatment of the politically less objectionable portfolio investments over direct investments in Western Europe and of providing advantages for direct investments in less developed areas. Government guarantees and the extension of preferential tax treatment for investments in developing countries would also serve the stated objectives.

[46] On the latter point, see the discussion of feedback effects in Chapter 4.

CHAPTER SEVEN

A Trade Policy for the Atlantic Area

The Relative Importance of Political and Economic Considerations

The purpose of this study has been to examine the political and economic objectives of trade liberalization and to indicate the interests of the industrial nations in trade liberalization in general, and in its various forms in particular. In this chapter, I shall summarize the principal findings of the study and provide an evaluation of alternative trade arrangements among the industrial countries. It should be recalled that the analysis extends to trade in industrial materials and manufactured goods but does not cover foodstuffs and fuels.

While political considerations assume increased importance in large countries, the economic advantages of trade liberalization tend to be inversely related to the size of the national markets. Thus, in relative terms, the continental member countries of the European Free Trade Association would expect to derive the greatest economic benefit from tariff reductions among industrial economies. Substantial gains could also be realized in Canada, Japan, and the United Kingdom; smaller benefits would accrue to the European Common Market and the United States.

In Chapter 4 I estimated that, under the static assumptions of unchanged production methods, the trade of the Continental EFTA countries would rise by 12 to 15 per cent if tariffs on industrial materials and manufactured goods were eliminated in the framework of an Atlantic Free Trade Area. The increase in trade would exceed 2 per cent of the combined gross domestic products of these countries; the relevant proportions for Canada and Japan are .8 and 2.5 per cent in the case of exports and 2.7 and 11.0 per cent for imports. In turn, the expansion of trade, calculated under the stated assumptions, would amount to approximately 1 per cent of the gross domestic product in the United Kingdom and the European Common Market, and .5 per cent in the United States.

The dynamic effects of multilateral tariff reductions—cost reductions due to economies of scale and improvements in production methods resulting from increased competition—would further benefit the Continental EFTA countries. While their relatively low duties permit some foreign competition in the domestic markets of these countries, the higher tariffs of other industrial nations limit the possibilities of exploiting economies of scale in their manufacturing industries. It is not surprising, therefore, that we find the Scandinavian countries, Switzerland, and Austria among the strongest advocates of trade liberalization.[1]

In this connection, mention may be made of the changing attitudes of Norway and Denmark toward the freeing of tariff barriers. Only a decade ago the two countries were reluctant to participate in a Nordic Union, largely because of the fear that competition from industrially more advanced Sweden would impede the development of their manufacturing industries. They have entered, however, the European Free Trade Association where a large part of Swedish export expansion is directed to other member countries, and their favorable experience with EFTA has led them to endorse a policy of free trade. In fact, since the establishment of EFTA, both Denmark and Norway have increased the share of manufactured goods in their exports to a considerable extent: by 1964 manufactures accounted for 35.8 per cent of Danish exports and 52.5 per cent of Norwegian exports to their EFTA partners, as compared to 25.9 and 44.3 per cent in 1959.

Similar changes have been observed in attitudes toward trade liberalization in Austria, whereas Sweden and Switzerland have long been the advocates of free trade in nonagricultural products. In all of these countries it is apparently understood that under modern conditions small nations are handicapped by the limitations of their domestic markets. Thus, for the sake of the enduring benefits of free trade, they are willing to accept whatever short-term sacrifices an adjustment to free trade may involve.[2]

[1] Portugal provides a special case but, by reason of its relative unimportance, it will not be considered here.

[2] Parenthetically one may note that in some of the smaller countries of Western Europe (e.g. in Sweden) it has been suggested that economic benefits

The effect on trade of tariff reductions by the industrial countries, estimated under static assumptions, would be smaller in the United Kingdom, which carries out a large proportion of its trade with non-industrial nations. The scope for economies of scale is also more limited in Britain than in the Scandinavian countries or in Switzerland, since the U.K. has a larger domestic market and British exports receive preferential treatment in most Commonwealth countries. Nevertheless, as indicated in Chapter 5, there is scope for increases in productivity through horizontal and vertical specialization in much of British industry. Moreover, Britain's growth performance can be expected to improve as a cut in the high U.K. duties increases competitive pressures in domestic manufacturing industries, provided that tariff disarmament is accompanied by the application of appropriate economic policies.

Exporters in the United Kingdom and in the Continental EFTA countries would also profit from the lessening of Common Market discrimination through multilateral tariff reductions. EEC exporters would derive similar benefits in EFTA markets, and the cost of protection associated with trade diversion would decline in both areas. In addition, while a decrease in the extent of discrimination against non-European countries would adversely affect the balance of payments of the EEC and EFTA, member countries in both groups would gain from a lowering of the cost of imports to the consumer as well as from technological improvements stimulated by increased foreign competition. Finally, although the combined national markets of the EEC countries may permit the exploitation of economies of scale in the majority of their manufacturing industries, it can be assumed that an increase in market size through multilateral tariff reductions would have beneficial effects in several of the modern branches of Common Market manufacturing.

Trade restrictions in the form of both tariffs and quotas have been used to protect domestic manufacturing industries in Japan. In connection with her admission to the OECD, quantitative restrictions

---

could be obtained by unilaterally abolishing tariffs. In the ensuing controversy few references have been made to the need for protecting import-competing industries; neither has there been much concern that adverse changes in the terms of trade would follow a unilateral removal of tariff barriers. Rather, the proposition has been objected to on the grounds that tariffs should be used as a bargaining weapon to obtain concessions from other industrial countries which, in turn, would make it possible to increase exports and to exploit economies of scale in the export industries.

were by and large abolished in the early sixties, but Japanese tariffs remain at levels exceeding those of any other industrial country. At the same time, Japan's gross domestic product is less than one-half of that of Britain and, given the disparities in per capita income levels, differences in the size of domestic markets for manufactured goods are even larger. The dynamic benefits of trade liberalization derived from economies of scale and increased competition can therefore be of considerable importance in Japan.

In Canada, high tariffs had been considered necessary to encourage the development of manufacturing industries in the face of U.S. competition. In recent years, however, attention has been given to the disadvantages of protectionist policies and it has been suggested that on balance these policies have had detrimental, rather than beneficial, effects for Canadian industrial development.[3] At the same time, the cost of protection has been estimated to amount to 3.5 to 4.5 per cent of Canadian gross private expenditure.[4] If we consider that an estimate of this kind cannot appropriately allow for the dynamic effects of trade liberalization, it would appear that the cost of protection accounts for a substantial part of the difference between U.S. and Canadian living standards. This disparity would tend to narrow if the limitations imposed on production methods by the size of the Canadian market were removed through the elimination of tariffs between the two countries, provided that the freedom of capital movements is maintained.

In relative terms, the gains from freer trade are likely to be smallest in the United States. Among the industrial countries, international trade accounts for the smallest proportion of the gross domestic product in the U.S., and the expansion of trade in an Atlantic Free Trade Area, estimated under static assumptions, would not exceed one-half of 1 per cent of GDP in this country. While this is not a negligible magnitude, it is only slightly smaller than the annual U.S. foreign aid expenditure the resulting welfare gain would be only a fraction of the increase in trade.

At the same time, the claim that the elimination of Common Market discrimination through multilateral trade liberalization would be of considerable importance for the United States balance of payments

[3] Cf. J. H. Dales, "Some Historical and Theoretical Comment on Canada's National Policies," *Queen's Quarterly,* Autumn 1964, pp. 297–316.

[4] J. H. Young, *Canadian Commercial Policy* (Ottawa: Royal Commission on Canada's Economic Prospects, 1957), p. 73.

appears to be exaggerated. In Chapter 4 I estimated that Common Market discrimination would entail a reduction in American exports of manufactured goods to the EEC countries from 1960 levels by about one-fifth, $311 million. A change of this magnitude would affect the U.S. balance of payments only slightly and could be fully offset by changes in trade flows between the two areas if the prices of manufactured products in the Common Market were to increase by about 3 per cent relative to U.S. prices.[5] Actually, in the period 1958–1963, national income statistics show an increase of 7.9 per cent in the average prices of manufactured goods in the Common Market as against 5.1 per cent in the United States—a change in relative prices of 2.8 per cent.[6]

Moreover, while a lengthening of production runs may bring gains in some new branches of industry, such as high-speed electronic computers and supersonic aircraft, most industries can already exploit all possible sources of economies of scale in the large U.S. market. The main benefits of trade liberalization for the American economy may, then, come as a result of intensified competition and by avoiding a shift toward protectionism at home and abroad. In Chapter 5 I noted the effects of foreign competition on production methods in several American industries; further reductions in tariffs would enhance the beneficial impact of this competition on the U.S. manufacturing sector. It would also appear that if no efforts are made to liberalize trade, the alternative is likely to be increased protectionism rather than the maintenance of the status quo. For lack of a better expression, we may speak of an "instability effect," according to which economic and political relationships are hardly ever in a position of stable equilibrium but have the tendency to move in one direction or the other. Thus, in the absence of pressures for the liberalization of trade, protectionist counterpressures may gain force in the United States as well as abroad.

While this conclusion is based on certain assumptions regarding political processes, account should further be taken of the political

[5] On the method of estimation, see note 23 in Chapter 4. In making calculations, I have neglected potential increases in Common Market imports from the United States that would result from an acceleration of economic growth in the EEC.

[6] Changes in the prices of manufactured goods have been measured by calculating implicit GDP deflators for the manufacturing sector. Cf. Organization for Economic Cooperation and Development, *General Statistics*, January 1965.

objectives of trade liberalization among the industrial countries. Given its concern with the world power balance, these objectives assume special importance for the United States. In fact, considering that the American economy is likely to derive relatively small economic benefits from multilateral reductions in duties, the political objectives of maintaining cohesion within the Atlantic alliance and raising living standards in less developed countries would have to assume first place in determining the position taken by the United States.

The political aspects of Atlantic trade arrangements are of great consequence for the United Kingdom and the Common Market, too. According to most observers, the principal motivating forces behind Britain's application for entry into the Common Market in 1961 were political rather than economic, and political considerations have played an important role in her renewed interest in EEC membership. The reasons are easy to find. In the postwar period, the disintegration of the Commonwealth and the weakening of Britain's "special relationship" with the United States have contributed to the deterioration of the power position of the United Kingdom, and the establishment of the Common Market has further reduced British influence in Western Europe. In turn, membership in the EEC would permit Britain to regain a leading role in European affairs and might even increase U.K. influence in world politics.

On the other side of the Channel, political considerations played a decisive role in De Gaulle's refusal to admit Britain to the EEC, as well as in his attempt to eliminate all elements of supranationality from the Common Market. The positions taken by the other five EEC members in favor of British membership and in support of the supranational elements of the Rome Treaty have also been largely politically motivated. In turn, in a choice among alternative trade arrangements in the Atlantic area, the objective of European unity and the desire to reduce the existing asymmetry in relationships with the United States are likely to assume considerable importance in the major countries of Western Europe.

There appears, however, to be little concern with European unification in the Scandinavian countries. While one cannot speak of a complete identity of views, these countries apparently take a pragmatic attitude toward trade liberalization. Thus, decisions on alternative trade arrangements will be made largely on the basis of economic considerations, with political objectives accorded second place. Nevertheless Sweden (and to a lesser or greater degree Austria and Switzerland) endeavors to avoid a conflict between economic advantage and the maintenance of neutrality.

The answer is less clear in the case of Japan. While it has often been argued that the Japanese tend to judge any trade arrangement chiefly on its economic merits, political considerations seem to have assumed increasing importance in recent years. On the one hand, participation in the OECD indicates Japan's desire to be a member of the councils of the West; on the other, Japan values its trade relations with the countries of Southeast Asia in large part because these permit maintaining—and strengthening—her influence in the area. Accordingly, Japan has an interest both in closer trade ties with the industrial countries of North America and Western Europe and in continuing trade relations with Southeast Asia.

I have noted the economic advantages that Canada would derive from freeing trade with the United States. Canada would also find it advantageous if the establishment of a free trade area in North America preceded that of an Atlantic Free Trade Area since, in such an event, she may expect an inflow of capital from the United States that would otherwise be largely directed to Western Europe. However, the political objective of independence from the United States has long obstructed the way toward economic integration in North America and may induce Canada to favor a wider arrangement where the asymmetry in power relations is less pronounced.

These considerations can be utilized in examining the desirability of alternative approaches to trade liberalization among the industrial countries. It will be recalled that four alternatives are considered in the present study: (a) an Atlantic Free Trade Area, (b) multilateral tariff reductions under the most-favored-nation clause, (c) a trade arrangement among the industrial countries with the exclusion of the Common Market, and (d) European integration.

An Atlantic Free Trade Area vs. Tariff Reductions under the Most-Favored-Nation Clause

In the introduction to this volume, I noted that the General Agreement on Tariffs and Trade allows an important exception to the application of the most-favored-nation clause: countries that agree to abolish duties on "substantially all trade" among themselves in the framework of a free trade area or customs union [7] are not required to extend these concessions to other nations. The establishment of free trade areas and customs unions thus conflicts with the principle of nondiscrimination, embodied in the most-favored-nation clause. This conflict is not resolved by provisions in GATT, according to which duties and other regulations of commerce in a newly established free trade area (customs union) should not be "higher or more restrictive" than beforehand, since the removal of internal, and the maintenance of external, tariffs automatically discriminate against imports from nonmember countries.

The exception made for free trade areas and customs unions in GATT has been the subject of much controversy. It has often been argued that it is illogical to allow 100 per cent discrimination against outsiders in a free trade area while proscribing preferential trading arrangements which involve a lesser degree of discrimination. Indeed, according to Harry G. Johnson, theoretical analysis "indicates some presumption that partial preferential arrangements are more likely to be beneficial than the complete preferences entailed in free trade areas or customs unions." [8]

But the conclusion that, on welfare grounds, *some* preferential arrangements are superior to establishing a free trade area or customs union [9] should not be used as an argument in favor of preferential arrangements *in general*. To begin with, no method has yet been devised to determine what kind of preferential arrangements would be more advantageous for the world economy than a free trade area or a customs union. There is no guarantee therefore that such an arrangement would actually be chosen even if this were the objective of the participating countries. And the latter assumption can hardly be made, since trade policies are designed to serve national interests, real or presumed, and governments often try to shelter domestic industries that may be adversely affected by reductions in tariffs.

Accordingly, while the elimination of tariffs in the framework of a free trade area or customs union will create new trade among the

[7] In a free trade area, the member countries maintain their own tariffs on imports from nonmembers and retain the right to follow independent commercial policies. Establishing a customs union entails in addition an agreement on a common external tariff and on the conduct of commercial policies.

[8] Harry G. Johnson, *The World Economy at the Crossroads*, p. 46.

[9] Cf. R. G. Lipsey and K. J. Lancaster, "The General Theory of the Second Best," *Review of Economic Studies*, No. 1 (1956–57), pp. 11–32.

member countries and divert trade from outsiders, selective tariff reductions undertaken on a preferential basis will often be predominantly trade-diverting because countries are less reluctant to increase trade at the expense of outsiders than at the expense of their own producers. Now, since trade creation is assumed to improve, and trade diversion to deteriorate, the allocation of resources in the world economy, there will be a *prima facie* case for free trade areas and customs unions in preference to discriminatory arrangements.[10] This conclusion is reinforced if we take account of the dynamic gains derived from the assumed permanence of economic integration schemes.

Different considerations apply to the choice between customs unions and free trade areas, on the one hand, and tariff reductions under the most-favored-nation clause, on the other. While the internal effects of these arrangements—i.e., the amount of new trade created among the member countries—will depend on the scope of tariff reductions actually undertaken, they will have contrary effects on outsiders: nonparticipating countries automatically benefit from tariff reductions under m.f.n. but are discriminated against in a customs union or free trade area. The repercussions of the two types of arrangements for third countries are especially important in cases where substantial differences in living standards exist between the "insiders" and the "outsiders"—in the present case, between the industrial and the less developed countries.

In claiming the superiority of free trade areas over reciprocal tariff reductions under m.f.n., the proponents of an Atlantic Free Trade Area have given emphasis to the internal effects of integration and have largely disregarded its impact on third countries. Since in a free trade area tariffs on substantially all goods are abolished (so the argument goes) the resulting increase in trade would be greater than in the case of less comprehensive tariff reductions. Furthermore, the simultaneous elimination of tariffs on all or most commodities allows for

---

[10] Jacob Viner writes in his classic *The Customs Union Issue:* "Customs union, if it is complete, involves across-the-board removal of duties between the members of the union; since the removal is non-selective by its very nature, the beneficial preferences are established along with the injurious ones, the trade-creating ones along with the trade-diverting ones. Preferential arrangements, on the other hand, can be, and usually are, selective, and it is possible, and in practice probable, that the preferences selected will be predominantly of the trade-diverting or injurious kind" ([New York: Carnegie Endowment for International Peace, 1950], pp. 50–51).

compensating changes in various industries, while pressure groups representing special interests may restrict the scope of reductions in duties if negotiations are conducted on an item-by-item basis. Finally, it has been suggested that the assurance against the reimposition of duties in a free trade area would induce producers to utilize fully the opportunities provided by the elimination of tariffs, but this would not be so in the case of tariff reductions under the most-favored-nation clause.

It is not to be denied that the establishment of a free trade area would create more trade among the industrial countries than would tariff reductions of a more limited scope. Protectionist pressures may also influence decision-making in the second case, and uncertainties will limit the expansion of trade as long as possibilities for the reimposition of duties exist. But, in judging the relative merits of the two alternatives, several further questions need to be raised—some political and others economic.

To begin with, it is questionable that the main industrial countries wish to have the degree of cohesion that the establishment of an Atlantic Free Trade Area would entail. André Marchal suggests that solidarity among the participating countries is a precondition of economic integration.[11] It would appear that, in U.S.–European relationships, we presently lack the degree of solidarity necessary to permit dispensing once and for all with the use of protective measures in the main sectors of the economy. Thus, the U.S. Congress does not seem inclined to accept the removal of duties on products where American producers are assumed to be uncompetitive, and a plan for an Atlantic Free Trade Area would run into similar objections in European parliaments. Moreover, in Western Europe many would consider the elimination of duties on trade with the United States a backward step in the process toward greater independence from the United States, on the grounds that the economic basis for the unification of Europe would thereby be undermined.

In the EEC itself, the external tariff is regarded as a unifying element, a sign of the Common Market's identity, and suggestions for abolishing tariffs are looked upon with suspicion. It has also been claimed that there is need for maintaining the common external tariff in the EEC in order to permit specialization to take place before confronting American competition. While this argument cannot be applied to *all* industries, differences in market size as well as direct and

[11] André Marchal, *L'Europe solidaire* (Paris: Editions Cujas, 1965).

indirect government support would favor American firms in research-intensive industries in case of a full and immediate removal of tariffs. On the other hand, periodic tariff reductions that maintained a balance between the requirements of protection and the need for foreign competition could contribute to the development of these industries in Western Europe.

Periodic tariff reductions have the further advantage of permitting a "learning process" to take place on the part of entrepreneurs, labor unions, and legislators with respect to the effects of trade liberalization on domestic industries. Their actual experience with tariff reductions may allay the fears of those who demand continued protection on the grounds that wages are lower in Western Europe than in the United States—or that productivity is higher in the United States than in Europe. Businessmen as well as governments will observe in practice that trade liberalization does not lead to the decline of national industries and that the adjustment to freer trade is considerably easier, and the losses suffered by domestic firms smaller, than commonly assumed.[12]

Changes in the attitude of French entrepreneurs toward trade liberalization provide an example of this learning process. While in 1958 the French Patronat had opposed the establishment of the EEC, a few years later it came to favor continued participation in the Common Market. At the time of the 1965 French presidential elections the majority of businessmen apparently joined the opposition largely because of their fear that De Gaulle's actions would lead to the breaking up of the Community. It has also been reported that entrepreneurs in France now object less to tariff reductions on trade with the United States—long considered the most formidable competitor of French industry—than they opposed the freeing of trade with neighboring countries a decade earlier.[13]

The arguments in favor of the gradual approach are further strengthened if we consider that the chances of reaching an agreement increase when especially sensitive industries can be excluded from the negotiations. At the same time, the procedural difficulties noted in connection with item-by-item tariff bargaining largely disappear if negotiations are carried out on an across-the-board basis. The procedure employed in the Kennedy Round conforms to these require-

---

[12] On this point, see pp. 189–91, in Chapter 4.

[13] Paul Fabra, "Le 'Kennedy Round' sert-il les intérêts de l'Europe?" *Le Monde,* May 3, 1964.

ments: the negotiating parties have reached a preliminary agreement on a flat rate of tariff cut applicable to all nonagricultural sectors, with exceptions to be determined at a later time.

But what of the advantages that free trade areas and customs unions are supposed to have over m.f.n.-type tariff reductions because the former—but not the latter—entail a commitment to refrain from reimposing tariffs and other forms of trade restrictions? Indeed, the uncertainty associated with the possibility that restrictions will again be employed makes it necessary to include an additional risk premium in entrepreneurial calculations, and this in turn limits the extent of international specialization. But the contrast between the two approaches should not be overdrawn, since entrepreneurial decisions will depend on the *credibility* of the commitment to forego the use of trade restrictions. In view of the use of import surcharges in the United Kingdom in the years 1964–1966, and the new British approaches toward the Common Market, the degree of credibility of this commitment is rather low in the European Free Trade Association, which fact restrains the adaptation of producing and marketing facilities to a larger area. In an Atlantic context, too, the credibility of any commitment will depend largely on the degree of solidarity among the participating countries. At the same time, procedures can be worked out that reduce uncertainty in trade relations among independent national economies without establishing a free trade area. In this connection, some comments on the relevant GATT rules and their practical application are in order.

The General Agreement contains provisions for escape clauses and for the renegotiation of tariff concessions, and permits raising duties on items that were not subject to negotiations. At the same time, the contracting parties have apparently taken a permissive attitude toward the application of escape clauses and of other forms of safeguards. According to an informed observer, "conflicts between pressing national interest and GATT obligations have generally been resolved in favor of the former," while in some instances "a country's desire for increased protection was satisfied by the successful search for a measure that achieved the desired result without technically violating the Agreement." [14]

The application of the across-the-board principle in tariff bargaining would effectively nullify the right of individual countries to increase duties on items not subject to negotiations. However, Article

[14] Irving B. Kravis, *Domestic Interest and International Obligations* (Philadelphia: University of Pennsylvania Press, 1963), pp. 133, 135.

28 of GATT, which permits the renegotiation of tariff concessions at three-year intervals, remains in effect. This provision contributes to uncertainty in international transactions, especially since the country that initiates the negotiations for modifying earlier concessions can act unilaterally if the concurrence of its trading partners is not obtained.

Further, the escape clause contained in Article 13 of the General Agreement empowers a country to reimpose trade restrictions in case "serious injury is caused or threatened to domestic producers" as a result of increases in imports. This clause was included in the Agreement at the insistence of the United States and has also been invoked chiefly by the United States. And while, on the occasion of its first application, an *ad hoc* working party was established to appraise the validity of the American claim, the working party has reportedly "accepted the primacy of the judgment of the country invoking the escape clause rather than attempting to make a fully independent assessment of the applicability of its provisions to the case at hand." [15]

The provisions for the renegotiation of tariff concessions and for escape clauses reflect a protectionist philosophy that does not accept changes in a country's production structure and aims at safeguarding narrowly defined domestic interests at the expense of foreign producers. The U.S. Trade Expansion Act of 1962 has brought about a change on both counts: it has redefined—and limited—the conditions under which the escape clause can be applied in the United States and has introduced the use of adjustment assistance in cases when this clause is invoked.[16] However, as long as escape clauses and the provision for renegotiating tariff concessions are part of the General Agreement, entrepreneurial decisions on entering foreign markets will take account of the possibility that tariffs will be raised above negotiated levels or quantitative restrictions will be imposed. It is suggested here that, to reduce uncertainty in international trade, it would be desirable to repeal these provisions of the Agreement and to substitute instead a "code of good conduct" which would regulate the actions of the trading partners in regard to tariffs, quotas, and subsidies.

Under the proposed code of good conduct, countries would relin-

[15] Same.

[16] Adjustment assistance can take the form of technical assistance, loans, and tax concessions to firms as well as readjustment allowances, retraining, and relocation for workers.

quish the right of raising tariffs or imposing other forms of trade restriction in the event that particular industries are adversely affected by increases in imports. Escape clauses would be provided only for cases when certain mutually agreed-upon conditions are fulfilled, and would permit applying temporary measures of adjustment assistance rather than tariffs and quotas. Aside from making explicit the cost to the domestic economy of measures taken in favor of a particular industry, the temporary character of financial assistance would ensure that the formerly protected industry does in fact adjust to the new situation. In this way, greater flexibility would be introduced in the economic structure, while the application of restrictive measures would tend to freeze the status quo. At the same time, a system of adjustment assistance does not penalize foreign producers as is the case when tariffs or other forms of trade restriction are reimposed on imports.

A code of good conduct should also strengthen existing provisions against domestic subsidies and dumping, the objective being to avoid the need for countervailing measures on the part of importing countries. Finally, a solution would have to be found to the problem of administering the code. In view of opposition from countries intent on safeguarding their national sovereignty, to the creation of an international authority with power to overrule decisions by individual governments the scheme would have to be largely self-policing. It would nevertheless be desirable to establish a committee, preferably within the framework of GATT, with the task of making recommendations on disputed issues, which would hopefully be capable of exerting moral pressure on governments in case of noncompliance.

By reducing uncertainty in trade relations among industrial countries and facilitating the process of domestic adjustments, the proposed scheme would both contribute to the expansion of international trade and increase the attractiveness of the gradual approach to the liberalization of trade. Uncertainty in international trade would be further reduced if tariff procedures were simplified and national tariff classifications unified. This is the case especially in the United States and Canada that do not use the Brussels Tariff Nomenclature. It is desirable that these two nations accept the BTN and that all countries achieve uniformity in regard to the subheadings of the Brussels Nomenclature. The simplification of U.S. regulations on customs valuation would further reduce uncertainties in international transactions.

Trade Arrangements without the EEC?

Another alternative would be to liberalize trade among the United States, Canada, and the EFTA countries on a preferential basis or in the form of a free trade area. Proposals to this effect were originally made for the eventuality that the Kennedy Round remained unsuccessful because of the resistance of the Common Market.[17] More recently, the establishment of a free trade area among these countries has been proposed as a genuine alternative, irrespective of the outcome of the Kennedy Round.[18]

In the event that negotiations in the framework of the Kennedy Round were to break down, the Committee for Economic Development has suggested that the United States reach a trade agreement with a smaller group of countries in such an event—even if this meant jettisoning the principle of nondiscrimination. Further, Henry Reuss, an influential member of the Joint Economic Committee of U.S. Congress, has raised the possibility of establishing a free trade area among the industrial countries that excluded the Common Market, or making the application of the most-favored-nation clause conditional on reciprocal concessions ("conditional" m.f.n.).

These proposals reflect the influence of various factors. For one thing, De Gaulle's refusal to admit Britain has created a certain disenchantment with the EEC in the United States and has prompted a reappraisal of the unqualified support given to the Common Market in the past.[19] There has also been concern with the rise in the EEC's bargaining power and with the problem of maintaining U.S. leadership in the Atlantic area. Finally, the opponents of the Administration's European trade policy have become increasingly vocal, and some of them have apparently taken a position in favor of "punishing" the Common Market.[20]

[17] Cf. Committee for Economic Development, *Trade Negotiations for a Better Free World Economy* (Washington: 1964), p. 41; and Henry S. Reuss, *The Critical Decade* (New York: McGraw-Hill, 1964), pp. 59–61.

[18] Canadian-American Committee, *A New Trade Strategy for Canada and the United States* (Washington: 1966)—the Committee considers this scheme as a first step towards the eventual establishment of an Atlantic Free Trade Area.

[19] Similar considerations explain the support for conditional m.f.n. by *The Economist* (February 16, 1963; p. 618) following the breakdown of the negotiations for Britain's entry into the Common Market.

[20] Congressman Reuss asks the rhetorical question whether the Common Market should "continue to mesmerize us," and suggests that the United States should take retaliatory action in case the Common Market adopts its announced agricultural policy. *The Critical Decade,* pp. 50–57.

Conditional m.f.n. is a flexible device since it would permit the exclusion of sensitive industries from the negotiations and would also allow for subsequent changes in the geographical scope and/or the commodity composition of tariff reductions. But while flexibility might facilitate reaching an agreement, this alternative has some important drawbacks. To begin with, in view of our previous discussion, there is a presumption that tariff reductions would take place mainly in industries where the participating countries have little to lose, thereby giving rise to trade diversion while limiting the creation of new trade.

A further consideration is that EFTA countries have much greater interest in freeing trade with the Common Market than with the United States. In 1964, the exports of these countries to the EEC amounted to $6.5 billion and imports to $8.8 billion, while the relevant figures for trade with the United States were $2.0 and $2.6 billion. Further, according to the calculations reported in Chapter 4, the direct effects of the elimination of duties would entail an increase in EFTA exports to the Common Market countries by $550 to $700 million and imports by $750 million to $1 billion, as compared to increases of $350 to $450 and $330 million, respectively, in trade with the United States. The EFTA countries would also benefit from the elimination of EEC discrimination that would permit an increase in their exports by $475 million.[21]

It appears likely, therefore, that if the member countries of the European Free Trade Association were to reach an agreement with the United States for reducing tariffs under conditional m.f.n., they would attempt to make similar arrangements with the Common Market. The EFTA countries would have the best of both worlds in such an event —just as the United Kingdom meant to have it in 1958 in proposing the establishment of an all-European free trade area while maintaining the Commonwealth preference system. On the other hand, the United States may ultimately lose, since the greater relative importance of their trade with the Common Market can be expected to induce the EFTA countries to enter into more comprehensive arrangements with the EEC than with the United States. Such an arrangement would also be attractive to the Common Market nations, since they fear the competitive power of the countries of the European Free Trade Association less than that of the United States.

In this connection, one may recall that in 1964 some commen-

[21] It will be recalled that the expansion of trade in an Atlantic Free Trade Area has been estimated from 1960 levels.

tators revived the idea of selective tariff-cutting among European countries, to be restricted to commodities that are of special interest to them. Given the similarity of export patterns among the industrial nations, such a scheme would hardly work as long as the most-favored-nation clause was applied. However, any move on the part of the United States to do away with this clause may be seized upon by the two European trade groupings as a justification for entering into preferential arrangements among themselves.

The objections to conditional m.f.n. further gain in strength if we consider that, once the Pandora's box of discriminatory tariff reductions is opened, individual countries may also enter into discriminatory agreements of varying scope and the specter of retaliation is raised. Finally, since the modification of Article 1 of GATT concerning the most-favored-nation clause requires the concurrence of all member countries, the possibility exists that the General Agreement would be abrogated and the progress toward free trade reversed.

To escape the latter result, Randall Hinshaw has suggested that countries entering into preferential arrangements should establish a two-tariff system: "a preferential tariff, bound by an agreed ceiling, which would apply to participants; and a nonpreferential tariff, not bound by the ceiling, which would apply to nonparticipants." [22] But, by permitting rates of duties on imports from participating countries to vary between nil and the agreed-upon tariff ceiling,[23] the two-tariff system would provide an opportunity to choose rates with a view to their trade-diverting effects. Moreover, countries or country groupings might negotiate tariff ceilings at varying levels with different trading partners.

Reuss and Hinshaw also consider the possibility of establishing a free trade area with the participation of the United States, Canada, the European Free Trade Association, and possibly Japan. While such an arrangement would be free of some of the objections levied against the application of the conditional m.f.n. clause, it is open to criticism on several counts. To begin with, in view of our previous discussion, the countries of the European Free Trade Association would find it more advantageous to enter into a trade arrangement with the Common Market than with the United States. This conclusion applies with especial force to the Continental EFTA countries

---

[22] Randall Hinshaw, *The European Community and American Trade* (New York: Praeger, 1964), p. 175.

[23] Hinshaw suggests the figure of 10 per cent.

whose exports to the EEC amounted to $3.9 billion and imports to $6.6 billion in 1964, while their trade with the United States was about one billion dollars in either direction. It stands to reason that the Continental EFTA countries would contemplate participating in a trade arrangement with the United States only if the chances for reaching an accommodation with the Common Market were nil.

Participation in a trade arrangement with the United States was proposed by the well-known Swedish economist Bertil Ohlin, in his capacity as the leader of one of the opposition parties in Sweden. This suggestion, in turn, has come under criticism from various quarters. The critics have pointed out that Ohlin has taken an overly pessimistic view regarding the possibilities for ending the division of Western Europe into two trading blocs. A further consideration has been that the chances for an accommodation between the two groups would probably be jeopardized if the EFTA countries entered into a trade arrangement with the United States that excluded the Common Market. It appears, then, that while political considerations may not deter the Continental EFTA countries from participating in a U.S.–Canada–EFTA free trade area, the limited economic benefits of such a scheme, and its implications for a future accommodation with the EEC, would make it an undesirable alternative for them.

For Britain, too, the Common Market countries are trading partners of greater importance than is the United States.[24] Moreover, in the case of the United Kingdom, political considerations militate against participating in a trade arrangement with the United States that excludes the Common Market. Participation in a truncated AFTA would increase Britain's dependence on the United States and would greatly reduce the chances for a European solution that appears to be the British objective. Aside from improving her power position in Western Europe, the United Kingdom may also be able to exert greater influence on American policy-making from within an enlarged Common Market than as a member of a U.S.-led free trade area.

The United States likewise has an interest, economic as well as political, in reaching an accommodation with the European Common Market. The EEC is the largest trading unit in the world economy and its importance as a trading partner for the United States over-

[24] United Kingdom trade with the EEC was nearly double the value of trade with the United States in 1964, and Britain will increasingly feel the effects of Common Market discrimination in years to come.

shadows that of the European Free Trade Association. In 1964, U.S. exports to the EEC were about double her exports to EFTA and imports were one-half larger; moreover, the potential discriminatory effects of the Common Market are considerably greater than those of EFTA. In Chapter 4 I estimated the decrease in U.S. exports due to discrimination to amount to $311 million in the former case and $78 million in the latter.

The question arises, then, whether a truncated Atlantic Free Trade Area would be directed against the EEC or designed to induce the Common Market to become a participant at some later date. While proposals of this kind are often motivated by anti-EEC sentiment, we may assume that the latter objective is being pursued. But can we accept the premise that the Common Market would ultimately join such an arrangement? A similar, and by hindsight unwarranted, assumption was made when the European Free Trade Association was established. A U.S.–Canada–EFTA free trade area might have a greater drawing power but chances are that it would instead create two hostile blocs and perpetuate the division—this time between North America and part of Western Europe on the one hand and the Common Market on the other.

Instead of serving the objective of greater cohesion in the Atlantic area, such a scheme would then contribute to a hardening of divisions within Europe and within the Western alliance. More generally, the asymmetry of power relations inherent in the U.S.–Canada–EFTA free trade area proposal makes it inappropriate for establishing an Atlantic alliance based on a bipolar relationship of two partners of comparable strength. The "building blocs" of the latter should be North America and Western Europe rather than a truncated Atlantic Free Trade Area and the European Common Market.

Implications of Alternative Trade Arrangements for the Developing Countries

Given the interest of the industrial nations in the well-being and political stability of developing countries, the potential impact of alternative arrangements on trade between these two groups of nations should further be considered. Under the most-favored-nation clause, tariff cuts are extended to all GATT members, and hence developing countries automatically benefit from reductions in duties undertaken by industrial economies. On the other hand, an Atlantic Free Trade

Area would discriminate against outsiders since the elimination of tariffs on intra-area trade provides an advantage to producers in partner countries over third-country producers.

Accordingly, while nonparticipating countries would automatically gain if the industrial nations reduced tariffs under the most-favored-nation clause, they would suffer discrimination in the event an Atlantic Free Trade Area were established. Some have suggested that the loss to developing countries would be small, since the volume of their exports of manufactures is also low. But, in judging the importance of this question, it is hardly sufficient to look at the present volume of trade. The exports of manufactured goods from developing countries increased rapidly during the fifties, reaching $1.1 billion, 5.5 per cent of their exports to industrial economies in 1960.[25] But quantitative restrictions limit the expansion of textile exports that account for a large proportion of the total, and the "graduated" tariff structure of the industrial nations provide a further disincentive to exportation from less developed areas.

In Chapter 3 I noted the tendency in the industrial nations to protect simple manufactures which are presently exported by developing countries or may become their export products in the future. Effective tariffs on these commodities, expressing the degree of protection of value added in domestic industry, often exceed 30 to 40 per cent in industrial economies. It is to be expected that the lowering of tariff barriers would improve the export possibilities of the developing countries to a considerable extent and would contribute to an acceleration of their industrial development. By contrast, discrimination against the exports of these countries in an Atlantic Free Trade Area would hinder the transformation of their economic structure by restricting demand for goods they actually export and by making it more difficult for them to introduce new export products.

The establishment of an Atlantic Free Trade Area would, then, run counter to the objective of raising living standards and encouraging economic growth in less developed areas. And, aside from its economic effects, such an arrangement would not fail to have unfavorable political repercussions since it would be regarded as a "rich men's club" in the developing countries. The adverse political effects may, in fact, overshadow the immediate economic consequences.

But could special concessions be offered to the developing nations

[25] Bela Balassa, *Trade Prospects for Developing Countries* (Homewood, Ill.: Irwin, 1964), p. 48.

to offset the losses due to tariff discrimination? I have doubts about the political feasibility of such a scheme. Experience indicates that the national legislatures of the industrial countries tend to regard compensatory measures as a form of foreign aid and are reluctant to increase commitments. Thus, while they may be prepared to accept the "side effects" of multilateral tariff reductions that automatically benefit third countries, it appears questionable that they would be willing to undertake unilateral obligations—even though these would serve the purpose of compensating for the discriminatory effects of AFTA.

At the same time, developing countries are likely to consider any compensation offered for the loss of potential future benefits inadequate. In fact, the underdeveloped world may find the establishment of an Atlantic Free Trade Area acceptable only if it is accompanied by the unilateral elimination of duties on the part of the industrial countries.[26] We would, then, arrive at a modified situation of worldwide free trade in nonagricultural commodities, with tariffs on manufactured goods being maintained in less developed areas. While this solution has much to commend it, national legislators are unlikely to find it acceptable. It could, however, be approached through a succession of Kennedy Round-type tariff reductions.

In effect, the merits of gradualism in trade liberalization, noted in connection with trade among the industrial countries, are even more pronounced in regard to the imports of manufactures from less developed areas. This conclusion is readily understood if consideration is given to the differences in the commodity structure of trade in the two cases. In Chapter 4 I indicated that trade in manufactured goods among the industrial countries is characterized by national product differentiation; reductions of tariff barriers on this trade would entail intraindustry specialization rather than the contraction of the activity of individual industries as postulated by the traditional theory of international trade. The traditional conclusions apply, however, to standardized products that are the actual and potential exports of developing countries. Since cost differences are of chief importance

26 It should be recalled that, on the occasion of the UN Conference on Trade and Development in 1964, Raul Prebisch suggested that the industrial countries give preferences to the exports of manufactures from less developed areas. On arguments pro and con of this proposal, see Gardner Patterson, "Would Tariff Preferences Help Economic Development?" *Lloyds Bank Review,* April 1965, pp. 18–30, and Harry G. Johnson, "Trade Preferences for Developing Countries," same, April 1966, pp. 1–18.

for this class of commodities, trade liberalization would lead to shifts in the location of production and would necessitate an adjustment in countries whose industries are adversely affected. The problems of adjustment can, in turn, be eased if the liberalization of trade takes the form of a gradual process.

More generally, in view of the decline in the share of primary products in world trade, manufactured goods will have to assume increasing importance in the exports of less developed countries if they are to accelerate the process of their economic development. The possibilities for expansion are the most favorable in the case of standardized products that are labor-intensive or utilize domestic raw materials. Aside from the cost of labor and material inputs, standardization provides important advantages to developing countries that lack entrepreneurship, technical skills, and marketing experience. On the one hand, the technological process and the organization of work are relatively simple in the case of standardized products; on the other, these commodities find ready markets in foreign countries.

With the shift in the comparative advantage of the less developed countries toward simple manufactures, these countries could provide a rising proportion of the domestic consumption of such products in the industrial nations. The lowering of duties under the most-favored-nation clause would contribute to this process, but tariff reductions would have to be supplemented by decisions regarding import quotas. Industrial countries use quantitative restrictions to limit the imports of textile products, and formal or informal quota arrangements also apply to some other manufactured goods exported by the developing countries. Moreover, the actual and potential export products of these countries were often excluded from the negotiations in the postwar period when tariff reductions were carried out on an item-by-item basis, and several of the commodities in question appear on the exception lists prepared in connection with the Kennedy Round of tariff bargaining. These actions reflect the intention of the governments of industrial nations to protect industries that may be adversely affected by an expansion of imports from less developed areas, an objective which is in conflict with the goal of contributing to economic progress and political stability in the developing nations.

Sooner or later, this conflict will have to be resolved and the importance of external political considerations indicates the need for a lowering of protective barriers in the industrial countries. In the long run, this solution would bring economic benefits to these countries since it would permit them to increase the share of sophisticated products in their manufacturing output in which they have a comparative advantage. However, the early elimination of trade barriers would create dislocation in domestic industries, and therefore the liberalization of trade would have to be undertaken in a gradual fashion. In this way, the process of adjustment can take the form of changes in the relative proportions of the increment in resources rather than an intersectoral shift of existing resources.

To begin with, the export earnings of the developing countries could increase by $7.5 to $9 billion if the industrial nations were to make additional purchases from these countries equivalent to 1 per cent of the increase in their gross national product between 1960 and 1975. While an expansion of trade of this magnitude would create few problems in the manufacturing sector of the industrial economies, it would help to deal with the projected $11.3 to $13.7 billion deficit of the developing countries and would contribute importantly to their economic transformation.[27]

The example of textiles, the imports of which from low-wage areas have been subject to much criticism in industrial nations, may be instructive in this regard. Although textile products already account for one-third of the imports of manufactures from developing countries, the share of these countries in the textile consumption of industrial economies remains small, and relatively modest increases in this share would bring a substantial expansion in trade. In the United States, for example, textile imports from less developed areas were valued at $145 million in 1960, amounting to about 1 per cent of domestic textile consumption.[28] With an approximately 4 per cent annual increase in consumption, by 1975 these imports would reach $1.2 billion if developing countries were to supply only one-tenth of the increase in consumption between 1960 and 1975. The adverse effects of such a change for American textile producers would be relatively small—for New England producers it would be negligible by comparison to the impact of the relocation of plants to the South. Should we assume, for example, that productivity in the U.S. textile industry is rising at a rate of 3.6 per cent a year, the adjustment process would not necessitate an absolute reduction in the number of workers employed in the U.S. textile industry.

[27] *Trade Prospects for Developing Countries*, pp. 35–36, 104.
[28] Same, pp. 117, 446.

Similar considerations apply to Western Europe except that, in view of the smaller projected increase of the working population, a reduction in the employment of textile workers would be called for. But this could be accomplished by not replacing the natural attrition in the textile industry's working force due to retirement, death, or change of occupation. At any rate, such a change in the composition of the labor force would be desirable from the point of view of Europe's economic growth since it would release labor for the more modern branches of manufacturing.

Nevertheless, to ensure that the real or presumed burden of adjustment be equitably shared by all industrial countries, it appears desirable that these countries should take concerted action with respect to tariffs and quotas on imports of simple manufactures. An agreement would have to be reached on reducing trade barriers on these products which would guarantee a steady rate of expansion of imports from the developing countries and a gradual process of adjustment in the industrial nations. These objectives might be served if the industrial nations established targets for the importation of manufactured goods from developing countries in a way similar to targets established for foreign aid.[29] Finally, as noted in Chapter 6, advantageous treatment accorded to foreign investments in developing countries would further contribute to the process of their industrial transformation.

Conclusion

The discussion in this and the preceding chapters leads one to reject certain policy alternatives proposed in recent years. To begin with, under present conditions, the establishment of an Atlantic Free Trade Area appears neither feasible nor desirable. The countries on the two sides of the Atlantic are not yet ready and willing to assume the real or imaginary risks such an arrangement may entail, and they do not possess the degree of solidarity that would be necessary for its coming to fruition. On the other hand, gradualism in lowering tariffs would make it possible to exclude especially sensitive industries from the negotiations and would permit a "learning process" on the part of business, labor, and national legislatures which promises to facilitate

[29] Such targets can be expressed as a proportion of the consumption, or the increment in the consumption, of particular categories of manufactured goods.

future reductions in duties. At the same time, the uncertainties associated with the possibility of a future reimposition of trade restrictions would decrease if a "code of good conduct" was instituted allowing for the use of adjustment assistance in case of transitional difficulties but precluding the employment of restrictive measures for this purpose.

Moreover, the major European countries are opposed to the establishment of an Atlantic Free Trade Area on the grounds that it would interfere with the political and economic process of integration in the European area. The developing nations, too, would oppose such a scheme—unless they were to enjoy the benefits of a unilateral elimination of tariffs by the industrial nations. While this would hardly be feasible at the present time, the gradual lowering of trade barriers would ensure a steady expansion of manufactured exports from less developed areas and permit the reallocation of the increment of resources in industrial economies.

In turn, preferential trade arrangements have decisive economic and political disadvantages and a U.S. proposal for the application of a conditional m.f.n. clause may provide an opportunity for other countries to enter into agreements detrimental to the economic interests of the United States. Nor does the plan for the establishment of a truncated Atlantic Free Trade Area—with the participation of the United States, Canada, and the European Free Trade Association—have much to commend it. For the EFTA countries, trade relations with the Common Market are of much greater importance than is trade with the U.S. and Canada. Also, membership in a U.S.-led free trade area would have decided political disadvantages for Britain; it would greatly reduce her chances of participating in a united Europe and she could easily be taken as a satellite of the United States.

But establishing a free trade area with the exclusion of the EEC would not serve the best interests of the United States either. Suggestions to this effect would be regarded by many as an effort to isolate the Common Market, and instead of increasing cohesion within the Atlantic alliance, the creation of a truncated AFTA would tend to create dissension by deepening the division of Western Europe. The political risks of such an arrangement would, then, far outweigh the modest economic gains it might possibly bring to the United States or to any other participants.

By contrast, the advantages of European integration for the participating countries are reasonably straightforward. Integration would contribute to the better utilization of resources and to economic growth in Western Europe by eliminating discrimination between the Common Market and EFTA that increasingly distorts trade flows in the area. Moreover, Europe needs to be unified to become an equal partner of the United States. As André Fontaine expressed it, a united Europe "constituted in the framework of the Atlantic alliance is the only partner who can seriously aspire to equality in all domains: political, military, and economic." [30]

It should be realized, however, that a united Europe is bound to follow its own objectives, which may often differ from those of the United States. Still, as I argued in Chapter 2, for the United States this risk is worth taking, in part because European integration is superior to other possible alternatives and in part because the basic interests of the United States and Western Europe in the world arena are by and large the same. This is not to say that the United States should actively interfere with the ways and means of European integration. Rather, U.S. actions in trade matters should concentrate in the field of multilateral trade liberalization. In this way the United States can avoid the charge—often voiced in the postwar period—that she favors integration in Western Europe on her own terms and insists on solutions that serve her own political and military objectives even if these conflict with the interests of European countries.

Tariff reductions under the most-favored-nation clause would serve the political objectives of the Atlantic alliance by making a European union more open and lessening discrimination against developing countries that would be adversely affected by integration in Western Europe. The discriminatory effects of European integration on U.S. exports would also decrease, and gradualism in multilateral trade liberalization would meet the European objection that removing tariffs would interfere with the consolidation of the Common Market. Finally, both the sensitiveness of the issue of U.S. investment in Western Europe and the interests of less developing countries would call for a policy that favors a shift in foreign investment from Europe to less developed areas.

But what of the interests of Canada and Japan? For Canada, the integration of Western Europe would increase the importance of trade ties with the United States. The loss of preferences on the British market and the discriminatory effects of a European union, as

[30] *Le Monde*, June 7, 1964.

well as the relatively small size of the Canadian economy, would provide an inducement for Canada to seek entry into one of the large markets. For political reasons it is unlikely that a Canadian application would receive favorable reception in Western Europe; a trade arrangement with the United States would hence appear the only feasible alternative. While such an arrangement has been objected to on political grounds in the past, in the event of integration in Western Europe, Canada's economic interest in trade with the United States may outweigh the political objections. From the economic point of view, the most desirable solution appears to be the establishment of a U.S.–Canadian free trade area. Aside from the question of conforming to GATT rules, only such a scheme would provide adequate assurance to investors to carry out the necessary transformation of the Canadian economy.

While her domestic market is larger than that of Canada, Japan would also derive important benefits from trade liberalization. Doubts arise, however, about the feasibility of Japan's participation in a free trade area with the United States. Given the existing differences in the level of industrial development and in wages, such a scheme would be strenuously opposed in both countries. Accordingly, Japan has a considerable interest in seeking tariff reductions under the most-favored-nation clause. This solution would also fit in with her objective of maintaining and strengthening her ties with the developing countries of Southeast Asia as well as with Australia and New Zealand.

The question remains: What policies should be followed in the event that the Kennedy-Round negotiations break down by reason of the intransigent position taken by the European Common Market? The arguments presented here point to the undesirability of establishing preferential arrangements or a truncated Atlantic Free Trade Area. However, as far as U.S. policy is concerned, they do not provide a positive answer. Rather, a wait-and-see attitude appears desirable, since a trade arrangement excluding the largest trading area of the world, the European Common Market, would offer small and uncertain economic gains and large potential political losses for the United States. Such a policy would maintain flexibility in U.S. policymaking and it would not jeopardize the chances of future agreements —economic and political—with the Common Market and other European countries.

APPENDICES

APPENDIX TABLE 1.1 World Trade Flows in 1964
(f.o.b. values, $ million)

	United States	Canada	Common Market	United Kingdom	Continental EFTA	Japan	Industrial Countries	Other Developed Countries	Less Developed Countries	Soviet-type Economies	Other	World
United States	0	4,660	4,530	1,510	1,040	1,900	13,640	1,990	8,230	335	2,035 [a]	26,230
Canada	4,120	0	520	1,120	140	310	6,210	290	610	565	5	7,680
Common Market	2,850	370	18,400	2,280	6,560	390	30,850	3,190	6,870	1,330	320	42,560
United Kingdom	1,140	530	2,520	0	1,560	165	5,915	2,775	3,340	325	5	12,360
Continental EFTA	830	110	3,940	1,590	2,160	135	8,765	955	1,330	632	8	11,690
Japan	1,870	165	370	200	195	0	2,800	500	2,990	386	−6	6,670
Industrial countries	10,810	5,835	30,280	6,700	11,655	2,900	68,180	9,700	23,370	3,573	2,367	107,190
Other developed countries	1,010	105	2,240	2,550	495	720	7,120	550	1,270	1,017	73	10,030
Less developed countries	6,360	710	8,410	3,960	1,080	2,600	23,120	1,790	7,080	1,905	455	34,350
Soviet-type economies	106	37	1,460	595	640	365	3,203	877	2,640	13,190	430	20,340
Other	4	3	0	−5	10	−15	−3	3	20	5	15	40
World	18,290	6,690	42,390	13,800	13,880	6,570	101,620	12,920	34,380	19,690	3,340	171,950

Source: United Nations, *Statistical Yearbook, 1965.*
Note: (a) Special-category exports, chiefly military.

APPENDIX TABLE 1.2 Commodity Composition of Trade among the Industrial Countries, 1963

EXPORTS	United States $ million	%	Canada $ million	%	Common Market $ million	%	United Kingdom $ million	%	Continental EFTA $ million	%	Japan $ million	%	Industrial Countries $ million	%
Food, beverages, tobacco	1,954	17.2	973	17.7	1,057	9.7	355	9.1	714	15.7	191	8.7	5,244	13.6
Fuels	638	5.6	351	6.4	645	5.9	180	4.6	36	0.8	2	0.1	1,852	4.8
Industrial materials	2,194	19.3	2,333	42.6	637	5.8	343	8.8	995	22.0	123	5.6	6,625	17.3
Manufactured goods	6,594	57.9	1,826	33.3	8,600	78.6	3,022	77.5	2,785	61.5	1,879	85.6	24,706	64.3
Total	11,380	100.0	5,438	100.0	10,939	100.0	3,900	100.0	4,530	100.0	2,195	100.0	38,427	100.0
IMPORTS														
Food, beverages, tobacco	919	9.9	403	8.4	1,726	16.4	1,078	25.4	688	9.7	430	16.9	5,244	13.6
Fuels	352	3.8	130	2.7	520	4.9	178	4.2	522	7.4	150	5.9	1,852	4.8
Industrial materials	1,870	20.3	441	9.1	2,079	19.8	822	19.4	527	7.5	886	34.7	6,625	17.3
Manufactured goods	6,087	66.0	3,839	79.8	6,197	58.9	2,165	51.0	5,333	75.4	1,085	42.5	24,706	64.3
Total	9,228	100.0	4,813	100.0	10,522	100.0	4,243	100.0	7,070	100.0	2,551	100.0	38,427	100.0

Source: United Nations, *Monthly Bulletin of Statistics*, March 1965; OECD, *Foreign Trade, Statistical Bulletins*, 1963.

Notes: Food, beverages, tobacco—SITC 0+1; Fuels—SITC 3; Industrial materials—SITC 2+4+unwrought metals; manufactured goods—SITC 5+6+7+8—unwrought metals. Data exclude intra-EEC and intra-EFTA trade as well as miscellaneous (SITC 9) and special-category exports.

APPENDIX TO CHAPTER THREE

The Measurement of Effective Duties

To calculate the effective rates of tariffs we need comparable data on nominal tariff rates and input-output coefficients, *net* of duties. Input-output tables using a common system of classification that also ensures comparability with trade statistics have been published for the five Common Market countries (Belgium, France, Germany, Italy, the Netherlands), pertaining generally to 1959.[1] Comparable tables for the other countries under consideration are not available, however, and I have chosen to use "standardized" input-output coefficients in all cases. In deriving these coefficients, I have relied largely on the input-output tables for Belgium and the Netherlands.[2] These countries were chosen because they had nil or low duties on most commodities in 1959 and hence the distortion in input-output relationships due to the existence of duties is relatively small.

The application of identical input-output coefficients for all countries is justified if the countries in question have identical production functions with unitary substitution elasticity in all industries, or if intercountry differences in efficiency are neutral in the sense that production functions differ only by a multiplicative constant. Under these assumptions, differences in the relative prices of inputs would not affect the coefficients.[3]

While the above assumptions have often been made in empirical research,[4] they may not be fulfilled in the real world. Still, one may argue that we can abstract from non-neutral differences in production functions, since firms in the industrial countries under consideration presumably have the same "technological horizon." At the same time, the use of standardized coefficients has the important advantage that the results will not be affected by international differences in the composition of output in individual industries.

Standardized input-output coefficients have been derived for thirty-six industries, including all of manufacturing except for food processing. The

[1] Office Statistique des Communautés Européennes, *Tableaux "Entrées-Sorties" pour les pays de la Communauté Européenne Economiqué,* October 1964.

[2] The input-output tables of the other three countries have served as a basis, however, in regard to automobiles, aircraft, and precision instruments, not produced in substantial quantities in Belgium and the Netherlands.

[3] The coefficients derived from input-output tables are expressed in value rather than in quantity terms and hence indicate relative shares.

[4] Cf., K. Arrow, H. B. Chenery, B. S. Minhas, and R. M. Solow, "Capital-Labor Substitution and Economic Efficiency," *Review of Economics and Statistics,* August 1961, pp. 225–50.

system of classification has been constrained by the breakdown used in the input-output tables of the Common Market countries, which provide a rather narrow definition of some industries (e.g., cleansing agents and perfumes) while a number of diverse commodities are included in others (e.g., miscellaneous chemical products). A more detailed breakdown has been employed for inputs whenever the use of a specific input could be ascertained. For example, from the category of synthetic materials I have selected synthetic rubber as an input for rubber goods.

In regard to every industry, separate consideration has been given to those inputs that contribute at least 4 per cent of the value of output. The number of such inputs in individual industries has been between one and six, with automobiles at the upper end of the range. Other material inputs and nonmaterial inputs (transportation, trade, etc.) have been included in separate categories. Within the group of other material inputs, fuels, paper, nonmetallic minerals, and metal manufactures predominate, hence I have calculated a weighted average of tariffs on these products. There are no duties on nonmaterial inputs.

In regard to tariffs, I have used the Brussels Tariff Nomenclature (BTN) employed by the European Economic Community, the United Kingdom, Sweden, and Japan. For the United States, tariff categories have been reclassified according to the BTN in *Comparative Tariffs and Trade;* [5] I have relied on this compilation while adjusting the results in the case of commodities (chiefly chemical materials and rubber footwear) where the American selling price is used as a basis for levying tariffs. To achieve international comparability, U.S. duties have been expressed as a percentage of the c.i.f. price.[6] Finally, in all instances, adjustments have been made for the tariff reductions undertaken in the Dillon Round of negotiations.

Since the industrial classification applied is less detailed than the BTN tariff nomenclature, it has further been necessary to average some tariff figures.[7] In averaging tariffs, the combined imports of the five industrial areas have been used as weights.[8] Subsequently, effective rates of duties have been calculated by utilizing the formula shown in Chapter 3.

[5] Frances Topping, *Comparative Tariffs and Trade* (New York: Committee for Economic Development, 1964).

[6] In effecting the adjustments, I have utilized information on the average ratio of freight and insurance to import values in B. Balassa, *Trade Prospects for Developing Countries* (Homewood, Ill.: Irwin, 1964), p. 369. Tariff rates are given on a c.i.f. basis in the countries of Western Europe and Japan.

[7] The correspondence has been established by the use of *Classification Statistique et Tarifaire* (Luxembourg: Office Statistique des Communauté Européennes, 1963).

[8] This solution is superior to weighting with own imports, or using unweighted averages, while data on world trade are not available in the appropriate breakdown.

APPENDIX TABLE 3.1 Nominal and Effective Tariff Rates, 1962
(per cent)

	United States		United Kingdom		Common Market		Sweden		Japan	
	Nominal	Effective	Nominal	Effective	Nominal	Effective	Nominal	Effective	Nominal	Effective
(21) Thread and yarn	11.7	31.8	10.5	27.9	2.9	3.6	2.2	4.3	2.7	1.4
(22) Textile fabrics	24.1	50.6	20.7	42.2	17.6	44.4	12.7	33.4	19.7	48.8
(23) Hosiery	25.6	48.7	25.4	49.7	18.6	41.3	17.6	42.4	26.0	60.8
(24) Clothing	25.1	35.9	25.5	40.5	18.5	25.1	14.0	21.1	25.2	42.4
(25) Other textile articles	19.0	22.7	24.5	42.4	22.0	38.8	13.0	21.2	14.8	13.0
(26) Shoes	16.6	25.3	24.0	36.2	19.9	33.0	14.0	22.8	29.5	45.1
(29) Wood products, incl. furniture	12.8	26.4	14.8	25.5	15.1	28.6	6.8	14.5	19.5	33.9
(32) Paper and paper products	3.1	0.7	6.6	8.1	10.3	13.3	2.0	−0.7	10.5	12.9
(33) Printed matter	2.5	2.2	2.7	0.2	3.3	−0.7	0.7	0.0	1.6	−4.2
(35) Leather	9.6	25.7	14.9	34.3	7.3	18.3	7.0	21.7	19.9	59.0
(36) Leather goods other than shoes	15.5	24.5	18.7	26.4	14.7	24.3	12.2	20.7	23.6	33.6
(37) Rubber goods	9.3	16.1	20.2	43.9	15.1	33.6	10.8	26.1	12.9	23.6
(38) Plastic articles	21.0	27.0	17.9	30.1	20.6	30.0	15.0	25.5	24.9	35.5
(39) Synthetic materials	18.6	33.5	12.7	17.1	12.0	17.6	7.2	12.9	19.1	32.1
(40) Other chemical materials	12.3	26.6	19.4	39.2	11.3	20.5	4.5	9.7	12.2	22.6
(42) Cleansing agents and perfumes	11.2	18.8	11.1	11.2	13.8	26.7	10.9	27.9	26.2	61.5
(43) Misc. chemical products	12.6	15.6	15.4	16.7	11.6	13.1	2.5	0.0	16.8	22.9
(45) Nonmetallic mineral products	18.2	30.4	13.6	20.9	13.3	19.8	6.0	10.0	13.5	20.8

(46) Glass and glass products	18.8	29.3	18.5	26.2	14.4	20.0	13.8	22.6	19.5	27.4
(48) Pig iron and ferromanganese	1.8	9.3	3.3	17.9	4.0	−13.8	0.0	−0.7	10.0	54.3
(49) Ingots and other primary steel forms	10.6	106.7	11.1	98.9	6.4	28.9	3.8	40.0	13.0	58.9
(50) Rolling mill products	7.1	−2.2	9.5	7.4	7.2	10.5	5.2	13.2	15.4	29.5
(51) Other steel products	5.1	0.5	17.0	46.8	9.9	20.9	5.4	9.5	13.4	14.1
(54) Nonferrous metals	5.0	10.6	6.6	19.4	2.4	5.0	0.4	0.6	9.3	27.5
(55) Metal castings	6.6	10.0	16.0	26.9	12.4	21.0	8.0	34.7	20.0	32.5
(56) Metal manufactures	14.4	28.5	19.0	35.9	14.0	25.6	8.4	16.2	18.1	27.7
(57) Agricultural machinery	0.4	−6.9	15.4	21.3	13.4	19.6	10.0	16.0	20.0	29.2
(58) Nonelectrical machinery	11.0	16.1	16.1	21.2	10.3	12.2	8.8	11.6	16.8	21.4
(59) Electrical machinery	12.2	18.1	19.7	30.0	14.5	21.5	10.7	17.7	18.1	25.3
(60) Ships	5.5	2.1	2.9	−10.2	0.4	−13.2	0.9	−5.8	13.1	12.1
(61) Railway vehicles	7.0	7.3	21.1	33.3	11.1	−0.2	8.7	13.8	15.0	18.5
(62) Automobiles	6.8	5.1	23.1	41.4	19.5	36.8	14.7	30.5	35.9	75.7
(64) Bicycles and motorcycles	14.4	26.1	22.4	39.2	20.9	39.7	17.1	35.8	25.0	45.0
(65) Airplanes	9.2	8.8	15.6	16.7	10.5	10.8	3.7	3.0	15.0	15.9
(66) Precision instruments	21.4	32.2	25.7	44.2	13.5	24.2	6.6	14.9	23.2	38.5
(67) Sports goods, toys, jewelry, etc.	25.0	41.8	22.3	35.6	17.9	26.6	10.6	16.6	21.6	31.2

Sources: Tariffs: National tariff schedules.
Trade: National and international trade statistics.
Input-output coefficients: Office Statistique des Communautés Européénnes, *Tableaux "Entrées-Sorties" pour les pays de la Communauté Européenne Economique,* October 1964.

APPENDIX TABLE 3.2 Rankings of Labor Input Coefficients and of Nominal and Effective Tariff Rates, 1962

	Standardized Labor Input Coefficient	United States Nom. A	B	United States Eff. A	B	United Kingdom Nom. A	B	United Kingdom Eff. A	B	Common Market Nom. A	B	Common Market Eff. A	B	Sweden Nom. A	B	Sweden Eff. A	B	Japan Nom. A	B	Japan Eff. A	B	Five Areas Together Nom. C	Eff. C
(21) Thread and yarn	29	1	19	1	8	2	30	2	19	3	34	4	32	5	31	3	29	4	35	5	35	32	27
(22) Textile fabrics	27	1	4	1	2	2	10	4	7	4	9	3	1	5	9	5	5	3	14	2	7	9	3
(23) Hosiery	17	2	1	3	3	3	3	2	7	4	6	5	2	5	1	4	1	1	4	1	3	1	1
(24) Clothing	26	3	2	3	5	1	2	2	9	4	7	4	14	5	5	5	14	2	5	1	10	2	7
(25) Other textile articles	24	3	7	3	19	1	4	1	6	2	1	2	4	5	8	4	13	4	25	5	32	8	14
(26) Shoes	22	4	11	4	17	2	5	2	12	3	4	3	7	5	6	5	10	1	2	1	8	4	8
(29) Wood products, incl. furniture	23	4	15	3	14	3	25	4	23	2	10	2	10	5	22	5	21	1	16	1	13	17	16
(32) Paper and paper products	18	4	33	4	33	3	32	3	33	2	27	1	26	5	32	5	35	1	32	2	33	33	34
(33) Printed matter	7	3	34	1	31	2	36	2	35	1	33	4	34	5	34	3	32	4	36	5	36	36	35
(35) Leather	32	3	23	3	16	2	24	2	15	4	29	5	24	5	21	4	12	1	13	1	4	24	12
(36) Leather goods other than shoes	13	3	12	3	18	2	15	2	21	4	12	4	15	5	10	5	15	1	8	1	14	11	17
(37) Rubber goods	16	5	24	5	22	1	11	1	5	1	11	2	6	4	12	3	8	3	30	4	24	16	11
(38) Plastic articles	21	2	6	4	12	4	17	2	17	3	3	3	8	5	3	5	9	1	7	1	12	3	4
(39) Synthetic materials	28	2	9	1	6	3	27	4	29	4	21	3	25	5	20	5	24	2	17	2	16	18	22
(40) Other chemical materials	25	2	17	2	13	1	13	1	10	4	23	4	20	5	27	5	27	3	31	3	26	25	21
(42) Cleansing agents and perfumes	30	3	20	4	20	4	29	5	32	2	16	3	11	5	11	2	7	1	3	1	2	15	13
(43) Misc. chemical products	12	3	16	3	24	2	23	2	31	4	22	4	27	5	30	5	33	1	21	1	25	26	25
(45) Nonmetallic mineral products	11	1	10	1	9	2	26	2	26	4	19	4	22	5	24	5	26	3	26	3	28	23	23

(46) Glass and glass products	5	2	8	1	10	3	16	3	22	4	14	5	21	5	7	4	11	1	15	2	22	12	19
(48) Pig iron and ferro-manganese	35	4	35	3	27	3	34	2	28	2	32	5	36	5	36	4	34	1	33	1	6	35	30
(49) Ingots and other primary steel	36	3	22	1	1	2	28	2	1	4	31	5	28	4	28	4	2	1	29	3	5	30	2
(50) Rolling mill products	33	4	26	5	35	2	31	4	34	3	30	3	30	2	26	2	23	1	22	1	18	29	32
(51) Other steel products	31	5	31	5	34	4	18	1	3	3	28	2	19	4	25	2	28	2	27	3	31	28	24
(54) Nonferrous metals	34	3	32	3	25	2	33	2	27	4	35	4	31	5	35	5	31	1	34	3	21	34	31
(55) Metal castings	3	5	29	5	26	2	20	3	20	3	20	4	18	5	19	1	4	1	12	2	15	19	18
(56) Metal manufactures	10	3	13	2	11	1	14	3	13	3	15	4	13	1	1	5	18	5	19	3	20	14	15
(57) Agricultural machinery	15	5	36	5	36	1	22	2	24	3	18	5	23	5	15	4	19	1	1	1	19	22	26
(58) Nonelectrical machinery	8	3	21	3	23	2	19	2	25	4	26	4	28	5	16	4	25	2	20	1	27	21	28
(59) Electrical machinery	4	4	18	4	21	1	12	1	18	3	13	3	17	5	13	5	16	2	18	2	23	13	20
(60) Ships	9	2	30	2	32	3	35	4	36	5	36	5	35	4	33	3	36	1	28	1	34	31	36
(61) Railway vehicles	6	5	27	4	29	1	9	1	16	3	24	5	33	4	17	3	22	2	24	2	29	20	29
(62) Automobiles	19	5	28	5	30	2	6	2	8	3	5	3	5	4	4	4	6	1	1	1	1	7	6
(64) Bicycles and motorcycles	20	5	14	5	15	2	7	3	11	3	2	2	3	2	2	4	3	1	6	1	9	5	5
(65) Airplanes	1	4	25	4	28	1	21	1	30	3	25	2	29	5	29	5	30	2	23	2	30	27	33
(66) Precision instruments	2	3	5	3	7	1	1	1	4	4	17	4	16	3	23	5	20	2	9	2	11	10	9
(67) Sports goods, toys, jewelry, etc.	14	1	3	1	4	2	8	2	14	4	8	4	12	5	14	5	17	3	10	3	17	6	10

Sources: See Appendix Table 3.1.

Notes: STANDARDIZED LABOR INPUT COEFFICIENTS

Ranking of industries according to the share of wages plus employer-financed social security payments in the value of output, derived from the input-output tables previously cited.

NOMINAL AND EFFECTIVE RATES OF DUTIES

A. Ranking of countries (country groupings) according to the rate of duty for individual industries.

B. Ranking of industries according to the rate of duty for individual countries (country groupings).

C. Unweighted average of the ranking of industries according to the rates of duty in the five areas.

APPENDIX TABLE 3.3   Rank Correlation Coefficients for Effective
Tariffs in 36 Industries, 1962

	United States	*United Kingdom*	*Common Market*	*Sweden*	*Japan*	*Five Areas Together*
United States	x	.481	.512	.506	.395	.737
United Kingdom	.481	x	.746	.650	.362	.770
Common Market	.512	.746	x	.827	.565	.907
Sweden	.506	.650	.827	x	.689	.867
Japan	.395	.362	.565	.689	x	.732
Five areas together	.737	.770	.907	.867	.732	x

Source: Table 3.2.

Note: All coefficients, excepting those calculated for the United States and Japan, and the United Kingdom and Japan, are statistically significant at the 1 per cent level; the latter are significant at the 5 per cent level.

APPENDIX TO CHAPTER FOUR

A. The Methodology of Estimating the Static Effects of Trade Liberalization

The Direct Effects of Tariff Reductions

The direct effects of trade liberalization have been defined to include changes in exports and imports that would result from multilateral reductions in duties if no account were taken of the potential discriminatory effects of the EEC and EFTA. Several factors will determine the magnitude of these direct effects: the height of original tariff rates, changes in these rates, and the responsiveness of the demand for, and the supply of, traded commodities to price changes in the individual countries. In turn, the elasticities of import demand and export supply will depend on the underlying elasticities of domestic demand and supply, the share of imports (exports) in domestic consumption (production), and the substitutability of domestic and foreign goods.

1. TARIFFS. The discussion in Chapter 3 indicates that nominal *and* effective duties should be used in estimating the probable effects of tariff reductions on trade flows. This has not been possible for the commodity classification employed in this chapter, however, because input-output data are not available in the appropriate breakdown. At the same time, the use of a detailed commodity classification has been judged necessary to estimate the direct and the discriminatory effects of tariff reductions for individual countries and country groupings. While this choice has given rise to errors in estimation, the results arrived at by the use of this method and by that employed in Chapter 3 are fairly close.

In regard to tariffs, I have used the Brussels Tariff Nomenclature (BTN), employed by all the industrial nations with the exception of the United States and Canada. For these two countries, tariffs have been reclassified according to the BTN and expressed in terms of c.i.f. prices.[1] The common external tariff has been used in the case of the European Common Market while an average of tariffs has been calculated for the Continental EFTA countries by using the total imports into these countries as weights. In all instances, adjustments have been made for reductions in duties undertaken in the Dillon Round of tariff negotiations.

Since the BTN headings largely correspond to the four- and five-digit items of the Standard International Tariff Classification (SITC), tariff averages had to be derived for the three-digit categories. In the calculation

[1] On the adjustments made in the case of the United States, see the Appendix to Chapter 3.

of these averages, the combined imports of each item into the industrial countries have been used as weights. As indicated in Chapter 3, this procedure avoids the downward bias imparted by weighting with the country's own imports. This method is also preferable to calculating an unweighted average of duties since it gives expression to the relative importance of individual commodities in the trade of the industrial countries.

2. IMPORT DEMAND ELASTICITIES. To indicate the responsiveness of import demand to decreases in import prices that result from reductions in tariffs, one may utilize estimates of price elasticities of import demand derived from data of past periods. Among time-series estimates of U.S. import demand elasticities, the recent calculations of Ball and Marwah appear the most reliable. These authors applied regression analysis to quarterly data covering eleven postwar years and estimated import-demand elasticities for five commodity groups, three of which are relevant for our discussion: crude materials, -0.26; semimanufactures, -1.38; and finished manufactures, -3.50.[2] But, as the authors note, by reason of the downward bias associated with the statistical method applied, these figures provide lower limits of possible values.[3] As "upper bounds" they suggest the use of -0.53 or -0.65 for crude materials, -1.89 or -2.15 for semimanufactures, and -4.74 or -5.28 for finished manufactures— obtained by adding two and three standard errors, respectively, to the estimated coefficients.

Ball and Marwah's estimates purported to measure the effects of changes in prices on imports over time. Measured changes in import prices, however, in part reflect changes in quality since import price indices are calculated by dividing an index of import values by an index of import volumes. Quality changes, then, contribute to errors in the independent variable that are known to cause a downward bias in the estimated coefficients. This source of bias can be avoided if we consider the relationship between changes in tariffs and in imports, since the rates of duties applied are known without error. Further sources of bias can be removed if cross-section estimates are made.

This procedure has been applied by M. E. Kreinin and L. B. Krause. Kreinin compared data for two groups of commodities, classified according to whether they had been subject to tariff reductions. The import-demand elasticities implicit in his results are -5 for all commodities, excluding textiles, in the period 1954–56 and -6 for finished manufactures

[2] R. J. Ball and K. Marwah, "The U.S. Demand for Imports 1948–1958," *Review of Economics and Statistics,* November 1962, pp. 395–401.

[3] On the statistical difficulties of applying the least-squares method to time-series data, see G. H. Orcutt, "Measurement of Price Elasticities in International Trade," *Review of Economics and Statistics,* May 1950, pp. 117–32, and Arnold C. Harberger, "A Structural Approach to the Problem of Import Demand," *American Economic Review,* Papers and Proceedings, May 1953, pp. 148–59.

in the period 1955–59.[4] In a cross-section analysis of ninety-one categories of manufactured goods, Krause obtained "tariff" elasticity estimates of −4.5 for the period 1947–54 and −5.6 for 1947–58. For both periods, the elasticity of demand for imports calculated with respect to tariff changes was considerably higher than the elasticities calculated with respect to price.[5]

Kreinin's and Krause's results point to the conclusion that a reduction of tariffs is likely to have a larger effect on imports than an equivalent change in import prices—a phenomenon that requires explanation. Aside from the downward bias in least-squares estimates of price elasticities, a possible explanation is that importers regard tariff changes as permanent and reallocate purchases accordingly, while changes in import prices are often considered transitory. A "ratchet effect" may also be operative in the second case: once purchases are accommodated to a lower import price, habit formation, or simply the acquired knowledge of foreign goods, may limit the shift back to domestic commodities if import prices rise again. On the other hand, we have few instances of increases in tariffs in the postwar period.

Further evidence of the responsiveness of imports to changes in tariffs is provided in a study by B. A. de Vries. De Vries calculated implicit "tariff" elasticities for 176 products on the basis of information supplied by commodity experts concerning the possible long-term effects on American imports of an assumed reduction, or increase, of the 1939 U.S. tariffs by one-half. For all commodities, taken together, the weighted average of elasticities is −2.2 for a reduction and −2.7 for an increase in duties.[6] For the three product groups of the Ball-Marwah study, the following elasticities were obtained: crude materials, −1.3; semimanufactures, −3.1; and finished manufactures, −3.9.

---

[4] M. E. Kreinin, "Effect of Tariff Changes on the Prices and Volume of Imports," *American Economic Review*, June 1961, pp. 310–24. Although in 1954–56 a large number of the tariff reductions had been in textile products, textiles have been excluded from the calculations relating to this period because shipments to the United States from Japan were subject to voluntary export quotas administered by the Japanese government.

[5] Elasticities calculated for the period 1954–58 provide an exception but tariff changes were relatively small during this period and the tariff elasticity was not statistically significant.

	Price elasticity	Tariff elasticity
1947–58	−1.77 (0.32)	−5.64 (2.11)
1947–54	−1.54 (0.31)	−4.49 (1.83)
1954–58	−1.32 (0.21)	−0.52 (0.28)

Cf. L. B. Krause, "United States Imports, 1947–1958," *Econometrica*, April 1962, pp. 221–38.

[6] B. A. de Vries, "Price Elasticities of Demand for Individual Commodities Imported into the United States," *International Monetary Fund Staff Papers*, April 1951, pp. 397–419.

These results suggest that, for the purpose of estimating the possible effects of tariff reductions on U.S. imports, the elasticities calculated by Ball and Marwah should be adjusted upward. Although available information does not provide a precise indication for selecting appropriate values within the range indicated, the addition of one standard deviation to the estimates may provide a reasonable compromise. This adjustment is also in conformity with De Vries' results for the commodity group that has primary importance for the present study—finished manufactures. The corresponding elasticities are crude materials, -0.39; semimanufactures, -1.63; and finished manufactures, -4.12.[7]

In making calculations on the possible expansion of imports into the United States following multilateral tariff reductions, I have accordingly assigned an elasticity value to each three-digit SITC commodity category, depending on whether it contained crude materials, semimanufactures, or finished manufactures. In regard to commodity categories that comprise products classified in two or three of the above groups, an average elasticity has been calculated by using U.S. imports of each product as weights.

Estimates on import demand elasticities for Western Europe, Canada, and Japan are few and far between. Among available calculations Harberger's results are subject to a substantial downward bias,[8] while the estimates of Scott[9] for the United Kingdom and of Wemelsfelder for Germany[10] are sensitive to conditions of capacity utilization existing during the periods under study. At any rate, estimates are not available for all the major countries of Western Europe and Japan, nor for the appropriate commodity categories. I have therefore chosen to derive the elasticity coefficients used for these countries from estimates pertaining to the United States in an indirect fashion.

In Chapter 3 I noted that, under the assumption of identical domestic demand and supply elasticities in all areas, import-demand elasticities will

[7] Estimates utilizing "lower limit" and "upper limit" elasticities can be derived from our results by reducing, or increasing, the latter by 15 per cent—the percentage difference between the two elasticities in the case of semifinished and finished manufactures. (The difference in the elasticities is larger in regard to crude materials, but this complication can be readily overlooked since most crude materials bear low duties or are imported duty-free into the industrial countries.)

[8] Arnold C. Harberger found elasticities of around unity for total imports into various European countries although higher values obtain if agricultural products are excluded from the calculations. See his "Some Evidence on the International Price Mechanism," *Journal of Political Economy,* December 1957, pp. 506–21.

[9] According to Scott's results, in the 1931–32 period a one percentage point rise in tariffs was accompanied by a 4.3 per cent fall in U.K. imports of manufactured goods (M. F. G. Scott, *A Study of United Kingdom Imports* [Cambridge: University Press, 1962], pp. 168–69).

[10] In a study of the effects of unilateral tariff reductions undertaken by Germany in 1956 and 1957, J. Wemelsfelder derived an import-demand elasticity of about 8 to 10. See his "The Short-term Effect of the Lowering of Import Duties in Germany," *Economic Journal,* March 1960, pp. 94–104.

be negatively correlated with the share of imports in domestic consumption (production). Empirical evidence of this relationship is provided by the results of the De Vries study. According to the latter, U.S. import demand elasticities average about −2.0 for commodities in the case of which the ratio of imports to domestic consumption exceeds 27 per cent (the average for all 176 products) while the corresponding figure is −3.4 for products where the import-consumption ratio is below the average.[11] Since the share of imports in domestic consumption is considerably smaller in the United States than elsewhere, import-demand elasticities are expected to be lower abroad than in the United States.

In 1960, the ratio of the imports of manufactured goods to value added in the manufacturing sector was 4.6 per cent for the United States, 50.9 per cent for Canada, 8.4 per cent for the European Common Market, 12.5 per cent for the United Kingdom, 34.7 per cent for Continental EFTA, and 9.3 per cent for Japan.[12] However, for various reasons, these values cannot be directly utilized to derive import demand elasticities for other industrial countries from the U.S. estimates.

To begin with, the relevant comparison is not between the value of imports and value added in manufacturing, but between the value of imports and the value of domestic consumption (production) of manufactures.[13] Accordingly, the above figures should be adjusted downward. The extent of the required adjustment will depend on the size of the country, because the ratio of imported inputs to the value of domestic consumption (production) tends to decline as the size of the country increases.[14]

On the other hand, various factors, including transportation costs, product differentiation, imperfect information, and intercountry differences in tastes, tend to restrict the substitutability of imports for domestic production and necessitate an upward adjustment in the figures referred to above. By reducing the amount of domestic output directly competing with imports, these influences contribute to a further narrowing of

[11] B. A. de Vries, "Price Elasticities of Demand for Individual Commodities Imported into the United States," cited, p. 413.

[12] Organization for Economic Cooperation and Development, *Statistics of National Accounts, 1955–1962,* Supplement (Paris, 1964), and United Nations, *Commodity Trade Statistics, 1960* (New York, 1963). In the case of the Common Market and the EFTA countries I have excluded intra-area exchange since tariffs on this trade will be eliminated whether or not trade is liberalized among the industrial countries.

[13] In addition to value added in manufacturing, the latter also includes the value of nonindustrial inputs and that of imports used as inputs.

[14] On the basis of information provided in input-output tables and production statistics, I have calculated the appropriate adjustment factors (the value of output divided by value added in manufacturing) for the Common Market countries and the United States. These are 2.5 for Belgium and the Netherlands, 2.1 for Italy, 1.8 for France and Germany, and 1.6 for the United States (cf. Bela Balassa, "Planning in an Open Economy," *Kyklos* 1966 [3], pp. 385–410, and U.S. Bureau of Census, *U.S. Commodity Exports and Imports as Related to Output* [Washington, 1962].)

intercountry differences in the relevant import shares. This conclusion can be readily understood if we consider that in larger countries a wider assortment of domestic goods is available to serve particular needs and transportation costs from the frontier to the place of consumption are also generally higher.

The latter factors are of special importance in the United States; I have followed J. E. Floyd in assuming that the ratio of the consumption of competing goods to imports is 4 in this country (an import share of 25 per cent).[15] I have taken this ratio to be 2 for Canada, on the assumption that the factors necessitating downward and upward adjustments with regard to the ratio of imports to value added approximately balance in this case. To derive import demand elasticities for Canada, I have divided the U.S. import demand elasticities by the United States consumption-import ratio and multiplied the results by the comparable Canadian figure. This procedure reflects the assumptions that consumption-import and production-import ratios are identical within each country and that domestic demand and supply elasticities are internationally identical. The underlying formula is the one used in Chapter 3:

$$(1) \quad \eta_m = \eta \frac{C}{M} + \epsilon \frac{P}{M}$$

when C denotes domestic consumption, P domestic production, and M imports; η and ϵ are the domestic elasticities of demand and supply and η_m the import-demand elasticity.

The estimates so obtained are roughly in conformity with the Canadian import-demand elasticity of -1.75 calculated by Chang for the interwar period.[16] In turn, on the basis of the data on import shares and the considerations noted above, I have assumed consumption-import ratios of 3 for the European Common Market and Japan, 2.6 for the United Kingdom, and 2.2 for Continental EFTA.[17] The import-demand elasticities calculated by the use of these ratios are:

	United States	Canada	Common Market	United Kingdom	Continental EFTA	Japan
Finished manuf.	-4.12	-2.06	-3.09	-2.68	-2.27	-3.09
Semifinished manufactures	-1.63	-0.82	-1.42	-1.06	-0.90	-1.42
Crude materials	-0.39	-0.20	-0.29	-0.25	-0.22	-0.29

[15] J. E. Floyd, "The Overvaluation of the Dollar: A Note on the International Price Mechanism," *American Economic Review*, March 1965, pp. 97–104.

[16] Cited in R. E. Caves and R. H. Holton, *The Canadian Economy—Prospect and Retrospect* (Cambridge, Mass.: Harvard University Press, 1959), p. 86. Note that finished manufactures predominate in Canada's imports; she hardly imports any foodstuffs and crude materials.

[17] The same ratios have been used with respect to industrial materials.

3. EXPORT SUPPLY ELASTICITIES. In most contributions dealing with the effects of multilateral tariff reductions on trade, it has been explicitly or implicitly assumed that the elasticities of export supply are infinite, i.e., every country can expand production at constant costs, and hence import prices will fall by the full amount of the tariff reduction.[18] Kreinin's calculations of the impact of tariff reductions on the prices of commodities exported to the United States in 1954–56 and 1955–59 led him to different conclusions, however. In his view, "it appears plausible that close to half of the benefit from tariff concessions granted by the United States accrued to foreign exporters in the form of increased export prices." [19]

This empirical result suggests the conclusion that export supply elasticities in the countries that provide the bulk of U.S. imports are less than infinite. In general, the size of these elasticities will depend on the share of exports in domestic production as well as on the conditions prevailing in the labor market. For one thing, export supply elasticities tend to be negatively correlated with the share of exports in domestic production; for another, in a tight labor market, wages in the export industries will have to be raised to attract labor from other sectors of the economy. However, the elasticities will be higher the longer the time period considered. For, despite the observed rigidity of prices and wages in the industrial countries, increases in productive capacity and in the labor force permit a certain degree of reversibility in relative prices in the long run.

These considerations can be applied to United States–Western Europe relationships. Given the small share of exports in production and the anticipated rapid rate of increases in the labor force, we can assume that an expansion of exports will not necessitate price increases in the United States. On the other hand, in Western Europe exports account for a larger proportion of production and future increases in the labor force will hardly remedy the tightness of the labor market. The reallocation of resources following reductions in duties may, then, lead to higher wages in European export industries. Nevertheless, in the process of long-term adjustment, the ensuing price increases will be mitigated and the rise in export prices can be expected to be smaller than Kreinin's results suggest.[20]

In the present study I have prepared two sets of estimates. Variant I

[18] Cf., e.g., H. G. Johnson, "The Gains from Freer Trade with Europe: an Estimate," *Manchester School*, September 1958, pp. 247–55; Lawrence B. Krause, "United States Imports and the Tariff," *American Economic Review, Papers and Proceedings*, May 1959, pp. 542–51, and Robert M. Stern, "The U.S. Tariff and the Efficiency of the U.S. Economy," *American Economic Review, Papers and Proceedings*, May 1964, pp. 459–79.

[19] M. E. Kreinin, "Effect of Tariff Changes on the Prices and Volume of Imports," *cited*, p. 317.

[20] In this connection, note that according to a study carried out by the EFTA Secretariat, "it appears that a large part of the tariff cuts has been passed on in lower prices than would otherwise have been charged." *The Effect on Prices of Tariff Dismantling in EFTA* (Geneva, 1966), p. 7.

assumes that European export prices of manufactured goods would rise by one-third of the reduction in tariffs while Variant II is calculated with unchanged European export prices. In all other exporting areas constant export prices have been assumed throughout and the same assumption has been made in regard to industrial materials, irrespective of their origin. If the original tariff rate, expressed as a fraction of the c.i.f. price exclusive of duty, is denoted by t and the rate of tariff reduction by $s,$ the price of imports will decline by $st/1 + t$ on the assumption that export prices remained unchanged (Variant II); on the alternative assumption, import prices would fall by two-thirds and export prices rise by one-third of this magnitude. Correspondingly, in calculating increases in the imports of individual commodities in constant prices in the case of Variant II, I have used the formula:

$$(2) \quad dM = \eta_m \, Mzt|1 + t$$

In turn, for manufactured goods imported from Western Europe under Variant I, equation (2) has been multiplied by 2/3, and the amount of new imports $(M + dM)$, expressed in terms of constant prices, has been adjusted for the assumed increases in export prices.

4. GEOGRAPHICAL BREAKDOWN OF THE ESTIMATES. Among industrial areas, separate estimates have been prepared for the United States, Canada, the European Common Market, the United Kingdom, Continental EFTA, and Japan. Intra-area trade in the EEC and EFTA has not been estimated, however, because tariffs within these two areas will be eliminated whether or not multilateral tariff reductions are undertaken by the industrial countries. In the calculations, the Common Market has been taken as a unit but for EFTA changes in the trade of the United Kingdom and Continental EFTA countries have been estimated separately. It has further been assumed that multilateral tariff reductions would not affect the balance of trade between the United Kingdom and Continental EFTA.

A different procedure has been followed in regard to British-Canadian trade, which is carried out in the framework of the Commonwealth preference system. In this case, preferences vary from zero to the full amount of the tariff, depending on the commodity and the exporter. With few exceptions (e.g., certain clothing articles, motor vehicles, and tractors), Canadian products enter the United Kingdom duty-free whereas British exporters enjoy a preferential advantage amounting, on the average, to one-third of the Canadian tariff.

I have assumed that Canadian exports of industrial materials ($340 million in 1960), paper, plywood, and veneer ($92 million) to the United Kingdom would not be affected by trade liberalization since Britain's m.f.n. tariffs are generally low on these products and Canada also exports them in substantial quantities to other markets. On the other hand, as a consequence of the loss of preferential advantages, Canada's exports of chemicals, crude steel, and their manufactured goods to the United Kingdom ($119 million in 1960) have been projected to decline, on the average, by one-third in an Atlantic Free Trade Area.[21] As regards British exports to Canada ($567 million) I have assumed that the gain derived from the removal of tariffs would be fully offset by the loss due to the attendant elimination in preferential advantages. In turn, the elimination of Commonwealth preferences would benefit competing suppliers in other industrial countries.

The Discriminatory Effects of EEC and EFTA

In considering the impact of Common Market discrimination on American exports of manufactures,[22] L. B. Krause has suggested that, to maintain their sales in the Common Market, U.S. exporters would have to reduce their export prices by the difference between the common external tariff and the national tariff that protected the "dominant supplier" [23] before the establishment of the Community. This proposition is based on the following assumptions:

a. The export prices of the dominant suppliers exceed U.S. prices by the amount of the tariff protecting their national markets;
b. The dominant suppliers can increase their output and replace U.S. exports, as well as inefficient domestic production in the partner countries, at constant costs.

These assumptions are subject to criticism on several counts. To begin with, while in the case of standardized products domestic prices may be said to equal the world market price *plus* the tariff, only a few manufactured goods (e.g., thread and yarn or pig iron) fall in this category. Most manufactured goods are differentiated products which are both exported *and* protected in individual countries. Correspondingly, producers who are "dominant suppliers" within the EEC also export appreciable quantities to the United States and other nonmember countries. This would not be possible if their prices exceeded those prevailing on the world market.[24]

[21] In this connection, note that Canada enjoys a 10 to 20 per cent preferential advantage on the British market in chemicals and steel where her competitive position is weak.

[22] Lawrence B. Krause, "The European Economic Community and the U.S. Balance of Payments," in W. S. Salant (ed.), *The United States Balance of Payments in 1968* (Washington, D.C.: The Brookings Institution, 1963), pp. 95–118.

[23] The country, that was the largest exporter in the intra-area trade of a given commodity group, was considered the dominant supplier.

[24] Except for the effects of geographical protection, neither would they have been able to export to other EEC countries before the establishment of the Community.

Further difficulties arise if we wish to measure the discriminatory effects of the Common Market on imports from EFTA countries and vice versa, since Krause's method would now imply different price ratios between, for example, German and British exports in the two calculations. Moreover, in the presence of product differentiation, all exporters in intra-area trade —not only dominant suppliers—would be able to make use of the full amount of protection provided by the tariff discrimination (the common external tariff in the case of the EEC and the tariffs on individual countries in EFTA) were they to expand production at constant costs.[25]

But is it realistic to assume that supply elasticities are infinite? I have noted that, in the event of a balanced expansion of trade among the industrial countries, increases in the prices of manufactured goods may take place in Western Europe. Pressures for cost-and-price increases will be stronger in a customs union encompassing only some of the industrial countries, since trade diversion resulting from tariff discrimination is equivalent to an *unbalanced* expansion of trade, and, correspondingly, excess demand is created on the national economy (union) level.

Moreover, even substantial price increases may not permit member-country producers to replace imports from third countries, when the former are small producers and exporters, by reason of comparative disadvantage, unavailability, or small size. It would make little sense, for example, to estimate the extent of discrimination against the United States in a Benelux union without taking account of capacity limitations in the latter. Given the present industrial structure of the member countries, this observation is of considerable importance for the European Free Trade Association, and—with respect to a number of industrial materials— pertains also to the European Common Market.

I have dealt with this problem by assuming that the possibility of replacing foreign suppliers depends on the share of member-country suppliers in each other's market. Accordingly, the rate of discrimination has been taken to be the following fractions of the tariff levied on products imported from nonmember countries (the common external tariff for the EEC and the national tariffs for EFTA): two-thirds in cases where the share of internal suppliers in total (intra- and extra-area) imports exceeded 30 per cent;[26] one-third where this share was between 10 and 30 per cent; and zero whenever the share of internal suppliers was less than 10 per cent.

[25] For example, in the Dutch market, American and British cars will be discriminated against not only in favor of German automobiles (the dominant supplier) but also in favor of French and Italian cars. In fact, the share of the dominant suppliers in intra-EEC trade has declined rather than increased since the Common Market's establishment (Cf. Bela Balassa, "Tariff Reductions and Trade in Manufactures among the Industrial Countries," *American Economic Review*, June 1966, pp. 466–73).

[26] In other words, the export prices of competing member-country suppliers have been assumed to rise by one-third of the external tariffs in this case.

Assuming that third-country exporters do not reduce their prices, the decrease in their sales due to the establishment of the Common Market and EFTA can be estimated by utilizing substitution elasticities between exports by the partner countries on the one hand and by the nonmember countries on the other. It has been shown that substitution elasticities are generally higher than import demand elasticities.[27] However, I have used the latter in the calculations in order to give expression to the fact that, as a result of increases in their export prices, member countries are bound to lose some foreign markets.

The Indirect Effects of Tariff Reductions

In the event that the industrial nations were to undertake tariff reductions under the most-favored-nation clause, their imports from nonindustrial countries would also rise, and the latter would further benefit from the lessening of EEC and EFTA discrimination. Now, assuming that industrial countries and Soviet-type economies accumulate (decumulate) reserves while nonindustrial economies spend all increases in their foreign exchange earnings, there will be a feedback in the form of higher imports from the industrial countries. Taking account of the cumulative effects of purchases by nonindustrial economies, it would appear that ultimately 95 per cent of the foreign exchange spent in these areas would return to the industrial nations in the form of higher exports. The remainder is assumed to "leak out" to Communist countries.[28]

The Welfare Consequences of Trade Liberalization

To indicate the welfare consequences of tariff reductions, let us consider first the case of a single homogeneous import good, produced under constant costs abroad and under increasing costs at home, the domestic output of which does not fall to zero as tariffs are eliminated. Let Op' be the tariff-inclusive domestic price before, and Op after, the removal of duties, t the rate of duty, and $t' = t/1 + t$ the percentage change in the domestic price in case tariffs are eliminated. Should we take Op', the tariff-free price of the imported good, to be 1, the fall in domestic prices following a tariff cut by 5 per cent can be expressed as

$$(3) \quad \frac{Op' - Op}{Op'} = \frac{t}{1 + t} = t'$$

[27] Cf. Arnold C. Harberger, "Some Evidence on the International Price Mechanism," cited.

[28] The results have been obtained through the inversion of a world trade matrix for 1960. For a description of the method of calculation, see W. Whitney Hicks, "Estimating the Foreign Exchange Costs of United Aid," *Southern Economic Journal*, October 1963, pp. 168–74.

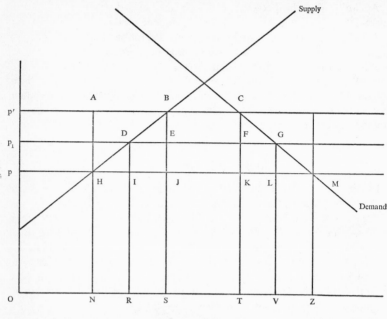

FIGURE 4.1

In Figure 4.1, the amount consumed and produced of the imported good is *OT* and *OS* before, as compared to *OZ* and *ON* after the removal of the tariff while imports will rise from *ST* to *NZ*. Employing the Marshallian concepts of consumer and producer surplus, the elimination of the tariff will result in an increase of consumer surplus by *pp′ CM*, of which *pp′ BH* is the decrease in producer surplus and *JBCK* the reduction in government tariff revenue. Accordingly, assuming compensation among producers, consumers, and the government, the net increase in welfare can be represented by the sum of areas *HBJ* and *KCM*. By reference to the change in the amount produced (dP_1) and consumed (dC_1) the improvement for commodity *i* can be expressed as

$$(4) \quad \frac{1}{2} t' dP_1 + \frac{1}{2} t' dC_1 = \frac{1}{2} t' dM_1$$

The formula has to be modified, however, if we assumed that tariffs are not completely eliminated. In case of a 50 per cent tariff reduction, the new price will be Op_1 in Figure 1 and the quantities consumed and produced *OV* and *OR*, respectively, with imports amounting to *RV*. Consumer surplus will then increase by $p_1p′CG$ and producer surplus fall by $p_1p′BD$. At the same time, government tariff revenue will decline by

EBCF on the old quantity of imports while tariffs equal to the sum of *IDEJ* and *KFGL* will be imposed on the increment in imports. Accordingly, assuming compensation among the three groups in the domestic economy, the increase in welfare can be represented by the sum of the areas *IDBJ* and *KCGL*. The total welfare improvement can then be expressed in terms of changes in production, consumption and imports under free trade as

$$(5) \quad \frac{3}{8} t' dP_i + \frac{3}{8} t' dC_i = \frac{3}{8} t' dM_i$$

Additional considerations need to be introduced if more commodities are considered. For one thing, some of the imported commodities may cease to be produced domestically after tariffs are reduced; for another, substitution and complementary effects will complicate the measurement of the consumer cost of protection. Let us, however, abstract from non-traded goods and assume that all imported commodities or their close domestic substitutes continue to be produced after tariff reductions and that the excess of domestic price over cost for these products is no greater than for the imports that replace them.[29] Under these assumptions, the welfare gain due to the elimination of tariffs can be approximated by

$$(6) \quad \sum_i \frac{1}{2} t' dP_i + \sum_i \frac{1}{2} t' dC_i = \sum_i \frac{1}{2} t' dM_i$$

But what will happen with the resources that are freed in the import-competing industries as reductions in tariffs lead to larger imports? If duties are reduced unilaterally by a single country, the export prices in this country would have to fall to permit the reallocation of resources into the export industries. In the case of multilateral tariff reductions, this reallocation does not require a fall in export prices and equation (6) can provide an indication of the welfare gain for the participating countries. The welfare gains under Variant II, estimated by the use of this formula, are shown in Appendix Table 4.5.

The calculations have to be modified, however, in the event that the expansion of exports in Western Europe entails increases in export prices (Variant I). In this case we have to consider the welfare effects of increases in imports measured at constant prices, and to allow separately for changes in the terms of trade. Domestic prices of goods imported from Western Europe will now fall by 2/3 *t'* if tariffs are eliminated while the terms of trade effect equals the amount of the new imports from Western Europe, multiplied by the increase in export prices.[30] In the exporting

---

[29] Cf., Harry G. Johnson, "The Cost of Protection and the Scientific Tariff," *Journal of Political Economy*, August 1960, pp. 327–45.

[30] It goes without saying that the terms of trade effects would not modify the amount of welfare gain on the world level, measured in constant dollars, but only its distribution.

countries, this gain would take the form of higher producer surplus and wages, while real incomes in the importing countries would be reduced through the rise in import prices.

I turn now to the welfare implications of a decrease in EEC and EFTA discrimination, associated with assumed reductions in duties. These changes can be considered in two parts: nonparticipating countries will benefit from the lessening of discrimination, and member countries will gain because their welfare losses due to trade diversion become smaller.

Faced with discrimination in EEC and EFTA markets, producers in nonmember countries would have to reduce their export prices in order to maintain exports at preintegration levels. If prices on all exports of the nonmember countries to these areas have to be reduced to maintain sales, this loss would equal the price differential times the total quantity sold. But, as I have noted above, the prices of competing products in the Common Market would tend to rise, thereby reducing the difference in prices. Should we assume, for example, that the prices of German and Italian automobiles would rise by one-third of the EEC tariff, Britain could maintain her position in the Common Market by reducing her export prices by two-thirds of the common external tariff.[31]

Correspondingly, the nonmember countries would improve their terms of trade as a result of the elimination of EEC and EFTA discrimination. In turn, the EEC and EFTA countries would derive a benefit in the form of a decrease in the cost of protection associated with trade diversion. For the latter purpose, a modified form of equation (6) has been utilized when dM_d (the changes in imports due to discrimination) has replaced dM_i and v' (the price difference due to discrimination calculated on the basis of assumptions referred to above) has replaced t'. The results of the calculations are shown in Appendix Table 4.5.

In interpreting the results, note should be taken of the inadequacies of the method applied. While expected changes in the terms of trade can be easily derived from the stated assumptions, the calculations of the cost of protection necessarily involve drastic simplifications that often bias the results downward. To begin with, I have disregarded the possibility that the domestic output of some protected commodities may fall to zero after duties are eliminated, or that wages and profits may be lower in protected industries, as appears to be the case in the United States.[32] Further, I have not taken account of the cost of protection incurred at various levels of manufacturing. Finally, and more importantly, the discussion has been confined to static effects and has not considered the dynamic benefits of

[31] Cf. the discussion on Common Market discrimination on pp. 193–94.

[32] See I. B. Kravis, "Wages and Foreign Trade," *Review of Economics and Statistics,* February 1956, and B. N. Vaccara, *Employment and Output in Protected Manufacturing Industries* (Washington, D.C.: The Brookings Institution, 1960), p. 24.

trade liberalization that are associated with greater competition, longer production runs, economies of scale, and technological improvements.

B. The Evaluation of Comparative Advantage

Comparative Advantage in Manufacturing: Industry Studies

Various methods have been suggested to ascertain where the comparative advantage of the industrial countries lies in their mutual trade in manufactured goods. An ideal solution would be to make comparisons on the basis of a production census undertaken simultaneously—and using identical methods of investigation—in all countries. In practice, production censuses have been conducted at different times, using different methods of inquiry, and sufficient information for making cost comparisons is not available.[33]

Alternatively, we may utilize the results of industry studies that provide cost comparisons for the manufacturing sector of the industrial countries. One such study, based on replies to a questionnaire by 147 companies conducting operations in the United States and abroad, was undertaken by the National Industrial Conference Board.[34] The NICB collected information on manufacturing costs (material costs, labor costs, plant overhead) and total unit costs (manufacturing costs, selling and distribution costs, general and administrative costs) in the domestic and foreign plants of these companies for 1960.

According to the findings of the study, material costs are generally lower in the United States than abroad, but labor costs and selling and distribution costs are higher here, while differences in plant overhead and general administrative costs are rather small. Within the material cost category, the U.S. cost advantage is greatest in regard to purchased components and fabricated inputs; the low cost of these products is explained by the availability of a vast network of specialized suppliers who enjoy economies of scale.[35] By contrast, higher labor productivity in the United

---

[33] An exception is the case of the United States and the United Kingdom, where interindustry cost comparisons have been made for 1950 in a study prepared by the Organization for European Economic Cooperation (Deborah Paige and Gottfried Bombach, *A Comparison of National Output and Productivity of the United Kingdom and the United States* ([Paris: OEEC, 1959]). But 1950 can hardly be regarded a "normal" year in any sense and, at any rate, the long time elapsed since this inquiry has reduced the value of the comparisons.

[34] Theodore R. Gates and Fabian Linden, *Costs and Competition: American Experience Abroad* (New York: National Industrial Conference Board, 1961).

[35] It may be suggested that comparisons of material (and labor) costs are affected by the degree of vertical integration. The NICB report did not find substantial differences in the average degree of integration in plants located in the United States and abroad, however. In more than half of the cases, the structure of the plants was identical, and while in some instances the degree of vertical integration was lower in

States does not fully compensate for differences in wage levels, so that labor costs are generally higher in domestic than in foreign operations. The report concludes that "those industries for which materials represented a major share of the cost dollar . . . stood a smaller chance of operating at lower cost abroad than at home; conversely, industries having operations heavily weighted with direct labor stood a better chance of faring better abroad." [36]

While these results provide some indication of the comparative advantage of the United States vis-à-vis other industrial economies, in the absence of a cross-classification according to countries and industries, the comparative advantage of foreign countries taken individually is not indicated. Moreover, the sample does not include national companies in foreign countries. We have to have recourse therefore to alternative explanations. Among these, prevailing theories of international specialization, are the Heckscher-Ohlin theory of factor proportions and the classical theory of comparative costs, suggest themselves.

International Trade Theory and Comparative Advantage

Eli Heckscher and Bertil Ohlin sought to explain international specialization on the basis of intercountry differences in factor endowments while assuming identical production conditions throughout the world.[37] In fact, in a two-country, two-factor world where production functions are identical internationally and the elasticity of substitution among the factors of production is zero or unity, the relative factor intensities of individual commodities will be uniquely determined, and international specialization will correspond to intercountry differences in factor endowments. If allowance is made for differences in tastes, relative factor endowments can be expressed in terms of relative factor prices, i.e., the country with the lower relative price of labor will be considered labor-abundant and its trade partner capital-abundant.

In a comparative study of nineteen countries, Arrow et al. have claimed to establish, however, that substitution elasticities are generally lower than unity and also differ among industries, so that relative factor intensities will not necessarily be independent of factor prices.[38] As wage rates rise

foreign plants, in others the unavailability of parts and components necessitated a greater degree of integration abroad (same, pp. 38–39).

[36] Same, p. 109.

[37] Eli Heckscher, "The Effect of Foreign Trade on the Distribution of Income," originally published in Swedish in 1919; reprinted in English in *Readings in the Theory of International Trade,* H. S. Ellis and L. A. Metzler (eds.), (Philadelphia, 1950), pp. 272–300; Bertil Ohlin, *Interregional and International Trade* (Cambridge, Mass.: Harvard University Press, 1933).

[38] K. J. Arrow, H. B. Chenery, B. S. Minhas, and R. M. Solow, "Capital-Labor Substitution and Economic Efficiency," *Review of Economics and Statistics,* August 1961, pp. 225–50.

in relation to the price of capital, the capital intensity of the industry with the higher elasticity of substitution will increase relative to the industry with the lower elasticity. Thus, if the latter industry was capital-intensive at lower wage levels, ultimately a switch in factor intensities will take place and relative factor endowments will not uniquely determine comparative advantage.

But irrespective of the possibility of factor reversal, a calculation of direct plus indirect labor and capital coefficients will not provide an appropriate indication of comparative advantage if intercountry differences in efficiency exist. On the assumption that these differences pertain equally to all industries, the countries at a higher level of efficiency—in the present case, the United States—can be expected to have comparative advantages in products at higher levels of fabrication where the efficiency advantages obtained at previous stages of production are cumulated. One should, then, consider separately direct labor and capital requirements and material inputs (intermediate products), when intercountry cost differences in the latter would give expression to relative efficiencies in intermediate stages of manufacturing.[39]

The important role played by material inputs has been noted by Arrow *et al.* in a comparison of the United States and Japan, where the Japanese advantage in direct costs appears to be offset by the lower cost of intermediate products in the United States.[40] The authors expressed the opinion, however, that differences in material costs are of special importance only between the United States and Japan whereas "between another pair of countries the variation in direct-factor cost might be more indicative of the variation in total cost of production." [41] But this statement is not based on a consideration of actual facts, and it appears to be contradicted

---

[39] These considerations may be of some usefulness in interpreting the Leontief paradox: the findings that the United States tends to export labor-intensive and import capital-intensive commodities (Cf. W. W. Leontief, "Domestic Production and Foreign Trade: The American Capital Position Re-examined," *Proceedings of the American Philosophical Society*, September 1953, and "Factor Proportions and the Structure of American Trade: Further Theoretical and Empirical Analysis," *Review of Economics and Statistics*, November 1956). For an ingenious effort to deal with the problem by introducing labor skills as a factor of production, see D. B. Keesing, "Labor Skills and International Trade: Evaluating Many Trade Flows with a Single Measuring Device," *Review of Economics and Statistics*, August 1965, pp. 287–94.

[40] "Actual price differences between Japan and the United States are affected as much by the cost of purchased inputs as by the value added component. Calculations for ten manufacturing sectors . . . give a range of direct costs in Japan of .3 to .95 of the United States value, but this element is only about 35 per cent of total cost on the average. The average price of purchased inputs in these sectors ranges from .93 to 1.70 of their cost in the United States, which more than makes up for the lower cost of the factors used directly. An adequate explanation of the differences in relative prices therefore requires an analysis of total factor use rather than of the direct use by itself" (cited, p. 244).

[41] Same, p. 244.

by evidence provided in the NICB report that points to the importance of material costs in determining comparative advantages between highly industrialized countries.

Difficulties arise in attempting to apply the Heckscher-Ohlin theory to the three-factor case, however. Whereas, in the absence of factor reversals, we can provide a unique ranking of industries according to their relative factor intensities in the case of two factors, in the three-factor case a unique ranking may be possible only with regard to pairs of factors. Thus one may rank industries, say, with respect to their labor and material requirements, but not necessarily with regard to labor, materials, and capital.[42] At the same time, we can hardly speak of a homogeneous material input, since the comparative advantages of industries using material inputs will also depend on the number of the preceding stages of transformation. A consideration of differences in natural endowments will increase the number of factors and compound the difficulties of establishing a unique ranking.

We encounter similar difficulties if two factors but more than two countries are considered. Although some conclusions can be reached in regard to industrial countries at the opposite end of the scale, such as the United States and Japan, less can be said concerning the countries of Western Europe that occupy the middle ground. The introduction of more countries *and* more factors further complicates the problem and if we also take into account interindustry differences in efficiency among the industrial countries, the Heckscher-Ohlin theory will hardly offer a guide in evaluating comparative advantages.

By contrast, the existence of intercountry differences in the efficiency of individual industries underlies the explanation given by the classical theory of comparative advantage, in the case of which labor productivity appears as a proxy for efficiency. The explanatory value of this hypothesis has been indicated in United States–United Kingdom comparisons.[43] But comparable data on productivity are not available for all industrial countries, and in U.S.–U.K. relationships too, changes over time would be of interest.

At any rate, the lack of consideration given to interindustry differences in capital costs and nonprice factors reduces the usefulness of the classical doctrine for purposes of the present study. Nonprice variables have been

[42] Take, for example, the case when in industries A, B, and C, labor requirements per unit of output are, 1, 1, 1, capital requirements 4, 3, 2, and material requirements 2, 6, 5. The ranking of industries with respect to capital and labor inputs will be A, B, C, for material and labor inputs B, C, A, and for material and capital inputs C, B, A.

[43] G. D. A. MacDougall, "British and American Exports: A Study Suggested by the Theory of Comparative Costs," Part I, *Economic Journal,* December 1951, pp. 697–724, and Bela Balassa, "An Empirical Demonstration of Classical Comparative Cost Theory," *Review of Economics and Statistics,* August 1963, pp. 231–38.

neglected in theoretical discussions and in empirical studies, even though quality differences, good will, servicing, the existence of repair facilities, and differences in weights and measures all have influence on the pattern of international trade among the industrial countries. Cost considerations will not be sufficient to explain the widespread use of British woollen goods or the success of Volkswagen, for example, and a complete explanation of comparative advantage would have to take account of the effects of nonprice factors.

"Revealed" Comparative Advantage

But is it necessary to explicitly take account of all influences that determine comparative advantage? This would be a rather laborious exercise and, in view of the difficulties of assigning numerical values to all the relevant variables, it might bring disappointing results. Instead, for purposes of evaluating the possible consequences of trade liberalization, it appears sufficient to provide information on "revealed" comparative advantage.

It is suggested here that "revealed" comparative advantage can be indicated by the trade performance of individual countries in regard to manufacturing products, in the sense that the commodity pattern of trade reflects relative costs as well as differences in nonprice factors. For one thing, comparative advantage would be expected to determine the structure of exports; [44] for another, under the assumption of uniformity in tastes and a uniform incidence of duties in every industry within each country, export-import ratios would reflect relative advantages.

The assumption of the uniformity of tastes and the uniform incidence of duties is not fulfilled in the real world, however. Imports are affected by differences in tastes as between countries, as well as by disparities in the degree of protection among individual industries. Moreover, in the case of intermediate products, export-import ratios are influenced by demand for purposes of further transformation in producing for export. To take account of these influences, separate consideration would have to be given to the special circumstances relating to individual products, which fact reduces the validity of the comparisons.

On the other hand, so long as all exporters are subject to the same tariff in foreign markets, data on relative export performance are not distorted

[44] Relative export performance has been used as an indicator of comparative advantage by H. H. Liesner in examining the possible effect of entry into the Common Market on British industry (H. H. Liesner, "The European Common Market and British Industry," *Economic Journal,* June 1958, pp. 302–16). In the present inquiry I have extended the scope of investigation to cover the main industrial countries, which fact has necessitated a reappraisal of the methodology used by Liesner.

by differences in the degree of tariff protection. Correspondingly, in evaluating "revealed" comparative advantage I have given greater weight to export performance than to export-import ratios, and, to exclude intra-area trade, I have regarded the European Common Market as a unit.[45] Other industrial countries included in the investigation are the United States, Canada, the United Kingdom, Sweden, and Japan. These countries, the largest exporters of manufactured goods, account for more than four-fifths of world exports of manufactures.

The inquiry has been limited to manufactured goods, partly because these provide the lion's share in trade among industrial countries and partly because a large number of primary products are subject to subsidies, quotas, and special arrangements, so that the ensuing trade pattern will hardly reflect comparative advantage. As in the preceding chapters, manufactured goods have been defined to include the products classified in commodity categories 5 to 8 of the SITC, less unwrought metals. With respect to these products, I have attempted to establish a commodity classification based on substitution possibilities in production. The point of departure has been the three-digit breakdown of the SITC; this has been supplemented by a four-digit breakdown whenever it appeared necessary and was made possible by the availability of statistical information.

Altogether, I have distinguished seventy-four commodity categories, having excluded from the investigation commodities that are not easily transportable, such as lime, cement, and fabricated building materials (SITC 661), clay construction materials (662), and mineral manufactures n.e.s. (663), as well as commodities where the countries under consideration, taken together, have an import surplus. This solution has been chosen because in such instances other exporters are likely to benefit from an over-all tariff reduction; less developed countries in regard to mineral tar and crude chemicals (521), dyeing and tanning extracts (532), wood and cork manufactures (631), jute fabrics (653.4), pearls and precious stones (667), silver (681), and miscellaneous metals (688.9), and Switzerland in the case of watches and clocks (864). Further, for obvious reasons, I have excluded developed cinematographic film (863), printed matter (892), as well as the motley collection of other miscellaneous manufactured articles n.e.s. (893—896, 898).

I have first calculated the relative shares of individual countries in the world exports of different commodity categories for the periods 1953–55 and 1960–62 that have been taken as representative of the mid-fifties and the early sixties. In both instances, the data have been made

[45] Note, however, that inasmuch as in the first period under consideration (1953–55), the trade pattern of the EEC countries was determined by their comparative advantage taken individually, a certain degree of "aggregation bias" has been introduced in the results.

comparable through appropriate "normalization." This has been accomplished by dividing a country's share in the exports of a given commodity by its share in the combined exports of manufactured goods of the ten industrial countries under consideration and expressing the result in index number form. Thus, for a given export commodity of a particular country, an index number of 110 will mean that the country's share in this commodity's exports is 10 per cent higher than its share in the total exports of manufactured goods. Further calculations have been made with regard to changes in shares between the two periods to provide an indication of developments over time.

Correspondingly, I have calculated (1) the relative share of country i's exports of commodity j in the years $1953-55$; (2) the relative share of country i's exports of commodity j in the years $1960-62$; and (3) the ratio of the relative share of country i's exports of commodity j in the second period to that in the first period. In all cases, the expression "relative share" refers to the ratio of the share of country i in the exports of commodity j to the share of country i in the exports of all manufactured goods.

In symbols,[46]

$$(1) \quad \frac{X^0_{ij}}{X^0_{nj}} \left| \frac{X^0_{it}}{X^0_{nt}} = \frac{x^0_{ij}}{x^0_i} \right.$$

$$(2) \quad \frac{X^1_{ij}}{X^1_{nj}} \left| \frac{X^1_{it}}{X^1_{nt}} = \frac{x^1_{ij}}{x^1_j} \right.$$

$$(3) \quad \frac{x^1_{ij}}{x^1_i} \left| \frac{x^0_{ij}}{x^0_j} \right.$$

---

[46] Explanation of symbols:

X = exports.
x = relative share of exports.

Superscripts:
o = average for the years 1953–55.
l = average for the years 1960–62.

Subscripts:
i = country i.
n = ten industrial countries taken together.
j = product j.
t = all products.

In evaluating relative advantages in the exportation of manufactured goods, various assumptions can be made. One may assume, for example, that relative shares observed in the most recent period will pertain also to the future, or relative growth rates may be taken as an indicator. Both methods have certain advantages and disadvantages. On the one hand, in considering relative export performance in a certain year or an average of several years, we neglect the trend factor; on the other, relative growth rates can give a misleading impression of comparative advantage since high growth rates are compatible with small exports in absolute terms, while a country that has a large segment of the export market in a given commodity can hardly be expected further to increase its share.

These considerations point to the need for using some combination of the two indicators to express comparative advantage. One possible solution would be to project the continuation of past trends in relative shares by multiplying equations (2) and (3) to obtain equation (4). I have decided against using this formula since it involves the questionable assumption that changes in relative shares take the form of a geometrical progression that can be extrapolated into the future. Instead, a compromise solution has been chosen by calculating the arithmetical average of equations (3) and (4).

$$(4) \quad \frac{x_{ij}^1}{x_i^1} \cdot \frac{x_{ij}^1}{x_i^1} \left| \frac{x_{ij}^0}{x_i^0} \right.$$

$$(5) \quad \frac{1}{2} \left[\frac{x_{ij}^1}{x_i^1} + \frac{x_{ij}^1}{x_1^1} \cdot \frac{x_{ij}^1}{x_i^1} \left| \frac{x_{ij}^0}{x_j^0} \right. \right]$$

This choice reflects the presumption that while past trends in relative shares can be expected to continue, they will do so at a declining pace as compared to the past. The results of the calculations are shown in Appendix Table 4.6.[47]

In the case of export-import ratios, indices of relative level and relative growth have been calculated, while the procedure of "normalization" has taken the form of dividing the export-import ratio of a country for a given commodity by that of the ten countries taken together. The calculations have been carried out on the basis of considerations similar to those relating to export shares and are shown in Appendix Table 4.7.[48]

While export-performance indices provide an indication of relative advantages (and disadvantages) for the individual countries, the dispersion of these indices will show the "markedness" of the comparative advantage of each country. In general, one would expect that large countries, as well as countries that occupy a middle position in terms of technological de-

---

[47] Any other average of the two figures could have been taken: my choice is based on the assumption that it is appropriate to give equal weights to the two indicators.

[48] The formula corresponding to equation (5) in the case of export-import ratios is:

$$(6) \quad \frac{1}{2} \left[\frac{x_{ij}^1}{m_{ij}^1} + \frac{x_{ij}^1}{m_{ij}^1} \cdot \frac{x_{ij}^1}{m_{ij}^1} \left| \frac{x_{ij}^0}{m_{ij}^0} \right. \right]$$

In the equation, *m* stands for relative export-import ratios.

velopment, would produce a great variety of commodities and hence show a relatively small dispersion of export-performance indices. On the one hand, large countries usually possess a more balanced resource endowment and will have a home market sufficiently wide to permit the production of most industrial goods; on the other, countries in the middle of the range among industrial economies are likely to export technologically less developed products to economies at higher levels of industrialization and more sophisticated products to countries at lower levels of industrial development.

These expectations are generally confirmed by empirical evidence. We find that the standard deviation of the export-performance indices is the lowest in countries that fulfill both conditions, such as the European Common Market (26.5) and the United Kingdom (55.5),[49] while it is somewhat higher in the United States (70.2), which is at the upper end of the range in terms of technological advance. In turn, the standard deviation of the export-performance indices is 119.6 in Sweden, the smallest of the countries under consideration in terms of home market for manufactured goods; it is 136.8 in industrially less developed Japan, and 205.1 in Canada—a country small in terms of domestic market and a relative newcomer among the industrial nations.

In the case of the Common Market, the indices also reflect lack of complete integration in the area. Despite the tariff reductions undertaken during the second period under consideration (1960–62), the trade pattern of the countries participating in the EEC is still determined to a large extent by their comparative advantages taken individually and, with the aggregation of national data, the dispersion of the indices is necessarily reduced. Nevertheless, differences in the relative position of Common Market industries are indicated by the fact that the export-performance indices fall outside the 80-to-120 range in the case of one-half of the seventy-four commodity categories under review.

The next problem concerns the similarities and dissimilarities shown in regard to the pattern of export performance and export-import indices in the individual countries. In the case of the majority of these countries, there appears to be a considerable degree of correspondence between the two sets of indicators: the rank correlation coefficients are 0.90 for Canada, 0.83 for Sweden, 0.78 for the United States, 0.75 for Japan, while lower values have been obtained for the United Kingdom (0.62) and the Common Market (0.57). Various factors explain the observed differences in the correlation coefficients: the "markedness" of comparative advantage, interindustry differences in the degree of protection and, in the case of the Common Market, the problems related to the aggregation of national data.

---

[49] The United Kingdom has been considered a "large" country because of the relatively easy access of British products to Commonwealth markets.

Other things being equal, the more marked are interindustry differences in trade performance, the greater the correspondence between the indices of export performance and of export-import ratios is likely to be. The results will be further affected by the degree of skewness in the pattern of protection; in general, a high degree of protection of selected industries will reduce the correlation between the export performance and the export-import indices. Finally, the aggregation of data for the six Common Market countries appears to have diminished the correspondence between the two indicators.

	Standard deviation of export performance indices	*Rank correlation coefficient between indices of export performance and of export-import ratios*
United States	70.2	0.78
Canada	205.1	0.90
European Common Market	26.5	0.57
United Kingdom	55.5	0.62
Sweden	119.6	0.83
Japan	136.8	0.75

Among the countries under consideration, Canada shows the greatest dispersion of the export performance indices as well as the highest correlation coefficient between the two sets of indicators. With the exception of shipbuilding, there is little evidence of the distorting effects of protection on export-import ratios; this result is explained by the fact that while tariffs are high in Canada, large interindustry disparities in duties are not observed.

Japan, the country with the second highest standard deviation of export-performance indices, occupies fourth place as far as the correlation coefficient between the two indicators is concerned. The explanation lies in the high degree of protection of selected manufacturing industries that has distorted the ranking of the export-import ratios. The effects of protection are manifest in the case of perfumery and cosmetics, paper, furniture, woollen yarn and textile machinery, as well as in regard to wrought lead and tin, where high tariffs and/or quotas have virtually excluded all imports.

In turn, low tariffs contribute to the high correlation observed between indices of export performance and of export-import ratios in Sweden, and the distorting effects of protection on export-import ratios are observable only in a few industries in the United States. The U.S. tariff appears to be nearly prohibitive for synthetic fabrics, while subsidies to domestic production restrict the importation of ships.

High tariffs on imports of selected commodities have contributed to the relatively low degree of correlation between the two sets of indicators in the United Kingdom, however. The 19 per cent tariff on glass and the 24 per cent duty on synthetic yarn are largely responsible for the small imports of these commodities; more importantly, the wide differences between indices of export performance and of export-import ratios for all kinds of steel products appear to be due to the fact that, among the industrial countries, Britain has the highest tariffs on steel.

Tariffs and quotas account for the relatively high export-import ratios for cotton fabrics and a few other products in the European Common Market. Nevertheless, a consideration of individual commodities indicates that, in the case of the EEC, the error possibilities introduced by the aggregation of national data have had a considerable influence on the observed differences between the two sets of indices. The export-import ratio was reduced by large German imports of woollen yarn and fabrics from the nonmember countries, for example, while after integration an increasing part of German demand may be satisfied by production in the partner countries.

Ranking of Products According to Export Performance and Export-Import Indices

Despite the observed differences between indices of export performance and of export-import ratios, the ranking of products at the top and at the bottom of the list is reasonably clear for all the countries under consideration. Taking account of import tariffs and other influences affecting export-import ratios, in Chapter 4 I indicated the "revealed" comparative advantage of the main industrial countries with respect to these products. No clear picture emerges, however, in regard to the majority of manufactured goods characterized by intraindustry specialization. Thus the tentative conclusions for individual commodity categories should be interpreted with caution. Still, the results derived in regard to these commodity categories may be of some interest in appraising changes in trade patterns in the event of trade liberalization.

In the chemical group, Canada appears to have comparative advantages with respect to organic and inorganic chemicals and manufactured fertilizers, the United Kingdom in synthetic dyes, paints and varnishes, medical and pharmaceutical preparations, perfumes and cosmetics, and explosives, while the United States has a leading position in the exportation of medical and pharmaceutical preparations, plastic materials, and other chemical materials and products. In turn, Sweden and Japan are at a comparative disadvantage in most chemicals, and Canada in the highly processed products of this group.

Among material-intensive commodities, Canada leads in leather and leather goods, with the United States at the bottom of the list. At the same time, the United Kingdom and Japan have relative advantages in the manufacture of rubber tires while in other rubber goods they are surpassed by Sweden. In both instances, Canada is at a disadvantage. In turn, Canada and Sweden are in a leading position with regard to paper, in the production of which the European Common Market and the United Kingdom have a comparative disadvantage. Finally, the EEC is in the most favorable position in the case of glass, Sweden leads in the exportation of glassware, and Japan in pottery.

Turning to textile products, we find that Japan has relative advantages in manufacturing cotton yarn and thread, cotton and synthetic fabrics, tulle and lace, made-up textile fabrics, blankets, and floor coverings; however, she cedes first place to the EEC in the case of wool yarn, to the United States in synthetic yarns, and to the United Kingdom in woven woollen fabrics. On the other hand, Sweden and Canada appear to be at a comparative disadvantage in regard to most textile products, the United States in cotton yarn, woollen yarns and fabrics, tulle and lace, blankets, and floor coverings, and the United Kingdom in cotton yarn and thread. The Common Market occupies the middle position in most cases.

By and large, the United States and the United Kingdom are at a disadvantage in iron and steel products. Within this group, Sweden leads in the highly manufactured forms of iron and steel (hoops and strips, tubes, pipes, and fittings) and shares first place with the Common Market in iron and steel bars and with Canada in railway-construction material. In turn, Canada has the lead in the case of pig iron and also in universals, plates, and sheets of iron and steel.

As to wrought ferrous-metals, I have indicated earlier the relative advantages for Canada and Britain in copper, the United States in nickel, Canada in aluminum and lead, the United Kingdom in zinc, and the United States and the United Kingdom in tin. Countries at a comparative disadvantage in these metals are the United States in regard to copper and lead, Japan in nickel, aluminum and zinc, Sweden in zinc and tin, and Canada also in tin.

We find further that the United Kingdom and the United States are in a favorable position with regard to much of nonelectrical machinery. The United Kingdom occupies first place in the exportation of power-generating machinery, textile machinery, and tractors, although Canada is ahead in other agricultural machinery. At the same time, the United States leads in metal-working machinery, office machinery, and other nonelectrical machinery, with Sweden occupying second place in the last two instances. Finally, with the exception of textile and office machinery, Japan and the EEC appear to be at a comparative disadvantage in this category of products, and Canada is also behind in several commodity groups.

The classification employed in this study in regard to electrical machinery is rather aggregated; owing to the lack of detailed statistics I have been able to distinguish only two commodity groups: electrical generators and other electrical machinery. The United Kingdom and the United States appear to have a comparative advantage in regard to the first while Japan is ahead in the second rather heterogeneous category. In both instances, Canada and Sweden are at a disadvantage.

In the transport equipment category, we find the United States in the lead in the case of aircraft and railway vehicles, but falling behind Japan in the exportation of bodies and frames of automotive vehicles, and at a decided disadvantage in shipbuilding, bicycles, and passenger automobiles. In turn, the countries of the Common Market have a strong lead in car exports, while Sweden and Japan appear to have a comparative advantage in shipbuilding, and the United Kingdom and Japan share first place in the case of buses and trucks, as in bicycles.

Among household accessories, Sweden possesses relative advantages in sanitary and plumbing equipment and in furniture, the United Kingdom being at a disadvantage in the former case and the United States and Canada in the latter. Turning to nondurable consumer goods, we find the United States, the United Kingdom, and Canada at a comparative disadvantage in regard to clothing, footwear, and leather goods; in all three instances Japanese producers have a leading position, with the Common Market a close second in the case of clothing and footwear.

By contrast, the United States has comparative advantages in the manufacture of different types of precision instruments, such as scientific, medical, and optical equipment, as well as photographic and cinematographic supplies. The United Kingdom appears to be at a disadvantage in the former case; Canada, Sweden, and Japan in the latter. Finally, Japan and the Common Market countries lead in the exportation of musical instruments and the EEC in jewelry; Canada, Sweden, and the United Kingdom are far behind.

APPENDIX TABLE 4.1 Trade in Manufactured Goods and Industrial Materials, 1960
(f.o.b. values, $ million)

		United States	Canada	Common Market	United Kingdom	Continental EFTA	Japan	Industrial Countries [a]
United States	IM	x	352	1,064	332	154	667	2,569
	MG	x	2,917	1,560	671	556	448	6,152
Canada	IM	1,095	x	208	430	84	65	1,882
	MG	1,210	x	55	211	25	12	1,513
Common Market	IM	159	12	(1,035)	136	230	17	554
	MG	1,850	263	(6,083)	1,065	3,349	162	6,689
United Kingdom	IM	91	29	174	x	(61)	17	311
	MG	728	538	1,057	x	(741)	67	2,390
Continental EFTA	IM	136	3	616	(316)	(124)	5	760
	MG	392	61	1,470	(408)	(854)	47	1,970
Japan	IM	47	2	34	17	11	x	111
	MG	976	105	84	35	71	x	1,271

Industrial countries [a]	IM	1,528	398	2,096	915	479	771	6,187
	MG	5,156	3,884	4,226	1,982	4,001	736	19,985
Other developed countries	IM	255	14	982	614	115	295	2,275
	MG	137	9	196	230	75	33	680
Less developed countries	IM	1,573	108	2,500	1,103	349	857	6,490
	MG	588	41	268	346	67	30	1,340
Soviet-type economies	IM	21	3	313	183	66	34	620
	MG	30	13	238	88	145	26	540
Total	IM	3,377	523	5,891	2,815	1,009	1,957	15,572
	MG	5,911	3,947	4,928	2,646	4,288	825	22,545

Source: National and international import statistics.

Notes: In the case of European countries and Japan that report imports on a c.i.f. basis, we have utilized the conversion ratios shown in B. Balassa, *Trade Prospects for Developing Countries* (Homewood, Ill.: Irwin, 1964), p. 369, to express the data on a f.o.b. basis.

IM—industrial materials; MG—manufactured goods.

[a] Totals exclude intra-EEC and intra-EFTA trade.

APPENDIX TABLE 4.2 Expansion of Trade in Manufactured
Goods and Industrial Materials, Atlantic Free Trade Area: Direct Effects [a]

($ million)

		United States	Canada	Common Market	United Kingdom	Continental EFTA	Japan	Industrial Countries
United States	IM	x	3	15	14	1	12	45
	MG I	x	680	458	235	80	168	1,621
	MG II	x	680	458	235	80	168	1,621
Canada	IM	27	x	8	—	0	2	37
	MG I	178	x	13	−42	3	3	155
	MG II	178	x	13	−42	3	3	155
Common Market	IM	9	0	x	6	2	1	18
	MG I	552	58	x	316	450	45	1,421
	MG II	677	68	x	403	578	56	1,802

United Kingdom	IM	4	—	2	x	x	0	6
	MG I	195	—	231	x	x	20	446
	MG II	254	—	294	x	x	25	573
Continental EFTA	IM	5	0	20	x	x	0	25
	MG I	157	14	317	x	x	16	504
	MG II	196	17	404	x	x	20	637
Japan	IM	1	0	1	1	0	x	3
	MG I	527	34	28	14	14	x	617
	MG II	527	34	28	14	14	x	617
Industrial countries	IM	46	3	46	21	3	15	134
	MG I	1,609	786	1,047	523	547	252	4,764
	MG II	1,852	799	1,197	610	675	272	5,405

Source: Appendix Table 4.1 and text.
Notes: ª Calculated on the basis of 1960 trade data.
Explanation of symbols:
IM—industrial materials; MG—manufactured goods, I—Variant I, II—Variant II.

APPENDIX TABLE 4.3 Expansion of Trade in an Atlantic Free Trade Area: Direct Effects and Discriminatory Effects
($ million)

	Exports			Imports			Trade Balance		
Variant	Direct Effect	Discrim. Effect	Together	Together	Direct Effect	Discrim. Effect	Direct Effect	Discrim. Effect	Together
United States									
I	1,666	389	2,055	1,655	1,655	—	+11	+389	+400
II	1,666	389	2,055	1,898	1,898	—	−232	+389	+157
Canada									
I	192	31	223	789	789	—	−597	+31	−566
II	192	31	223	802	802	—	−610	+31	−579
Common Market									
I	1,439	297	1,736	1,907	1,093	814	+346	−517	−171
II	1,820	297	2,117	2,057	1,243	814	+577	−517	+60
United Kingdom									
I	452	198	650	685	544	141	−92	+57	−35
II	579	198	777	772	631	141	−52	+57	+5
Continental EFTA									
I	529	275	804	811	550	261	−21	+14	−7
II	662	275	937	939	678	261	−16	+14	−2
Japan									
I	620	26	646	267	267	—	+353	+26	+379
II	620	26	646	287	287	—	+333	+26	+359
Industrial countries									
I	4,898	1,216	6,114	6,114	4,898	1,216	—	—	—
II	5,539	1,216	6,755	6,755	5,539	1,216	—	—	—

Sources: Direct effects: Appendix Table 4.2 and text.
Discriminatory effects: Table 4.2.

APPENDIX TABLE 4.5 Welfare Effects of an
Atlantic Free Trade Area
($ million)

[*Note.* Appendix Table 4.4 will be found on the following pages.]

		Direct Effects			Discriminatory Effects			Total
		Cost of Protection	Terms of Trade Effects	Total	Cost of Protection	Terms of Trade Effects	Total	Welfare Gain (loss)
United States	I	+71	−142	−71	—	+198	+198	+127
	II	+108	—	+108	—	+198	+198	+306
Canada	I	+47	−16	+31	—	+16	+16	+47
	II	+51	—	+51	—	+16	+16	+67
Common Market	I	+44	+138	+182	+42	−229	−187	−5
	II	+65	—	+65	+42	−229	−187	−122
United Kingdom	I	+28	+20	+48	+16	+28	+38	+86
	II	+43	—	+43	+16	+28	+38	+81
Continental EFTA	I	+15	+15	+30	+13	−20	−7	+23
	II	+28	—	+28	+13	−20	−7	+21
Japan	I	+15	−15	—	—	+13	+13	+13
	II	+20	—	+20	—	+13	+13	+33
Industrial countries	I	+220	—	+220	+71	—	+71	+291
	II	+315	—	+315	+71	—	+71	+386

Source: Appendix Table 4.3 and text.

APPENDIX TABLE 4.4 The Expansion of Trade in Manufactured Goods and Industrial Materials in Case of a 50 Per Cent Tariff Reduction under n.f.n.

($ million)

		Exports				Imports				Trade Balance
	Variant	Direct	Discrim. Effects	Feedback	All	Direct	Discrim. Effects	Feedback	All	
United States	I	833	195	118	1,146	1,008	—	—	1,008	+138
	II	833	195	118	1,146	1,130	—	—	1,130	+16
Canada	I	96	15	11	122	403	—	—	403	−281
	II	96	15	11	122	410	—	—	410	−288
Common Market	I	719	149	96	964	625	455	—	1,080	−116
	II	910	149	96	1,155	699	455	—	1,154	+1
United Kingdom	I	226	99	101	426	334	82	—	416	+10
	II	289	99	101	489	378	82	—	460	+29

Continental EFTA	I	265	137	26	428	291	136	—	427	+1
	II	331	137	26	494	355	136	—	491	+3
Japan	I	310	13	48	371	149	—	—	149	+222
	II	310	13	48	371	158	—	—	158	+213
Industrial countries	I	2,449	608	400	3,457	2,810	673	—	3,483	−26
	II	2,769	608	400	3,777	3,130	673	—	3,803	−26
Other developed countries	I	99	35	—	134	—	—	127	127	+7
	II	99	35	—	134	—	—	127	127	+7
Less developed countries	I	262	30	—	292	—	—	273	273	+19
	II	262	30	—	292	—	—	273	273	+19
Total	I	2,810	673	400	3,883	2,810	673	400	3,883	—
	II	3,130	673	400	4,186	3,130	673	400	4,203	—

Source: Appendix Table 4.3 and text.

APPENDIX TABLE 4.6 Indices of Export Performance

SITC		United States Index	United States Rank	Canada Index	Canada Rank	Common Market Index	Common Market Rank	United Kingdom Index	United Kingdom Rank	Sweden Index	Sweden Rank	Japan Index	Japan Rank
512	Organic chemicals	109.9	27	418.8	4	116.7	26	69.4	55	39.0	50	51.3	51
513,4,5	Inorganic chemicals	126.7	21	186.5	12	96.1	48	94.0	38	41.0	49	62.7	46
531	Synthetic organic dyestuffs	50.0	50		72	128.8	13	145.7	14	1.6	73	30.9	63
533	Pigments, paints, varnishes	107.4	29	28.7	45	90.8	59	239.8	3	32.7	52	20.3	65
541	Medical & pharmaceutical	144.2	16	34.3	41	95.6	49	127.7	23	26.6	55	38.5	58
551	Essential oil & perfumes	187.3	8	10.2	60	114.2	28	84.4	44	5.5	67	7.0	70
553,4	Perfumery & cosmetics	128.0	20	17.9	54	93.1	56	160.5	11	44.2	45	42.2	56
561	Fertilizers, manuf.	87.6	33	240.7	8	127.9	15	6.8	75	2.5	71	107.0	35
571	Explosives & pyrotechnic	72.6	44	6.5	65	95.5	51	217.3	4	113.8	21	73.4	45
581	Plastic materials	142.8	18	29.2	44	104.0	39	86.1	43	84.7	31	77.2	43
599	Chemical material & products	288.6	2	43.7	33	67.4	69	119.0	26	35.4	51	7.2	69
611	Leather	84.4	35	120.8	18	112.8	31	136.1	19	43.5	46	32.5	62
612	Manufactures of leather	57.5	48	200.2	11	125.2	20	105.2	32	74.1	33	94.2	39
613	Fur skins	221.1	4	92.6	20	96.8	47	87.6	42	47.7	42	7.3	68
621	Materials of rubber	26.5	63	36.6	40	112.9	30	136.8	17	155.4	15	139.0	26
629.1	Rubber tires & tubes	78.1	40	40.0	36	100.6	43	133.9	21	102.2	25	163.5	23
629.0	Other rubber articles	209.1	6	18.3	53	50.9	72	115.4	29	323.5	6	118.1	31
641	Paper & paperboard	76.0	42	1430.2	1	29.4	73	28.9	71	502.3	2	47.3	53

Code	Item												
642	Articles made of paper	118.9	23	50.5	30	95.6	50	118.0	28	87.6	29	135.4	28
651.2	Yarn of wool	0.7	74	5.5	66	157.7	2	98.1	34	13.8	64	54.8	50
651.3	Cotton yarn, unbleached	18.1	66	—	72	103.0	40	43.8	67	0.5	74	545.9	2
651.4	Cotton yarn, bleached	16.6	68	4.2	67	136.2	7	118.6	27	22.8	56	243.4	16
651.6	Yarn of synthetic fibers	124.7	22	40.4	35	105.1	37	80.9	48	8.6	65	107.1	34
652	Cotton fabrics	61.9	46	78.3	22	79.5	62	54.7	65	45.6	43	442.0	5
653.2	Woollen fabrics	1.0	73	21.1	49	120.6	23	200.1	6	4.5	70	137.9	27
653.5,6,8	Synthetic fabrics	50.3	51	18.7	52	92.4	58	21.4	72	43.5	47	469.9	3
653.0	Other woven textile fabrics	36.0	58	58.9	23	110.9	33	78.2	49	53.8	40	361.9	7
654	Tulle, lace, embroidery	37.5	55	10.0	61	111.4	32	88.6	40	22.4	58	312.6	11
655	Special textile fabrics	60.2	47	57.4	24	94.1	54	139.4	16	68.9	35	184.2	21
656.6	Blankets	14.5	69	6.7	64	127.1	16	63.0	60	22.5	57	250.3	14
656.0	Made-up textiles	165.5	11	33.5	42	79.5	63	74.2	52	51.7	41	157.2	24
657	Floor coverings	21.8	64	4.0	68	118.7	25	136.6	18	30.7	54	190.2	19
664	Glass	49.4	53	9.1	62	147.1	5	72.2	54	18.9	61	55.1	49
665	Glassware	102.4	30	2.9	69	115.8	27	66.4	57	102.8	24	77.5	42
666	Pottery	2.6	72	—	72	76.0	65	135.5	20	31.9	53	458.8	4
671	Pig iron	31.4	60	258.6	7	148.2	3	32.6	70	149.9	17	50.2	47
673	Iron & steel bars	17.3	67	40.0	37	133.3	10	59.1	62	114.8	20	99.9	37
674	Universals, plates, & sheets	49.8	52	172.3	14	125.1	21	82.5	46	91.8	27	126.5	30
675	Hoops & strips	37.1	57	—	72	135.2	8	57.6	63	227.2	8	103.1	36
676	Railway constr. material	75.2	43	396.2	5	95.4	52	83.5	45	558.1	1	153.2	25
678	Tubes, pipes, & fittings	37.3	56	51.9	29	127.0	17	94.1	37	178.4	12	116.6	32

APPENDIX TABLE 4.6 Indices of Export Performance (continued)

SITC		United States		Canada		Common Market		United Kingdom		Sweden		Japan	
		Index	Rank	Index	Rank	Index	Rank	Index	Rank	Index	Rank	Index	Rank
682.2	Copper, wrought	19.6	65	281.7	6	108.0	34	169.7	9	223.2	9	33.3	61
683.2	Nickel, wrought	174.7	9	160.4	16	60.5	71	180.4	8	116.6	19	2.0	74
684.2	Aluminum, wrought	78.6	39	214.6	10	119.5	24	110.9	31	101.2	26	33.9	60
685.2	Lead, wrought	48.5	54	852.7	2	128.6	14	97.2	35	411.7	4	45.2	54
686.2	Zinc, wrought	118.7	24	48.6	31	107.6	35	146.7	13	2.4	72	2.8	73
687.2	Tin, wrought	270.1	3	—	72	129.5	12	149.7	12	17.8	62	50.2	52
691.8	Manufactures of metal	81.5	37	46.8	32	101.8	42	111.9	30	106.6	23	128.7	29
711	Power-gen. machinery	99.0	31	228.0	9	64.9	70	248.0	2	78.2	32	40.2	57
712.0	Agricultural machinery	139.4	19	476.9	3	87.3	61	76.5	51	151.2	16	11.8	67
712.5	Tractors	214.7	5	53.7	26	25.9	74	301.3	1	42.9	48	3.8	71
714	Office machinery	157.0	14	132.8	17	92.5	57	62.1	61	170.8	13	77.0	44
715	Metal-working machinery	173.2	10	20.9	50	97.2	46	72.3	53	56.6	39	22.5	64
717.1	Textile machinery	85.9	34	26.8	47	113.9	29	128.7	22	21.1	59	83.4	41
718.9	Other machinery	143.6	17	40.0	38	93.4	55	99.5	33	149.9	18	35.4	59
722.1	Electric power machinery	113.6	25	52.6	28	99.9	44	120.7	25	91.7	28	98.2	38
72.0	Other electric machinery	109.3	28	57.1	25	94.9	53	92.1	39	72.7	34	309.6	12
731	Railway vehicles	200.2	7	30.9	43	71.5	68	65.5	59	166.8	14	215.8	18

Code	Item												
732.1.6	Automobiles	28.8	62	17.8	55	162.5	1	124.7	24	317.8	7	42.7	55
732.2,5,7	Buses, lorries, trucks	110.4	26	17.1	56	87.9	60	205.1	5	183.7	11	385.0	6
732.0	Bodies, chassis, frames	164.4	12	37.7	39	79.2	64	140.7	15	63.8	36	226.9	17
733	Bicycles	52.8	49	53.3	27	98.7	45	191.9	7	62.5	37	113.3	33
734	Aircraft	331.4	1	169.0	15	72.0	67	55.9	64	4.7	68	3.5	72
735	Ships & boats	14.5	70	13.0	59	102.0	41	82.4	47	423.6	3	347.1	8
812	Sanitary, plumbing, heating	97.3	32	100.6	19	104.2	38	77.4	50	407.1	5	92.9	40
821	Furniture	63.5	45	43.1	34	134.7	9	88.3	41	210.8	10	57.7	48
831	Travel goods, handbags	31.6	59	8.2	63	124.7	22	42.6	69	59.0	38	321.9	10
841	Clothing	29.5	61	20.0	51	136.6	6	43.3	68	87.2	30	245.9	15
842	Fur clothing	77.5	41	88.6	21	122.6	18	163.7	10	109.7	22	262.7	13
851	Footwear	7.2	71	26.5	48	147.4	4	47.9	66	15.9	63	601.4	1
861	Scientific, medical, optical	159.6	13	184.8	13	75.7	66	68.5	56	45.1	44	189.7	20
862	Photographic & cinematographic	148.1	15	28.1	46	106.5	36	95.3	36	4.7	69	20.3	66
891	Musical instruments	80.0	38	13.4	58	130.7	11	66.3	58	19.1	60	329.5	9
897	Jewelry & goldsmith	83.5	36	14.5	57	126.5	19	15.8	73	6.8	66	169.1	22

Sources: Organization for European Economic Cooperation (later OECD) *Foreign Trade Statistical Bulletins*, and United Nations, *Commodity Trade Statistics*, various issues.

APPENDIX TABLE 4.7 Indices of Export-Import Ratios

SITC		United States		Canada		Common Market		United Kingdom		Sweden		Japan	
		Index	Rank	Index	Rank	Index	Rank	Index	Rank	Index	Rank	Index	Rank
512	Organic chemicals	324.3	15	1478.6	3	83.0	55	68.3	60	37.3	37	46.4	59
513,4,5	Inorganic chemicals	113.3	34	109.1	9	106.6	33	123.4	39	16.2	57	184.8	50
531	Synthetic organic dyestuffs	109.1	36	0.0	72	121.5	19	201.1	26	1.2	72	20.7	66
533,4	Pigments, paints, & varnishes	545.4	10	7.3	51	66.9	66	773.6	8	14.2	60	45.2	60
541	Medical & pharmaceutical	169.6	24	16.7	32	82.6	58	686.0	9	13.1	62	43.1	61
551	Essential oils & perfumes	166.1	25	7.2	52	112.8	26	76.3	56	13.5	61	5.5	69
553	Perfumery & cosmetics	241.0	18	4.7	60	75.5	60	474.8	13	23.8	51	592.3	34
561	Fertilizers, manuf.	93.0	39	174.1	7	176.8	4	6.2	74	1.5	71	61.8	56
571	Explosives & pyrotechnic	63.1	48	2.0	64	146.0	12	6627.5	2	31.9	45	495.0	37
581	Plastic materials	1683.6	4	8.2	47	95.2	42	82.7	53	39.4	35	76.0	55
599	Chemical material & products	1367.8	5	7.8	49	76.3	59	104.7	46	23.3	52	4.6	71
611	Leather	88.4	41	107.4	10	104.6	34	100.0	47	43.4	32	241.9	46
612	Manufactures of leather	49.5	56	80.2	12	165.8	8	64.7	61	59.3	21	307.9	43
613	Fur skins	163.1	26	46.1	17	108.8	30	64.1	62	34.0	42	87.4	54
621	Materials of rubber	1379.8	3	16.8	31	112.2	27	109.9	44	49.5	25	313.1	42
629.1	Rubber tires & tubes	74.6	43	22.2	26	88.1	46	279.4	19	28.6	47	2093.1	21

Code	Description												
629.0	Other rubber articles	91.1	40	4.3	61	64.5	68	1216.5	6	403.3	4	375.6	41
641	Paper & paperboard	36.6	59	1498.0	2	38.4	73	22.0	72	2683.1	2	2386.6	18
642	Articles made of paper	153.3	28	11.1	44	90.4	45	179.5	31	54.6	22	21109.2	31
651.2	Yarn of wool	2.0	72	7.8	48	102.5	37	251.0	22	15.8	58	1320.8	29
651.3	Cotton yarn, unbleached	50.3	54	0.3	72	110.1	28	22.1	71	0.2	74		1
651.4	Cotton yarn, bleached	35.3	60	35.6	69	146.1	11	186.2	29	12.8	63	10766.3	9
651.6	Yarn of synthetic fibers	504.6	11	22.7	20	72.0	62	219.9	25	2.7	69	1121.2	30
652	Cotton fabrics	65.9	46	11.7	25	139.8	13	22.6	70	50.9	24	11142.8	8
653.2	Woolen fabrics	1.1	73	7.0	42	64.1	68	424.5	16	4.1	68	449.4	38
653.5,6,8	Synthetic fabrics	152.0	29	20.4	53	72.0	63	26.2	69	17.6	56	674.5	33
653.0	Other woven textile fabrics	22.3	63	3.2	28	83.8	51	123.3	41	77.0	18	5876.2	11
654	Tulle, lace, & embroidery	51.9	52	12.7	62	100.1	38	75.2	51	34.8	40	3252.8	16
655	Special textile fabrics	49.9	55	12.7	40	104.2	36	232.5	24	38.6	36	2008.2	23
656.6	Blankets	50.7	53	1.9	65	84.6	50	119.1	42	40.6	33	3581.6	14
656.0	Made-up textiles	156.0	27	6.9	54	104.3	35	56.9	54	45.1	30	2193.5	20
657	Floor coverings	18.0	66	3.0	63	108.1	31	145.6	36	21.1	55	3989.2	13
664	Glass	23.4	62	1.8	67	172.1	6	258.4	21	10.8	64	283.2	45
665	Glassware	103.9	38	0.5	68	129.6	17	73.5	58	155.3	7	417.4	40
666	Pottery		74		72	130.0	16	94.4	40	48.5	26		2
671	Pig iron	68.3	45	622.4	4	114.4	24	84.7	51	131.5	10	11.5	68
673	Iron & steel bars	10.8	70	27.2	21	114.6	23	434.5	15	141.9	9	1638.1	25

APPENDIX TABLE 4.7 Indices of Export-Import Ratios (continued)

SITC		United States		Canada		Common Market		United Kingdom		Sweden		Japan	
		Index	Rank	Index	Rank	Index	Rank	Index	Rank	Index	Rank	Index	Rank
674	Universals, plates, sheets	150.9	30	170.8	8	82.8	57	276.6	20	40.1	34	5018.8	12
675	Hoops, strips	53.1	51		72	87.1	48	2756.0	4	175.9	5	125.8	53
676	Railway constr. material	424.4	12	569.0	5	54.6	69	5633.1	3	2749.4	1	177.4	52
678	Tubes, pipes, & fittings	17.7	67	24.3	24	139.3	15	347.4	17	77.8	17	1516.3	27
682.2	Copper, wrought	14.1	69	212.7	6	91.2	44	576.1	10	98.4	13	417.5	39
683.2	Nickel, wrought	2671.2	2	26.9	22	87.8	47	77.1	55	21.8	54	2.8	73
684.2	Aluminum, wrought	61.0	50	89.9	11	154.4	9	95.3	48	47.1	28	13.5	67
685.2	Lead, wrought	40.6	58	35212.1	1	93.4	43	234.2	23	105.3	12	2442.3	17
686.2	Zinc, wrought	299.3	16	19.2	30	68.3	65	298.2	18	14.6	59	36.6	63
687.2	Tin, wrought	1340.1	6	0.0	72	83.3	54		1	4.5	67	500.0	36
691.8	Manufactures of metal	62.9	49	8.6	45	121.0	20	187.2	28	74.7	20	787.4	32
711	Power-gen. machinery	403.7	14	46.4	16	71.6	64	182.5	30	44.3	31	51.1	57
712.0	Agricultural machinery	119.0	32	52.4	15	107.6	32	168.4	32	168.1	6	184.2	51
712.5	Tractors	194.4	22	4.9	58	34.6	74	2054.6	5	26.5	49	24.5	64
714	Office machinery	219.2	20	62.4	14	109.7	29	81.1	54	79.2	16	40.9	62
715	Metal-working machinery	780.9	8	15.2	34	98.8	39	111.9	43	34.6	41	5.0	70
717.1	Textile machinery	147.1	31	12.8	39	97.5	41	144.0	37	26.7	48	10444.2	10
718.9	Other machinery	807.5	7	8.5	46	83.4	53	108.2	45	94.6	14	48.4	58

Code	Commodity												
722.1	Electric generators	224.2	19	15.0	35	83.5	52	199.8	27	45.2	29	200.8	49
72.0	Other electric machinery	112.9	35	22.1	27	86.1	49	160.8	34	36.2	38	1397.2	28
731	Railway vehicles	648.8	9	11.7	43	43.3	71	147.9	35	51.5	23	557.5	35
732.1,6	Automobiles	15.1	68	4.8	59	789.8	2	508.7	12	33.6	43	0.3	74
732.2,5,7	Buses, lorries, trucks	4209.3	1	5.2	56	72.7	61	1030.3	7	33.0	44	11177.5	7
732.0	Bodies, chassis frames	284.4	17	13.2	37	39.2	72	451.4	14	93.0	15	21329.9	5
733	Bicycles	29.6	61	14.0	36	120.8	21	527.3	11	35.5	39	1997.3	24
734	Aircraft	405.3	13	37.6	19	53.2	70	166.1	33	6.8	66	3.6	72
735	Ships & boats	104.0	37	13.0	38	124.1	18	43.1	66	153.9	8	222.7	48
812	Sanitary, plumbing, heating	212.2	21	24.8	23	82.9	56	89.1	50	412.4	3	2083.2	22
821	Furniture	68.4	44	15.6	33	114.1	25	127.2	40	126.8	11	3541.6	15
831	Travel goods, handbags	18.6	65	1.9	66	210.2	3	42.5	67	48.4	27	1609.8	26
841	Clothing	18.7	64	12.0	41	175.8	5	39.8	68	76.1	19	32751.2	4
842	Fur clothing	74.9	42	63.0	13	115.9	22	83.6	52	22.7	53	16686.4	6
851	Footwear	3.6	71	20.1	29	895.4	1	47.5	65	10.4	65	194489.9	3
861	Scientific, medical, optical	189.3	23	41.6	18	98.5	40	58.5	63	25.5	50	223.3	47
862	Photographic, cinematogr.	114.5	33	7.7	50	139.5	14	140.7	38	2.2	70	22.7	65
891	Musical instruments	65.7	47	5.2	57	149.8	10	70.0	59	30.2	46	2311.4	19
897	Jewelry & goldsmith	44.4	57	6.2	55	170.3	7	16.2	73	0.8	73	306.4	44

Sources: Organization for European Economic Cooperation (later OECD), *Foreign Trade Statistical Bulletins*, and United Nations, *Commodity Trade Statistics*, various issues.

APPENDIX TO CHAPTER SEVEN

The Policy Implications of Trade Liberalization

In this study I have examined the economic and political objectives of trade liberalization among the industrial countries and its possible effects on resource allocation and economic growth. By increasing the degree of interdependence of national economies, the expansion of trade will also bear influence on domestic policy-making in the individual countries. On the one hand, fluctuations in the economic activity of any one country will be transmitted to the partner countries through trade; on the other, national economic policies will interact to an increasing extent and the effectiveness of the measures employed by each country will be reduced.

In the event a country undertakes expansionary policies, for example, the ensuing rise in domestic incomes will be accompanied by increases in purchases from abroad, and imports will further rise—and exports decline—as higher domestic prices induce the substitution of foreign products for domestic goods. In turn, the increased demand for export- and import-competing goods produced by the trading partners will raise incomes and prices abroad and will lead to a rise in demand for the products of the country where the expansion originated. The process of adjustment will further continue until the force of the original stimulus is spent. Under the present system of fixed exchange rates and assuming full employment everywhere, the cumulative changes will entail a deterioration in the balance of payments of the first country, providing thereby a restraint to the unilateral application of expansionary measures.[1]

The question arises, then, whether the transmission of fluctuations in economic activity would necessitate a coordination of economic policies by the industrial countries in the event of trade liberalization. The answer to this question will depend on the extent of interdependence through trade as well as on the responsiveness of trade flows to changes in relative prices. It is suggested here that the degree of interdependence among trading partners is reflected in the "spillover" of increases in incomes in the form of higher imports. Under the assumption that spending on foreign goods out of an increment in income is roughly proportional to spending out of total income, and excluding nontraded goods from our purview, the ratio of trade among the industrial countries to value added in the production of traded goods can be used to indicate the extent of this interdependence. Thus, in cases when mutual trade is a large proportion of domestic output, a change in the economic activity of any one country

[1] However, the amplitude of the transmission of fluctuations would be reduced and balance of payments equilibrium would be continuously maintained if exchange rates were free to fluctuate.

will be immediately transmitted to other countries, and this impact will be magnified if import demand is responsive to price changes.

There are substantial differences among the industrial countries in regard to the ratio of their mutual trade to value added in the production of traded goods; these ratios range from 6 per cent in the United States to 45 per cent for the Continental EFTA countries.[2] The differences are even larger in bilateral relationships. Thus, while U.S.–Canadian trade amounts to nearly 35 per cent of value added in industries producing traded goods in Canada, the corresponding ratio hardly exceeds 2 per cent in the United States. A similar pattern is shown in U.S.–Japanese relationships, although the relevant magnitudes are smaller here.

In case of an asymmetry indicated by these ratios, economic fluctuations in one country will be transmitted to the other, while changes emanating from the latter will have little effect on the former. In the event of an extreme asymmetry, the relationships are unidirectional and, under free trade and fixed exchange rates, the smaller country will be frustrated in its efforts to follow independent economic policies. So far as its economic policies are concerned, it will thus become a satellite of the larger country.

On the other hand, when bilateral relationships are symmetrical, policies followed by the trading partners will interact and decisions taken by national authorities will become mutually interdependent. Nevertheless, if a trading group includes a large number of countries, the position of a single country is in some respects similar to that of a small nation facing a large trading partner. Thus the possibilities for any one member country to follow independent economic policies will be reduced, although it will not become a satellite of others—unless all of its trading partners carry out identical policies.

Relationships among the countries participating in the European Common Market are more or less symmetrical, and we also observe a considerable degree of interdependence among these countries, inasmuch as their mutual trade exceeds 15 per cent of combined value added in the production of traded goods.

An empirical demonstration of the policy implications of this interdependence has been provided by Robert Triffin and Herbert Grubel, who have indicated the extent of "spillover" among the countries in question with respect to their monetary financing.[3] These authors have shown that, in the open economies of the EEC countries, increases in monetary financing and import surplus are highly correlated, while the relationships

---

[2] Calculations refer to the average share of exports and imports in 1964. For sources, see Table 1.2.

[3] Monetary financing has been defined to include increases in the quantity and in the velocity of money as well as net foreign borrowings by the nonbank sector of the economy.

between monetary financing and domestic prices and production are far less pronounced.[4]

Instead of monetary variables, Stephen Resnick has considered the effects of fiscal policies followed by individual countries in the Common Market on the economies of the other member nations.[5] The results indicate a considerable degree of interdependence among the EEC countries. For example, a 10 per cent increase in government expenditure undertaken by any one country is shown to lead to an average rise of 1 per cent in the gross domestic product of the partner countries, while the impact of this measure on the domestic economy of the countries where the expansion originated is correspondingly reduced.

In conformity with our expectations, the effectiveness of domestic economic policies in the individual countries tends to decrease with a rise in the ratio of exports and imports to value added in the production of traded goods. Thus an increase in their government expenditure has the smallest effect on domestic incomes in Belgium and the Netherlands, where the ratio of trade to value added is the highest; moreover, the stated relationship is also observed among the larger member nations. For the period 1948–1961, the long-run multiplier, indicating the cumulative change in domestic incomes associated with a one dollar increase in government expenditure, was estimated as 1.46 in Belgium and 1.37 in the Netherlands,[6] while the proportion of intra-area trade to value added in the production of traded goods in the two countries was 38.7 and 36.4 per cent respectively.[7] The relevant magnitudes for the larger Common Market countries are: Germany, 2.38 and 7.2 per cent; Italy, 2.71 and 5.2 per cent; and France, 3.66 and 3.1 per cent.

The results of the two studies provide evidence of the conflict between economic interdependence and national policy-making in a closely knit trade group. Since the effects of any change originating in one country are transmitted to its trading partners, the effectiveness of national monetary and fiscal policies is reduced and economic activity in the individual member countries is affected by policies undertaken by others. It is noteworthy that, according to Resnick's calculations, an increase in government spending in the individual EEC countries is not sufficient to raise domestic incomes if the partner countries reduce their government expenditure in the same proportion.[8]

---

[4] Robert Triffin and Herbert Grubel, "The Adjustment Mechanism to Differential Rates of Monetary Expansion among the Countries of the European Community," *Review of Economics and Statistics,* November 1962, pp. 486–91.

[5] S. A. Resnick, *An Econometric Study of the Common Market* (to be published by The Brookings Institution).

[6] Cf. Resnick, cited.

[7] Data refer to 1958. For sources, see Table 1.2.

[8] The net change in domestic incomes due to a simultaneous increase of domestic government expenditure and a contraction of expenditure in the partner countries

Aside from frustrating the efforts of the individual countries to carry out independent economic policies, a country that unilaterally employs expansionary measures will incur a balance of payments deficit that cannot be sustained for a protracted period. But balance of payments considerations introduce an element of asymmetry in the policy responses of the member countries: while the constraint provided by the availability of foreign exchange reserves does not permit a country to sustain an expansion at a higher rate than its trading partners, there is less incentive to avoid accumulating reserves through balance of payments surpluses. Given this asymmetry and the desirability of maintaining fixed exchange rates within an integrated area, some degree of coordination of economic policies will be called for.[9]

The conclusions pertaining to the Common Market would also apply to a European union. Intra-European trade amounts to over one-fifth of value added in the production of traded goods in Western Europe, indicating the need for policy coordination in the area. The degree of interdependence is also high within North America although, as noted above, relationships between the United States and Canada are characterized by a considerable degree of asymmetry. Accordingly, trade liberalization would further reduce the autonomy of Canadian policy-makers and increase the need for aligning policies with the United States.

But the conclusions need to be modified in U.S.–European relationships where the extent of interdependence through trade is considerably smaller than within North America or within Western Europe. Thus in 1964 trade between the United States and Western Europe amounted to less than 3 per cent of value added in the production of traded goods in the United States and this ratio was only slightly higher for Western Europe taken as a whole. The liberalization of trade between the two areas would increase this ratio, but even a doubling of trade would make little difference in absolute terms.

With the relatively low degree of interdependence indicated by the low ratio of mutual trade to domestic production, the spillover of an expansion in either area would be relatively small. And although disparate changes in prices would lead to the substitution of foreign goods for domestic products, the influence of various nonprice factors reduces the extent of short-run substitution. For one thing, tastes and consumption habits differ to a considerable extent on the two sides of the Atlantic; for another, the short-term response is limited by the scarcity of information on foreign goods and by the need for components, repair facilities, and

---

by 10 per cent has been estimated as follows: Belgium −0.31 per cent; France −0.15 per cent; Germany −0.08 per cent; Italy −0.25 per cent; and the Netherlands 0.05 per cent. Same.

[9] On various aspects of this coordination, see my *Theory of Economic Integration,* chap. 12.

selling outlets. While changes in these variables will occur in the long run, they will tend to limit the short-run impact of price changes on trade between North America and Western Europe more than within either of the two.

Given the relatively low degree of interdependence through trade and the limitations of price-induced substitution, the interaction of national economic policies will be considerably smaller between North America and Western Europe than inside these areas. Thus, while the national autonomy of France, Italy, or the Netherlands in carrying out economic policies is narrowly circumscribed by reason of the spillover to other countries of the Common Market, a considerable degree of independence in policy-making can be preserved in North America and in Western Europe, taken as a unit. These conclusions are supported by the results of Triffin and Grubel: whereas increases in monetary financing were accompanied by changes in domestic prices in the Common Market, taken as a unit, and by changes in production in the United States, the link between monetary financing and import surplus was rather weak in both cases.

I have considered here the implications for trade flows of differences in the economic policies followed on the two sides of the Atlantic. A further question relates to the international transmission of structural changes, such as shifts in demand patterns, technological improvements, and the introduction of new products. It has often been argued that, in a closely knit trade group, the process of adjustment to such changes would approximate that observed in interregional relationships. Thus, just as a fall in demand for its export products leads to a decline in a region's economy, structural changes due to demand shifts or any other courses would cause serious imbalances in an integrated area. Should this be the case, a considerable degree of coordination in economic policies would be necessary.

But the analogy is hardly appropriate. Given the differences in the economic structure of regions within a national economy and that of developed industrial countries in a European union, the effects of structural changes will be rather different in the two cases. The vicissitudes of a region with a concentrated production (and export) pattern are often due not so much to the decline in demand for its main export product as to the absence of other profitable opportunities and the lack of external economies that make it difficult to expand along new lines. However, most developed countries possess a differentiated industrial structure and hence the effects of a disturbance in any one industry will be relatively small. At the same time, as long as the disturbances are more or less randomly distributed, their effects will overlap and they will tend to offset each other over time. Accordingly, there appears to be little need for policy coordination to offset the effects of structural changes between national economies in an integrated area.[10] This conclusion applies with especial force to U.S.–European relationships, where the degree of interdependence through trade is small.

We may thus conclude that although some coordination of domestic economic policies would be necessary within the European area and within North America, trade liberalization would not necessitate policy coordination between the two areas. Aside from the problems related to differences in national tax regulations,[11] similar considerations apply to direct foreign investment. And while divergences in monetary policies will influence the flow of portfolio capital, this is largely independent of trade and hence it falls outside the scope of this study.

[10] It is a different question that the coordination of regional policies is often desirable. On this point see Chapter 9 of my *Theory of Economic Integration.*

[11] For a detailed discussion, see Douglas Dosser's contribution in *Studies in Trade Liberalization,* (Bela Balassa, ed.), Johns Hopkins University Press, 1967.

Index

COUNCIL ON FOREIGN RELATIONS

PUBLICATIONS

FOREIGN AFFAIRS (quarterly), edited by Hamilton Fish Armstrong.

THE UNITED STATES IN WORLD AFFAIRS (annual). Volumes for 1931, 1932 and 1933, by Walter Lippmann and William O. Scroggs; for 1934–1935, 1936, 1937, 1938, 1939 and 1940, by Whitney H. Shepardson and William O. Scroggs; for 1945–1947, 1947–1948 and 1948–1949, by John C. Campbell; for 1949, 1950, 1951, 1952, 1953 and 1954, by Richard P. Stebbins; for 1955, by Hollis W. Barber; for 1956, 1957, 1958, 1959, 1960, 1961, 1962 and 1963, by Richard P. Stebbins; for 1964, by Jules Davids; for 1965 by Richard P. Stebbins.

DOCUMENTS ON AMERICAN FOREIGN RELATIONS (annual). Volume for 1952 edited by Clarence W. Baier and Richard P. Stebbins; for 1953 and 1954 edited by Peter V. Curl; for 1955, 1956, 1957, 1958 and 1959 edited by Paul E. Zinner; for 1960, 1961, 1962 and 1963 edited by Richard P. Stebbins; for 1964 by Jules Davids; for 1965 by Richard P. Stebbins.

POLITICAL HANDBOOK AND ATLAS OF THE WORLD (annual), edited by Walter H. Mallory.

THE CHINESE PEOPLE'S LIBERATION ARMY, by Brig. General Samuel B. Griffith II, U.S.M.C. (ret.) (1967).

THE ARTILLERY OF THE PRESS: Its Influence on American Foreign Policy, by James Reston (1967).

ATLANTIC ECONOMIC COOPERATION: The Case of the O.E.C.D., by Henry G. Aubrey (1967).

TRADE, AID AND DEVELOPMENT: The Rich and Poor Nations, by John Pincus (1967).

BETWEEN TWO WORLDS: Policy, Press and Public Opinion on Asian-American Relations, by John Hohenberg (1967).

THE CONFLICTED RELATIONSHIP: The West and the Transformation of Asia, Africa and Latin America, by Theodore Geiger (1966).

THE ATLANTIC IDEA AND ITS EUROPEAN RIVALS, by H. van B. Cleveland (1966).

EUROPEAN UNIFICATION IN THE SIXTIES: From the Veto to the Crisis, by Miriam Camps (1966).

THE UNITED STATES AND CHINA IN WORLD AFFAIRS, by Robert Blum, edited by A. Doak Barnett (1966).

THE FUTURE OF THE OVERSEAS CHINESE IN SOUTHEAST ASIA, by Lea A. Williams (1966).

ATLANTIC AGRICULTURAL UNITY: Is It Possible?, by John O. Coppock (1966).

TEST BAN AND DISARMAMENT: The Path of Negotiation, by Arthur H. Dean (1966).

COMMUNIST CHINA'S ECONOMIC GROWTH AND FOREIGN TRADE, by Alexander Eckstein (1966).

POLICIES TOWARD CHINA: Views from Six Continents, edited by A. M. Halpern (1966).

THE AMERICAN PEOPLE AND CHINA, by A. T. Steele (1966).

INTERNATIONAL POLITICAL COMMUNICATION, by W. Phillips Davison (1965).

MONETARY REFORM FOR THE WORLD ECONOMY, by Robert V. Roosa (1965).

AFRICAN BATTLELINE: American Policy Choices in Southern Africa, by Waldemar A. Nielsen (1965).

THE CONSCIENCE OF THE RICH NATIONS: The Development Assistance Committee and the Common Aid Effort, by Seymour J. Rubin (1966).

NATO IN TRANSITION: The Future of the Atlantic Alliance, by Timothy W. Stanley (1965).

ALTERNATIVE TO PARTITION: For a Broader Conception of America's Role in Europe, by Zbigniew Brzczinski (1965).

THE TROUBLED PARTNERSHIP: A Re-Appraisal of the Atlantic Alliance, by Henry A. Kissinger (1965).

REMNANTS OF EMPIRE: The United Nations and the End of Colonialism, by David W. Wainhouse (1965).

THE EUROPEAN COMMUNITY AND AMERICAN TRADE: A Study in Atlantic Economics and Policy, by Randall Hinshaw (1964).

THE FOURTH DIMENSION OF FOREIGN POLICY: Educational and Cultural Affairs, by Phillip H. Coombs (1964).

AMERICAN AGENCIES INTERESTED IN INTERNATIONAL AFFAIRS (Fifth Edition), compiled by Donald Wasson (1964).

JAPAN AND THE UNITED STATES IN WORLD TRADE, by Warren S. Hunsberger (1964).

FOREIGN AFFAIRS BIBLIOGRAPHY, 1952–1962, by Henry L. Roberts (1964).

THE DOLLAR IN WORLD AFFAIRS: An Essay in International Financial Policy, by Henry G. Aubrey (1964).

ON DEALING WITH THE COMMUNIST WORLD, by George F. Kennan (1964).

FOREIGN AID AND FOREIGN POLICY, by Edward S. Mason (1964).

THE SCIENTIFIC REVOLUTION AND WORLD POLITICS, by Caryl P. Haskins (1964).

AFRICA: A Foreign Affairs Reader, edited by Philip W. Quigg (1964).

THE PHILIPPINES AND THE UNITED STATES: Problems of Partnership, by George E. Taylor (1964).

SOUTHEAST ASIA IN UNITED STATES POLICY, by Russell H. Fifield (1963).

UNESCO: ASSESSMENT AND PROMISE, by George N. Shuster (1963).

THE PEACEFUL ATOM IN FOREIGN POLICY, by Arnold Kramish (1963).

THE ARABS AND THE WORLD: Nasser's Arab Nationalist Policy, by Charles D. Cremeans (1963).

TOWARD AN ATLANTIC COMMUNITY, by Christian A. Herter (1963).

THE SOVIET UNION, 1922–1962: A Foreign Affairs Reader, edited by Philip E. Mosley (1963).

THE POLITICS OF FOREIGN AID: American Experience in Southeast Asia, by John D. Montgomery (1962).

SPEARHEADS OF DEMOCRACY: Labor in the Developing Countries, by George C. Lodge (1962).

LATIN AMERICA: Diplomacy and Reality, by Adolf A. Berle (1962).

THE ORGANIZATION OF AMERICAN STATES AND THE HEMISPHERE CRISIS, by John C. Dreier (1962).

THE UNITED NATIONS: Structure for Peace, by Ernest A. Gross (1962).

THE LONG POLAR WATCH: Canada and the Defense of North America, by Melvin Conant (1962).

ARMS AND POLITICS IN LATIN AMERICA (Revised Edition), by Edwin Lieuwen (1961).

THE FUTURE OF UNDERDEVELOPED COUNTRIES: Political Implications of Economic Development (Revised Edition), by Eugene Staley (1961).

SPAIN AND DEFENSE OF THE WEST: Ally and Liability, by Arthur P. Whitaker (1961).

SOCIAL CHANGE IN LATIN AMERICA TODAY: Its Implications for United States Policy, by Richard N. Adams, John P. Gillin, Allan R. Holmberg, Oscar Lewis, Richard W. Patch, and Charles W. Wagley (1961).

FOREIGN POLICY: THE NEXT PHASE: The 1960s (Revised Edition), by Thomas K. Finletter (1960).

DEFENSE OF THE MIDDLE EAST: Problems of American Policy (Revised Edition), by John C. Campbell (1960).

COMMUNIST CHINA AND ASIA: Challenge to American Policy, by A. Doak Barnett (1960).

FRANCE, TROUBLED ALLY: De Gaulle's Heritage and Prospects, by Edgar S. Furniss, Jr. (1960).

THE SCHUMAN PLAN: A Study in Economic Cooperation 1950–1959, by William Diebold, Jr. (1959).

SOVIET ECONOMIC AID: The New Aid and Trade Policy in Underdeveloped Countries, by Joseph S. Berliner (1958).

NATO AND THE FUTURE OF EUROPE, by Ben T. Moore (1958).

INDIA AND AMERICA: A Study of Their Relations, by Phillips Talbot and S. L. Poplai (1958).

NUCLEAR WEAPONS AND FOREIGN POLICY, by Henry A. Kissinger (1957).

MOSCOW-PEKING AXIS: Strength and Strains, by Howard L. Boorman, Alexander Eckstein, Philip E. Mosely, and Benjamin Schwartz (1957).

RUSSIA AND AMERICA: Dangers and Prospects, by Henry L. Roberts (1956).

ABOUT THE AUTHOR

Dr. Bela Balassa is presently Professor of Political Economy at the Johns Hopkins University and an Adviser to the Economics Department of the International Bank for Reconstruction and Development. In the period of writing this book he was Associate Professor of Yale University; he also taught at Columbia University and the University of California (Berkeley). A native of Hungary, he holds doctor's degrees from the University of Budapest and Yale University. At various times, he was consultant to national and international agencies, including the U.S. State Department, the Treasury Department, the Organization for Economic Cooperation and Development and UNCTAD.

Professor Balassa has published widely in economic periodicals. His books include *The Hungarian Experience in Economic Planning* (1959), *The Theory of Economic Integration* (1961), *Trade Prospects for Developing Countries* (1964), and *Economic Development and Integration* (1965). He edited *Changing Patterns in Foreign Trade and Payments* (1965) and *Studies in Trade Liberalization* (1967).